**4,000 years
under the sea**

ALSO BY PHILIPPE DIOLÉ:

The Undersea Adventure

4,000 years under the sea

by Philippe Diolé

Promenades D'Archéologie Sous-Marine

Translated by Gerard Hopkins

JULIAN MESSNER, INC., NEW YORK

TO
Alfred Merlin
Permanent Secretary
of the
Académie des Inscriptions et
Belles Lettres, who, at Mahdia,
won the first victory
for undersea archaeology
I dedicate this book in gratitude

Translator's Note

The French have two words for diver, *scaphandrier* and *plongeur*. The *scaphandrier* wears the *scaphandre*, or hermetically sealed suit, of the professional, a spherical helmet of metal screwed onto a gorget, and weighted boots. A life line and breathing tube keep him in constant communication with the surface, but limit his movements. The *plongeur*, on the other hand, works independently. He breathes by means of compressed-air cylinders strapped to his back, he wears a mask, and rubber extensions on his feet, and can swim freely beneath the surface of the sea.

I have made use of the terms "helmet diver" and "free-diver" wherever there seems to be a risk of confusion.

G. H.

Author's Note

I could never have brought this book to a successful conclusion without the co-operation of friends and masters. To all of them I owe a debt of gratitude.

To Monsieur Alfred Merlin, Secrétaire perpétuel de l'Académie des Inscriptions et Belles Lettres, I am indebted for more than guidance and advice. From him I have learned the lesson of scientific honesty, and in him I have found a true teacher of caution and proportion in all things. He has ever been for me a model of exemplary virtue.

Monsieur Raymond Lantier, membre de l'Institut, Conservateur en chef du Musée des Antiquités Nationales, has suggested a number of modifications. These may win for me from readers a degree of indulgence which I do not deserve.

In Monsieur Fernand Benoit, Directeur de la XIIᵉ Circonscription archéologique, I have long found not only an accurate but also a kindly guide. Once again he has not failed me.

Monsieur Louis Leschi, Directeur des Antiquités de l'Algérie, who took much interest in the diving operations at Cherchel, has kept a watchful eye on my account of them.

Finally, I owe much to Monsieur Jean Babelon, Conservateur des Médailles de la Bibliothèque Nationale, to Monsieur Jacques Heurgon, professeur à la Sorbonne, to Monsieur Denizet, Directeur des Archives et des Bibliothèques de la Marine, to Commandant Guilleux La Roërie, whose knowledge in all matters pertaining to the sea is equaled only by his generosity in putting it at the service of enquirers, to Monsieur Meile, professeur à l'École des Langues Orientales, to Monsieur l'Ingénieur en chef de la Marine Brunel du Service Central hydrographique de la Marine, and to Monsieur Thevenot, whose admirable studies on the subject of Gallo-Roman life are well known. I should like to express my thanks to all these friends who have been, throughout, so eager to assist me.

Contents

Preface

I was like a ship sinking in a closed world of waters.

PAUL ELUARD

Remember, we rendezvous at the anchor!"—such is the ritual phrase used by the divers of the Club Alpin Sous-Marin when they go overboard, those the words with which they take a temporary farewell of their life upon the earth. It is a formula which has already set its seal upon many leave-takings, the last spoken interchange between man and man. It rings out, and from then onwards, all is silence, all is solitude, in a world of waters which seems so terribly too wide. Even when they move cheek by jowl, these adventurers into the depths can do very little for one another. The signs they make, as of deaf-mutes, the soundless messages of their closed lips, are powerless against the overwhelming loveliness of a universe of waters. Like men buried alive they are condemned to carry on a series of monologues. Each can think only for himself, can bring to the surface only such treasures as he can acquire singlehanded. To be initiated into the life of the ocean bed is a test in which "cribbing" is impossible, in which each man is entirely on his own.

ix

But though the presence of others can be of little practical avail, it has its value. The anchor rendezvous is religiously observed. In that blue underwater world, the anchor of the boat which has brought the divers to their point of departure shows as a familiar landmark, biting deep into the sand and weed. The cable climbs obliquely upwards to a sky which hangs above a human universe. There is comfort in clinging for a moment to that tenuous thread before plunging with one's fellows into the great caverns of the deep. It is there, at the anchor, that daring hardens into courage, and friendships become firmly knit. Just for a moment glances are exchanged through goggle windows. And on the return journey, too, it is the anchor that first brings a message from the solid earth as one prepares to emerge from the coldness of a land of dreams. It is from the anchor cable that one says a last farewell to the motionless kingdom of half-lights, to that twenty-fathom zone in which the diver dreams rather than moves.

I remember a time when the dividing line between two worlds lay only just beneath the surface, on, as it were, the backside of the mirror. Today, it is rather further down, at anchor level. In the space of a few years we have gained perhaps a dozen yards, have "humanized" the sea to a depth equal to the height of a two-storey house. I leave it to others to decide whether that is much or little.

⚡ ⚡ ⚡

I HAVE spoken in another book (*The Undersea Adventure*; New York: Julian Messner, 1953) of the vivid sense of delight which takes hold of one when, for the first time, one penetrates beneath the surface. After thousands of years of fear and effort man has at last succeeded in getting beneath the top layer of the sea, winning a long battle against asphyxia and terror. The palace untouched by human hand, with its gardens of rock and water where living creatures play the part of flowers, is the goal of all our striving. But scarcely have we crossed the threshold than we are dazzled and bewildered. In very fact we stand beneath the crystal vaults which form the entrance to a "Wonderland," but still embarrassment has hold of us. We cannot shed our earlier timidity. So far from expanding, our bodies seem still further to contract. We remain mere creatures of the earth, intruders into, obsequious and awkward visitors in, a world where we do not belong. The sea has conquered man.

Are we to rest content with being tourists intent only on taking home mementoes and photographs to stick into an album? It would be an outrage against the human spirit and the destiny of man to think of the sea as of some foreign land to which it is praiseworthy to make an occasional trip with a load of ready-made and superficial enthusiasm. No: into that journey we must put every ounce of what strength we have. We must make full use of all our resources. We must be as emigrants setting sail in search of a fortune. To leave our luggage at the frontier would be plain absurd. The moment has come for us to settle down for good and all at the very heart of the deep sea, using for that purpose all the knowledge at our command, and finding in this new world a true delight. The capital we have is no great sum, when all is said, but already, scarcely knowing what we do, we have sunk some part of it in the enterprise. Our science and our skill have put out feelers into the world of waters not unlike those submarine valleys which carry the rivers of the earth across wide stretches of the sea bed, marking the lines and masses of a geographical system for centuries known only to the fishes.

Biological and mineral resources, for long unknown, await us. But that is not all, for we may well find in the depths new sights, new categories of thought. Until man recognizes that new world as his natural domain, his condition will remain unchanged. He will be as he has always been, with his age-old load of familiar images, his earth-bound competence, a dweller on one quarter only of the world's surface.

❧ ❧ ❧

IT is not enough for us to see the goal. We must acquire a knowledge of the roads that lead to it. It remains for us to map out in the oceanic mass, and in the mass, no less vast, of our gigantic ignorance, the areas to be cleared, the tracks to be followed. To prove that he was Poseidon's son, Theseus had only to bring a golden ring from under the sea. That was an easy task. The divers of today have a far more difficult one confronting them if they are to show themselves worthy of the unfathomable depths. If they would play their part successfully they must train as specialists in a hundred and one branches of knowledge. They are like those African pioneers who, fifty years ago, settled in the bush, and found that they must learn many crafts and many callings. They had to know how to kill wild animals, build bridges, administer justice, vaccinate children, fell trees, and plant vegetables. We, the first arrivals in the virgin forests of the sea, must improvise a working knowledge of ichthyology, algology, and hydrography. Others, coming later, will improve on our achievements with far less merit than is due to us.

Only for certain men of science is the line of duty straight and plain. Diving for them is a matter of professional obligation. Naturalists, for instance, like Professor P. Drach or Professor J. M. Pérèz have explored the depths in order to study marine life which is their chosen field. For them diving is merely laboratory research carried one step further. A time will most certainly come when diving will become more important than research.

But not everyone is fortunate enough to be a naturalist. For most of us the path of duty is less clearly marked. Those who find mere trips beneath the surface not sufficiently satisfying look in the deep places of the sea for more definite tasks to undertake, only too soon to realize that such things demand a knowledge which they have not got, and a scientific training which they have not acquired.

ᴍ ᴍ ᴍ

WE rendezvous at the anchor, but with whom, with what? With vague hopes or with the certainties of science? With poetry or biology?

It is questions of this kind that I have put to myself while swimming beneath the surface. They have been set moving half unconsciously in my mind and to them this book is due. Did I have to write it? Maybe the simple fact that one finds happiness in diving is sufficient excuse for putting it on record. Whether such an occupation is useful or idle matters little. Must we forever be seeking the warm glow of satisfaction in doing useful things, like boy scouts getting a kick out of a daily "good deed"?

Let there be no mistake. Had only some moral consideration been at issue I should have done far better to stay silent, to go back with a clear conscience to the simple, pointless pleasure of week-end diving. But I thought that I was on the track of something. To exercise the intelligence is not so frequent, nor so easy, an activity as it would seem to be, and I have found that immersion in salt water stimulates the mind. What I came to realize in the course of the years, as I adjusted the straps of my air-containers and gripped between my teeth the salty mouthpiece of my breathing tube, was that diving involved not only the human body, but the human spirit as well: that it provided a satisfying employment for that little dancing, flickering flame within the brain that never ceases to seek sustenance.

At the risk of appearing pretentious, I will say this: that in my worst moments, when I found it impossible to decide what to do or what to write, I have always taken to the deep waters. They act upon me like a cleansing bath. They are a sort of slimming cure for the mind, a reducing process which strips thought to its essentials without in any way producing a feeling of impoverishment. As I sink down, down, not merely with an eye open for animals and weeds, but as one turning upon himself a searchlight that can reveal a world of complicated truths, I believe myself to have discovered, not perhaps a method, but at least a contrivance.

It may be a golden key: it may, on the other hand, be nothing at all. I have tested it on matters of archaeology and history, because they are within my range, are, as it were, familiar victims.

Tiny though the result may seem to be, I am far from regretting the effort needed to achieve it. The lesson was too beautiful for that.

A poor diver, vulnerable and ill-provided, I have set out on a risky venture which may well result in the discovery of a world. I have seen opening before me long vistas of the deep, down which, always ahead of me, I seem to catch the shadowy shape of man. I am a late member of a long line of living creatures who may have had their distant origin in water. The image of the sea's profundities was with me even before I was aware of it. It haunted thousands of my ancestors. The ghosts which I have started in the very heart of the waters, from the dark secrecy of wrecks, are eloquent to me not so much of death as of continuity, not so much of drowned life as of a determination to continue the adventure of living. Each has been the bearer of a message, eager to make it plain: symbols, religions, secrets of forgotten skills or simple processes of trade, a Gorgon's head, or the stopper of a wine jar. All these things, lost in the sea for two thousand years or more, have something to offer.

The man of the twentieth century, like an ungrateful heir, has turned his back upon his past. The ancient triumphs of his forebears now scarcely interest him. Nothing seems to rouse his admiration but technical efficiency, and those sciences to which he has long applied the word "exact." In a sudden outburst, tinged with bitterness, Salomon Reinach once gave it as his opinion that "in 1950 no one will any longer take the slightest interest in Greek sculpture."

There are, I believe, certain strange and important matters which the seas are making ready to reveal to man—who has grown forgetful of himself. For his spirit, maybe, is formed in the image of the waters, a fluid element with strong attachments to the past.

Doubtless a day will come when there will no longer be any depths unplumbed. Technical improvements will make it possible for the diver, clad in a new form of armor, to reach the lowest of the ocean beds. Of one great depth, and of one alone, will he have to take account—the huge abyss which, since the beginning of time, has yawned within himself.

4,000 years
under the sea

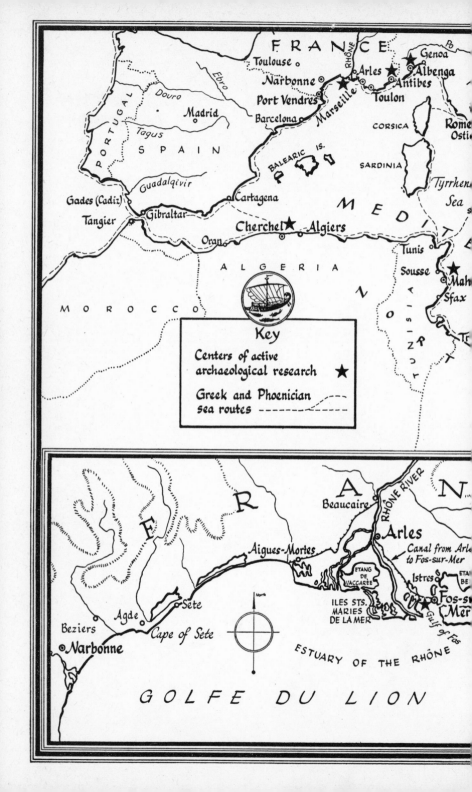

1. Archaeology Is Young

*Archaeology in the first half of the
19th century had great hopes but
little technique.*
                    CHARLES PICARD

U NTIL OUR EXPLORATIONS CAN BE SYSTEMATICALLY CONDUCTED,
until we can be assured of adequate means, financial as well as
technical, we must rest content with a mere glimpse of what the
sea can offer in the way of archaeological riches. All we know is
that they must be considerable.

Let me start by making one thing quite clear. We have heard
much in recent years about *undersea archaeology*. The phrase
carries with it a somewhat simple-minded prestige, and a pretext
for a good deal of fishing for wine jars. But fishing—even when
it results in a miraculous haul—remains just fishing.

There is among laymen, and even among certain people who
go on "digs," a genuine misunderstanding of what the word
"archaeology" really means. The mere practice of digging does
not make a man an archaeologist, nor does digging in the sea
give a man the right to style himself an undersea archaeologist.
No matter how sound the methods adopted, no matter to what
1

extent the searcher can give the guarantees nowadays required for competence in this kind of work, it can never be satisfactorily carried out unless it is based upon complete knowledge of the various problems presented by the site.

It must, therefore, be definitely stated that digging is not archaeology. It is merely a means of discovery; one aspect, and one aspect only, of the work in hand. It can never be an end in itself. The fact is that digging presents us with more problems than it solves. To hope that it will give us a number of simple truths is to court disappointment. If "dissection" of this kind is to be carried to a successful conclusion it must be undertaken with full knowledge of the case on which we are operating. It should be regarded as the reward for a tremendous amount of preparatory work.

I feel that I should apologize for enunciating so elementary a truth. But everything goes to show that it has been neglected in this matter of undersea archaeology. How, otherwise, can archaeologists bring themselves to hand over to a lot of well-meaning but essentially amateurish divers the responsibility for laying the foundations of a brand-new branch of their science?

The idea of a naturalist undertaking to describe the lives of marine animals in their native element merely on the strength of the tales told by professional divers would provoke us to laughter. Why, then, should we show greater indulgence to archaeologists? Gone are the days when underwater exploration could be carried out only at second hand. Diving no longer requires exceptional qualities of physique. Any young man in good health can penetrate beneath the surface of the sea, provided he possesses a rudimentary knowledge of the art of swimming. (I know of one diver belonging to the Research Group who could barely swim at all. He had several times been to a depth of twenty fathoms before he knew how to move about comfortably on the surface.) The conditions met with in the sea are such as any normal archaeologist may face with confidence. Many of them, in other circumstances, have given proof of a far greater degree of physical endurance and courage.

All the same, a man can be a resourceful diver, and yet not necessarily fitted for the kind of work I am describing. No matter how much learning an archaeologist may have, he has got to be able to examine under water the evidence which he has set him-

self to study. On the other hand, be he never so daring, a diver
has no right to formulate disputable hypotheses and fanciful
theories merely on the strength of his skill. Archaeology is a science. Before he can become proficient in it a man must serve an
apprenticeship. To train archaeologists in diving is neither a
difficult nor a lengthy process, whereas to hope that divers will
one day develop into archaeologists may well lead to disappointment.

There was a time when I wondered whether undersea archaeology might not claim to be a self-sufficient and separate science,
whether the special conditions in which it is conducted and a
working knowledge of a number of complementary branches,
such as physical oceanography and marine biology, might not
justify it in a claim to independence. I know now that I was
approaching the problem from the wrong end. It is essential to
realize that all archaeology is one. The fact that it is a work containing many chapters does not mean that it can be broken up.
Whether conducted on dry land or in the water, it draws its life
from a shared mastery of sources, texts, and disciplines. To know
a lot about the sea is no sufficient excuse for a man who knows
nothing at all about epigraphy or history.

In the course of this book I have tried to test my beliefs by
applying the yardstick of reality, and to bring to the examination
of certain sites a concentrated effort of endurance which shall
involve qualities of mind as well as of body. The first thing I
had to do was to sketch out a method. Whether that method
was valid only the future can say. Because it can deal with certain
necessities does not mean that it can deal with all, and I have
approached the subject in a manner sufficiently provisional to
leave the field open to other possible explanations.

The limited nature of my ambitions as an author should
emerge clearly from my use of the word "excursions" in describing my activities in this book. I have said already that by limit-
ing oneself to such casual enterprises, one does, to some extent,
diminish the extent of those promises which the world of the sea
makes to us. But at present we are little more than beginners. We
may set our sights high, but it is better to begin by creeping toward the target. It is dangerous to claim too much, for by doing so
we may well prejudice such possibilities as the future may hold.

PERHAPS I had better, before conducting the reader on a tour of specific "sunken sites," give him a general sketch of the undersea world, and familiarize him—if he is not already familiar—with the physical and spiritual contingencies with which the diver has to cope. True, the life of the depths is now to some extent easily accessible, but it does not follow that the conditions to be found there resemble those of dry land, or that our manner of dealing with them is the same as it would be in utterly different circumstances. A great deal more is involved than wanting to work beneath the surface, even if that means no more than being a mere observer. Though the exercise of free-diving demands but a brief period of training, a considerably longer time is necessary before we can hope to acquire an experience of life in deep waters and to train our powers of vision and observation so that they will be at home in a strange medium. A supplementary course of training is required before we can hope to become proficient in the type of work we have undertaken, and it is essential that we acquire an accurate knowledge of the capacities and limitations of the human body when submerged. Only experience can teach us these things. We must distinguish clearly from the beginning between diving and the power to turn diving to effective uses.

So long as we confine ourselves to "strolling" and dreaming, the diving habit does certainly bring us a sense of leisure and an illusion of freedom beyond anything we have previously known. But—and we must face the fact squarely—that sort of diving is no more than a species of slow-motion dawdling, in which the body, freed from its own weight, ceases to feel the need of any fulcrum. The mind, cut loose from the world of solids, becomes the passive recipient of a stream of images. Such a state is not favorable to any kind of action. We are unprepared by our physical and psychological heredity for life in a fluid universe. We are accustomed on dry land to employ many variations of leverage: we habitually lift weights and handle masses. Once under the water, however, we realize that we need machines and contrivances with which to supplement our own unaided efforts. We need some counterbalance to the weight of any object we may wish to move. We try to raise a rock, only to find that it drags us down. We try to lift a mass of weed and are entangled in it. The only course open to us is to pit our wits against the machinations of this strange world, to develop new reflexes. Only by the use of the imagination can we acquire an efficient response to new stimuli. Merely to take a firm stance under submarine conditions involves a degree of ingenious adaptation, to gain the proper amount of ballast, to adjust our human muscles to a strange kind of effort. No matter how skillful he may be, the free-diver inevitably finds his strength reduced, his field of activity restricted. But what matters most to him is not so much having the power of movement, as being able to see what he is looking for—worked stone or wreck, anchor or wine jar. The only serious disadvantage of which he is conscious is the difficulty of distinguishing in the tangle of marine vegetable life the evidence of what he seeks. At a deep level the scene, more often than not, has, to his eyes, a uniform appearance. No matter whether what he sees is a rock, a cliff face, or a sunken ship, the surface is disfigured by a living growth of molluscs, of coral, of sponges, or of sea mosses. Sometimes, as at Saint-Tropez, he will find that clumps of *Lithodomus*, the date-mussel, have eaten deep into the Carrara marble, and so eroded it as to give it the look of worn pumice, so that it is only with difficulty that the eye can pick it out from the rock formations among which it lies. Elsewhere, as off the coast of Brittany, for instance, seaweed covers everything with an impenetrable marine fleece which makes accurate examination impossible. At Anthéor, the searchers found themselves defeated by a luxuriant growth of *Posidonia*—which is not a seaweed but a flowering plant—on a wreck dating from the classical period. In other places mud is the trouble. All objects abandoned to the mercy of the sea have become overlaid with a thick, viscous layer. That is the case at Port de Bouc, where the Rhône silt has formed a top layer of anything from eighteen to twenty-one feet in depth, which only a dredger could shift.

No matter how slowly the marine prospector may swim in the blue depths, the chances of a "find" are pretty slim, and he is more often than not reduced to hoping for a stroke of luck. All the same, the human mechanism is so responsive that it adapts itself with quite extraordinary efficiency to conditions of excessive difficulty. The human body and the human spirit, each, when so tested, gives a good account of itself. It may be recalcitrant at first, but sooner or later it comes to heel, and the results are not too bad.

Training in undersea archaeology is based upon the ability to recognize the tiniest scraps of evidence and to turn to account sudden glimpses which are often of the most fugitive description. I do not mean that it is either vague or indefinite. After all, medical students can be taught, through the recognition of symptoms, to master the subtle skill of the diagnostician. A bronze anchor ring half buried in the sand, the rather too rectilinear outline of a rock—such things are enough to prick the curiosity, even at a depth of ten fathoms. There are aquatic as well as terrestrial intuitions. An object strange to the landscape of the depths, though the sea may have laid a conquering hand upon it, though the constant wash of the tides may have made it unrecognizable, and the fish used it as their home, strikes a familiar note and never wholly loses the traces of man's handiwork.

I should, however, be the last to deny that psychological difficulties play their part and add to the problems caused by weed growths and the depredations of marine fauna. This explains how it is that many a diver has passed unseeing above a site from which later visitors may reap an ample harvest. But it would be foolish to exaggerate this difficulty, which is caused by the fact that man's condition is not, to any great extent, acclimatized to the sea. A psychologist has said that "the cognition of the external world began as *re*-cognition." We are strangers to the ocean depths. Before we can recognize them we have much to learn. Our first sensations when plunged beneath the surface are vague and shapeless. They force themselves upon us before we are sufficiently experienced to pick and choose. All that we are aware of in the early stages is a colored fluidity, meaning little, and providing next to no information. Into this compact mass the intelligence thrusts with varying degrees of success, separating, sorting, retaining. Perception, imagination, and memory are all brought to bear by the 'prentice diver. His power to distinguish is about on a par with what he might learn from a textbook of psychology designed for use in the upper grades of schools.

☙   ☙   ☙

WOULD it be fair to say that such conditions of scientific exploration are in any way exceptional; that they are more rigorous than

those imposed by archaeology on dry land? I cannot answer that
question with any degree of certainty. The sands of the desert, no
less than the mud of the sea bed, long concealed the archaeological wealth of Egypt and the evidence which made it possible
to construct the pattern of oriental prehistory. In order to bring
into the light of day certain Mesopotamian "finds" it was necessary to burrow into a surface layer of ninety feet of earth and to
clear away a mass of rubbish, all of which had to be passed
through a sieve. There are certain sites in Asia Minor which are
more difficult to approach, even today, than is the submarine
dockyard of Saint-Tropez, which lies no more than two hundred
yards from the shore at a depth of little more than three fathoms.
That our masters—who, for the most part, are now in their sixties
—should not indulge in the practice of diving—much though they
would like to—is understandable enough. But that the young
pupils of the École des Hautes Etudes, of the École Normale,
of the École des Chartes, and of the Schools of Rome and Athens
should show a reluctance to venture beneath the surface implies
a degree of indifference which is hard to explain—and is somewhat disturbing. The wild fig trees which concealed the temples
and palaces of the Khmers were no less dense than the vegetation of the ocean depths, but that did not prevent scholars from
studying a civilization which had been overgrown by forest. The
same might be said of the Mexican jungle, which has not stood
in the way of those who wished to explore the ruins of Punta, or
made it impossible to bring to light a culture dating back thousands of years, a system of hieroglyphic writing, a complex
calendar, a whole pattern of astronomical and mathematical science "heavy with the scent of flowers and the stench of blood."

When we take this sort of bird's-eye view of archaeology, it is
borne in upon us that the obstacles which shut us off from the
past are due less to physical difficulties than to mental cowardice,
to lack of method, to an insufficiency of means. Whenever research in this field has acquired a certain discipline, the results
have exceeded expectation. It is natural to assume that the
further we are removed in time from the objects of our search,
the less decipherable become the traces of the past, and the
harder to follow. Such, in fact, is not the case. The twentieth
century has found it easier to reconstruct the ancient world than
did the nineteenth. The explanation of this seeming paradox is

that in the course of a hundred years improved techniques have
come into use and the general theory of archaeological research
has been more firmly established.

য়   য়   য়

ARCHAEOLOGY is a recent science. Egyptology, the oldest of its
departments, is little more than a hundred years old. Its beginning has been dated to September 14, 1822, when Champollion
read the name of Rameses and succeeded in deciphering the
Rosetta Stone. At the beginning of the twentieth century, all
that men knew about the ancient peoples of the East was what
was contained in the Bible. Mesopotamian archaeology goes
back no further than Botta and Place—1840-1845. It was only
in 1850 that Boucher de Perthes, in face of official skepticism,
produced the essential proofs which led to the establishment of
a science of prehistory. In 1860 Renan conducted the first "digs"
in Phoenicia. Schliemann started work at Hissarlik (Troy) only
in 1870. It was not until 1900 that Sir Arthur Evans established
himself in Crete, and only in 1933 that André Parrot turned the
first sod at Mâri.

It is, in the main, since the war of 1914 that our efforts of
research have produced solid and numerous results. These have
been due no less to an intelligent examination of documents
than to material discoveries. The triumphs of archaeology have
been achieved by a combination of brain and pickaxe. The strati-
graphical method, which alone supplies reliable chronological
evidence, was brought to perfection precisely thirty years ago.

The most surprising fact of all, but also, from the point of
view of the present book, the most encouraging, is that the greater
part of this new knowledge has come from a relatively poor
area of research, or, if not poor, at least inferior in extent when
compared with the number of traces which it is reasonable to
suppose exist in the world. We have nothing like exhausted the
documentary evidence which archaeology may hope to assemble.
Field work is far from being complete in the countries of the
world, including France. As to the exploration of the subsoil,
excavation, properly so-called, has so far been carried out in a
ridiculously restricted field. There are numerous sites as yet un-
examined in Macedonia, Asia Minor, and Syria. Aerial photogra-

phy is constantly bringing new facts to light in England no less
than in North Africa.

It is safe, therefore, to say that the science of archaeology has
not by a long way exhausted its possibilities. Not yet has it
mastered all the material evidence of which it stands in need,
nor surveyed all the available territory. It is in no position to
claim that it can now at last, in the light of long experience,
establish an orthodox method from which no divergence may
be permitted. Its technique is likely to be extensively modified
as a result, not only of aerial observation, but of the newest improvements in metallurgical analysis.

Since, then, the science of archaeological research is still far
from complete, why should it be confined to dry land? Why
should it not extend its inquiries to the sea? Wherever man has
left traces of himself, it is the duty of archaeology to extend its
operations.

What we today call undersea archaeology is, for the time being,
no more than a curiosity of casual trippers whose enthusiasm is
comparable to that which urges travelers to bring back "mementoes" of their journeys. Why should that be a matter for surprise?
That was how archaeology began. We of the sea are at a stage
comparable with that of the Rosetta Stone and Michaux stones.
If our efforts have so far produced little, the reason lies not in
the difficulties presented by marine conditions, nor in the absence
of suitable sites. It can more reasonably be blamed on our mental
approach to the problem, and to our lack of the necessary funds.
It is for the twentieth century to take the needed step forward.
In the words of Monsieur Robert Demangel, "the future of
archaeology lies in the sea."

¥   ¥   ¥

FROM creek to creek along the coast of the Mediterranean, in
North Africa, on the Riviera, in Italy, and in Spain, I have set out
to explore the ocean depths as the result of some chance phrase
read in a textbook, some tale told by a fisherman, some item of
news given me by a diving colleague. I can still recapture the
thrill which has come to me at the sight of some barely noticed
block of masonry, a Roman tile, a fragment of pottery, lying
perhaps fifteen or so fathoms beneath the surface.

But I know, too, the futility of this sort of rag picking. What does it all amount to? The necks of a few amphorae, an occasional piece of marble (as at Cherchel), some sherds, and the handles of a vase smoothed by the sea; a cumbersome mass of small booty to be packed in a haversack after wrapping it in an old pullover; a collection of rubbish which will later have to be sorted carefully. The net result is a little heap of stuff for which there is no name in any language other than that special jargon concocted for the identification of these odds and ends of history. A tiny chip of pottery, perhaps from some bowl which once was the apple of its owner's eye, amounts to no more than "a sample of Campanian ware"—which has its value, all the same, because it may help to establish a date; or, perhaps, a fragment of a Graufesenque, a scrap of red-glazed earthenware with part of a garland or the torso of a goddess worn smooth by the waves.

It is in the course of such modest investigations that I have learned to come to terms with those obstacles which the world of the deep sea puts in the way of the archaeologist who works alone without any lifting tackle to help him, without any means of dredging and, more often than not, without a boat. I have realized what an enormous difference quite elementary equipment would make to him.

The lesson I have learned is that none of the normal obstacles encountered in this kind of exploration is insurmountable—not seaweed nor molluscs, nor even mud so long as it is not too thick. A day will come when these things will be seen as no more important than the Punta cactuses, the Angkor fig trees, or the sand of the Egyptian desert.

At the present stage of our knowledge and our resources we must resign ourselves to the necessity of making a modest beginning on the great hoards of the past which the sea has covered. Those who come after us will conduct a more authoritative search on the very spots where we have fumbled. Only by feeling with our hands, by gripping an object and pulling it free, can we hope, at present, to make even the smallest discovery. Some compound of rock and encrusted shellfish which has roused our curiosity because the edge looks suspiciously straight may turn out to be the first step toward reconstructing a whole segment of the past. On the other hand it may, after examination, prove to be nothing —a scrap of stone, a lump of brick transformed by the action of

the waves into something we were rather too ready to see as a
museum piece.

On one occasion I carried out diving operations off the coast of
Algiers in water which had the very color of those masterpieces
of Persian ceramic art dating from the sixteenth and seventeenth
centuries—that deep blue which we find in the tiles of the Mosque
of Achmet in Constantinople. Yet in spite of its promise, in spite
of the presence of a sea bed sown thick with "remains," my every
gesture was fraught with disappointment. I felt quite convinced
that I had stumbled on a treasure trove which had been cemented
into a solid mass by a calcareous formation in no more than five
fathoms of water. I broke off a piece of the hard outer crust, tearing my hands in the process on its sharp points of gray and pink.
It cracked as soon as I put pressure on it, and yielded me a tool
which was better than nothing, a spike composed partly of rock,
partly of animal parasites. I proceeded to rout about with it in the
open wound which I had contrived in a colony of animal life. A
thick cloud of mud poured out and spread. My liquid sky grew
dark, and it was a quarter of an hour before this disturbance
settled down. There was no point in hanging about in a dense
fog. I must move further on, try my luck somewhere else, start all
over again. The sum total of my efforts was an amphora of rather
inferior design—or rather part of an amphora, because there was
nothing left of it but the body. Even the neck had gone. I am as
sure today as ever I was that there is a great deal more to be
found in that particular spot. But a considerable effort will be
needed before any result of value is achieved. The process of
recovery will be a long one.

☙   ☙   ☙

Like all other undersea activities, archaeology can, for the most
part, claim only very modest successes. A great deal of obstinacy,
much attention to detail, and the constant following of false
clues, is the price one pays for mediocre results; or that is so at
present. When we know more about the sea over the greater part
of its extent, we shall waste much less time. But even so, I very
much doubt whether we shall ever come upon those massive ruins
chock-a-block with marvels of which we sometimes dream.

I am not at all sure that all this talk about drowned cities does much to help our cause. We have got beyond the stage of bolstering up such empty hopes, which are no sooner formulated than they have to be abandoned. They serve to show how persistent are those ancient visions which went to the making of *La Ville d'Ys* and *Twenty Thousand Leagues Under the Sea*. Those sunken cities with their broken columns, their population of enormous octopuses, their weed-choked streets, and their golden statues still haunt the imagination of mankind. Men's minds cling obstinately to a dream which flatters their affinity with the sea and links the romance of ruins with the poetry of the ocean depths—the dream of an Atlantis waiting to be found by divers.

It is for us to submit to a stricter discipline and to refuse admission to such facile illusions. Just conceivably there may exist, somewhere or other, ruins of sufficient importance to merit exploration at some future date. But I should be very much surprised if any complete city ever came to light. Earthquakes, which so often find mention in books devoted to this subject, produce *first* destruction, *then* submersion. What they leave to the sea can only be a tumbled chaos which is soon engulfed in mud. Helike, a Greek city which sank abruptly in the fourth century B.C., has raised many high hopes. But it lies under a solid twenty feet of slime. If ever it is reached, the divers will have had plenty of time in which to prepare their minds for such surprises as its discovery may have in store. Months of hard work will be necessary, and the employment of powerful mechanical aids, before this new Pompeii can be freed from its accumulation of submarine ashes.

About Ys I had better say nothing, if I want to retain the friendship of my Breton acquaintances. All through one winter I received a flood of letters and telegrams, all of them full of information. Either one does or does not believe in Ys. The actuality of that drowned city is a matter of faith, not of reasoned argument. One of my friends, whose duties kept him for a long time in Brest, was a firm believer. He was eager to know where precisely the place was situated: he wanted to see it. Well, the first thing he found out as a result of his preliminary investigations was that there was not *one* city of Ys but two, three, four cities. He eliminated the least promising, pinned his faith to one, and sat down, as it were, to lay siege to it. He went in to the attack with picked troops of evidence and inquiry, threw about it a

trench system of plausibilities, plotted its exact position on the
Antonine Itinerary and the *Peutinger Map*, and mapped the
point of intersection of those ancient highways which today stop
short at the coast of the mainland. The place was at his mercy.
The report of a diver which he turned up in the archives delivered
it over to him lock, stock, and barrel. This diver had actually
seen the city ten years previously, but Brittany had shown not the
slightest sign of excitement. In the Bay of Douarnenez, at a depth
of ten fathoms, he had touched walls. That was where the place
was situated.

We planned to carry out an operation in the water above the
City of Ys. By great good luck the diver in question was found,
and by great good luck also he had a perfectly clear recollection
of the incident—*only* what he had actually seen on the date
recorded had been not blocks of masonry, not walls, but massive
rock formations. A geologist was consulted and talked learnedly
of "the dorsal ridge" and "summits." The City of Ys still careens
madly about the Breton sea bed, with the Devil in the saddle,
and only the Devil knows where. . . .

What would be really comic would be to find that the City of
Ys really had been all the time in the precise spot where the
diver had failed to see it! A fine finish, that, to a legend born in
the fifth century! We know perfectly well that Ys *is* a legend:
all the same, there must be more than one ruin at the bottom of
the Breton seas, by whatever names they may go. But such relics
as there are can bear very little resemblance to the popular idea
of what *ought* to be found. I can envisage the reality only too
clearly: huge growths of *Saccorhiza bulbosa* clinging to a few scattered pieces of masonry with tendrils as hard and curved as a
vulture's claws, their stems as thick round as a wrestler's arms,
standing up like oriental palms in a sea the color of lead or un-
polished pewter. The place would be just one of those endless
Atlantic jungles. There are thousands of them, and they may well
conceal such remains as there may still be of streets and human
habitations—and not one single octopus! At ten fathoms the
ground swell keeps the diver lolloping about as though he were
being rocked in a hammock by somebody with a very strong
grip. The trunks of the rooted seaweed scarcely move at all; but
man is too light for his surroundings when he has got below the
surface. He hangs there, swinging to and fro. The treacherous

currents of the ocean depths very soon cure him of any desire he may have felt to loiter on the bottom in order to find out whether or no the City of Ys lies in ruins in the grip of tangled weeds. Still, Brittany does have its fine days, and on one of them, maybe, some neophyte of our craft may find himself in luck's way, and come upon the palace of King Gralon or the bedchamber of Dahut of Armorica.

On the other hand, that adventurous young man may find nothing but maërl (a mixture of sand and weed), specimens of the Sea Hare—so evocative of the Devil, Dead Men's Fingers, and Razor Shells which rear up with a rattle that sounds like the clash of jaws. The deep waters of Brittany are a deal more disturbing than her legends!

※   ※   ※

THE Mediterranean, on the other hand, is a smiling sea. It hampers the intruder with only a very few patches of weed. It is sometimes lively, but rarely boisterous, and its waters, once one has gone below the surface, are, to all intents and purposes, without movement.

It takes no long time to make the round of the known hoards of amphorae between Marseille and Nice, by way of Port Cros, so long as one's activities are confined to a quick dive, a superficial survey, and a prompt return to the surface.

Those who return, year after year, to the same sites, get a fondness for them. There is a bond of friendship which links the undersea landscapes—where there is "something"—and the men who have learned to know them well. One develops a nostalgia for the deposits of sherds, for the expanses of sand littered with the bric-a-brac of broken vases, tufted with vegetable seagrowth. Time and time again, in Paris, I have found myself welcoming divers with their packet of news from Fos or Anthéor, with something of the warmth I might extend to colonists just back from Abidjan or Gao.

Not all underwater sites are beautiful. The ones which are richest in promise, the ones where the traces of man's passing are best preserved, suffer from a superfluity of mud. The water is often thick with the alluvial deposits of rivers—as at Fos-sur-Mer. Often, as at Cherchel, the columns, the hewn and sculptured

masonry, lie cheek by jowl with all the refuse of a modern port—
rusty cables, hoops of casks, and even worse. Not that it really
matters. One quickly forgets the sewage dumps in one's eagerness
to go in search of older things. But the marks left by the past
beneath the sea differ a great deal in different places. Off the
coast of Provence they have a certain lightness about them, are
intermittent; almost, one is tempted to say, unobtrusive. In North
Africa they are heavy rather than sharply defined, massive under
their pelt of short-stemmed weed. There is something rustic about
them: they lack nobility. I have never, there, seen anything to
compare with the blocks of Carrara marble which lie upon the
sea bed in the Bay of Saint-Tropez, but only columns of modest
dimensions, showing evidence of provincial workmanship, and
cut from the limestone quarries of the mainland. As soon as one
gets deep into that African water, the mass of Roman rubble
spreads on every side with a prodigality unknown upon the coasts
of France. One realizes that one is far from the world of dredgers.
Such recent harbor works as have been carried out have been
confined to a limited area. They have barely touched those great
hoards which the sea has kept for us in almost the same confusion
as when they went to the bottom so long ago.

The memory of one particular day of diving—too short by
half—at Port-aux-Poules, near Arzew, comes back to me endowed
with an especial charm. It was on a cool morning of African
spring. There was something of the freshness of a mountain
valley about the cold, translucid water, the great stone slabs, and
the familiar fishes flitting in and out of holes in the Roman
cement.

The sea treats kindly the relics of our man-made world. It
covers the poor dead, vanquished, broken objects in an envelope
of liquid cellophane. It gives them a sort of "museum look," and
even when they are brought to shore and the bright colors of the
tiny marine beasts fade in the harsh sunlight, there remain the
graffiti made by the worms, the traces of coral-colored borings,
an arabesque superimposed by the sea upon the neck of an
amphora.

The landscapes of past centuries live on beneath the water.
Sometimes the sea retains the appearance of the coast line in its
most typical forms. It is as though the earth had there preserved
behind the glass of a showcase the old human dream of security

in this world, and life eternal in the next. In just such a way has
the Tipasa creek enclosed within the crystal of its waterlogged
quarries, still unfinished columns, and all the African mysticism
of a certain St. Salsa who was so tenderly in love with martyrdom.

In the transference from dry and rocky land to the transparency
of water, nothing seems to have changed: time has stood still.
That is true of almost any place along the Algerian coast. Beyond
reckoning are the landfalls which my friends and I have made
when setting out on an idle car run, ready at any moment to stop
for a bathe or a ruin. Tiny sites picked out in Gsell's *Atlas*,
simple seaside villas with walls half buried in the vines. Five
minutes in the water were enough to show their counterparts.
We would come on weed-smothered stones which marked the
position of some ancient jetty, or, in a neighboring creek, the
shaft of an unfluted column, calling to mind some building on
the water's edge, a temple or a summer house where we would
lie in the sun, mechanically picking at fragments of mosaic with
our fingers. In such spots both earth and sea are quietly, effort-
lessly eloquent of the wisdom which is bred of a life devoted to
the culture of the vine, long before the copper sulphate of the
plants we know today, a wisdom which saw good sense in comfort.

What a disappointment, after all that, to go back to our modern harbors with their scraped sea beds, their dredged channels,
their unbreached quays.

The sea reveals, too, at times what the coast has long forgotten.
Many a trace of antiquity remains only in the water. That is the
case on the seaboard of Provence, toward Agay, Anthéor, Nice,
and Monaco. The coast road is now no more than a death-dealing
racing track filled with young women with too much suntan, and
cars with too much chromium plating. The sea which is scored
by the surfboards of young goddesses in Bikini bathing suits
hides shy relics in deep privacy, out of the range of undersea
sportsmen, beneath a screen of marine vegetation.

Toward the west, toward Fos, toward Narbonne, the muddy
water is thick with the dust of history. Those murky bottoms are
suited to the ghost of Marius, the conqueror of the Cimbri and
the Teutones. At Narbonne, the coast is flat and far from lovely.
Where it touches the sea the ground is soft, and it is easy to
imagine that it is thick with amphorae and leaden anchors. A

whole civilization might well lie buried there. But seen through
a diving mask the plain is gray and hopeless, an undersea Sahara,
with, as its only oasis, a wreck.

🝚   🝚   🝚

I, ALAS, have no first-hand knowledge of the sea about Tyre and
Sidon, nor of the waters of Minet-el-Beida, the "White Harbor,"
half a mile from Ras Shamra, where lies Ugarit, the most aston-
ishing discovery of dry-land archaeology in recent times. The
splendid work done by R. P. Poidebard at Tyre and Sidon has
proved that those eastern seas no less than our own have been
faithful to the memories of mankind. Who knows but that we
may not find in the tiny bay which guards the ghost of the White
Harbor the mingled traces of the people of the Aegean, the
Egyptians, the Hittites, and the Hurrites who passed that way?
On the wall of the room devoted to Oriental antiquities in the
Louvre there is a photograph which has often set me dreaming
for long periods. It shows the "mound" of Ras Shamra, at its
feet a cove very similar to one of the creeks of our own Provence,
with here and there a spike of rock peeping above the surface,
and a strip of yellow sand. Ras Shamra means "Cape of the Fennel"—that same fennel which Provençal housewives use in cooking perch. It was beneath a tangled mass of that fennel that Cl. A.
Schaeffer and G. Chenet found five successive cities, the last of
which was destroyed by the "People of the Sea" and never rebuilt. That occurred in the twelfth century B.C. The sea must
hold some memory of the event, however small.

🝚   🝚   🝚

THE coastal fringe of the Mediterranean, where the works of
men's hands, and their ships—in a sort of eroded and petrified
existence—still survive, is neither a capricious chaos nor yet a
voiceless landscape. This withdrawn world has, to be sure, its
puzzles, but they are not insoluble. As the light of an extinct star
reaches us long after that star has died, so do the voices of a vanished people echo in the silence of the sea. One would dearly like
to understand them.

A day comes when one dreams of breaking free from the mud

and the melancholy harvests of scattered sherds, when one longs to bring together all those many fragments, all those gaping wrecks and shattered bits of earthenware, and build a visible scene.

It is then that the real difficulties begin. To raise an amphora from the sea bed is nothing. To plumb the secrets of an underwater site, to understand its archaeological importance, to set it in historical perspective, is a very different matter. We can always, of course, make a preliminary study of the relevant books, or emerge from the water to plunge into a library; but real efficiency lies in the ability to move beneath the surface with a brain fully furnished, so that at two or twenty fathoms we may be able to summon to our memory, just when we want it, the revealing passage from Grenier, Gsell, or Cagnat, to pick on the illuminating sentence from Strabo, the geographer of Ravenna, Stephanus of Byzantium, or the Pseudo-Scylax. For what matters is a knowledge of the past and the revelation of those discoveries to which that knowledge leads us when confronted by some unexpected segment of reality.

It is not always possible to resist such a temptation. The doctrine of our special pursuit encourages us to yield to it. There would be little value in archaeology if it did not contribute to the evocation of dead forms of life. It would otherwise remain an aimless science, a mere catalogue. There would be no point in struggling with the difficulties of so unusual a medium if we were not animated by the hope of finding a new angle from which to view the past.

I have carried this search for new angles as far as I have been able. I have not been content, as the result of certain discoveries here recounted, to try my powers in the creating of new syntheses or modifying accepted views. As a result of wandering in deep waters I have come to hope that one day the sea will "stop the gaps" in history. In the blue light of the sea's underworld I have come to see this matter of history in a rather different manner from that in which the seekers on dry land have regarded it.

History, too, has a "rendezvous at the anchor." Undersea archaeology will never be of much use until it has been fully developed. Research on land and research in the waters must be tightly bound together. Both must be ruled by the same traditions and the same disciplines. They must form a united front before

too many submarine sites have been irremediably ruined. Archaeology, whether on land or in the sea, cannot be self-sufficient. It
must seek aid from tributary sources which, as it advances, it may
help to enrich—epigraphy, numismatics, and the history of religions. "Whenever archaeology works in a vacuum," George Dax
has said, "the knowledge which it brings us of the past is strangely
incomplete."

That is why the reader will find in this book many references to
ancient texts and classic manuals; that is why he may find that
at times it leads him far from the sea bed. It must be so if we
would remain faithful to a method which may be described in the
formula "by plummet and the printed word"—the plummet
which takes us into the depths, the printed word which enables
us to understand what we find there.

To those who would criticize me adversely, on the ground that
I have said too much or too little about a subject which is still
new, a subject of which the raw material is, in the words of a
specialist, "meager," I would reply in the words of Marc Bloch:
"Previous to Boucher de Perthes there were as many flints in the
alluvial deposits of the Seine as there are today. But the inquiring
mind was absent. There was no such thing as prehistory . . .
All historical research needs from the start a discipline of direction. In the beginning is the Word . . . When the explorer sets
out upon a journey he begins by mapping an itinerary. He knows
perfectly well that he will not follow it in every detail. But if he
did not have it, he would be in grave danger of falling a victim
to the dangers of casual wandering."

I do not for a moment claim to be the Boucher de Perthes of
undersea archaeology. I am only an explorer who has made up
his mind, once and for all, not to waste his efforts in aimless
wandering.

2. A Cargo of Masterpieces
at Twenty Fathoms

*The richest Museum of antiquities
in the whole world is still inaccessible. I mean the sea bed of the
Mediterranean. . . . We can
explore without much difficulty
both earth and air, but beneath the
surface of the sea we are far from
being able to compete with the
fishes who, as Saint Augustine put
it, saunter at will along the path-
ways of the Deep.*
SALOMON REINACH

THE OLDEST IN DATE, AND TILL NOW THE MOST REWARDING OF
all our deep-sea explorations, was carried out from 1907 to 1913,
off Mahdia, which is a small Tunisian port. (The submarine
undertakings at Cerigotto in 1900—to which I refer in Chapter
Eight—admirable though they were of their kind, can scarcely be
regarded as an example of undersea archaeology proper.) It
brought to light a sunken ship which had been carrying a cargo
of works of art. The story of this adventure is instructive in more
ways than one, and deserves detailed narration.

Mahdia is the name of an Arab town in the Gulf of Gabes,
situated between Sousse—the ancient Hadrumetum, and Sfax—
formerly known as Taparura. It is a small, sheltered harbor hu-
manly contrived in the living rock. The workmanship is Punic.
The word used to describe a place of this description is *cothon*,
doubtless derived from a Semitic root meaning to cut or carve.

20

Mahdia has seen the passage of several cultures, migrant peoples and conquering armies. It is now no more than a fishing village spread out upon a promontory jutting into a sea which is often rough and unwelcoming. The Arab houses are massed on one side, the rest of the peninsula being overrun with cropped grass. High walls stand in close juxtaposition with Punic masonry, Roman cement, and Berber buildings, the confusion being eloquent of a complicated past which had this in common, that those who lived here were forever pinched between a harsh mainland and an angry sea.

𝔐   𝔐   𝔐

WHEN, on the cursed soil of Carthage, Scipio had discharged his debt to history by quoting two lines of Homer, Mahdia was annexed by Rome along with the rest of the Punic legacy. Caesar visited it after having dawdled away nine months at Cleopatra's side, and before driving Cato to suicide at Utica. Later, the port enjoyed a period of prosperity as the flourishing city of a proconsular province, before becoming a haunt of Barbary pirates. A day came when Roger II, King of Sicily, and the first European sovereign to set foot on the continent of Africa after the Moslem conquest (the Pisans had stolen a march on Roger by taking Bône in 1034), dispatched a fleet of twenty ships to assist his friend, El Hassam, Emir of Mahdia, when that place was besieged by the Prince of Bougie in 1123. In this way it came about that Norman pride gained a foothold in this tiny corner of Africa which had already been familiar with the trade of Carthage and the might of Rome.

Mahdia, then, is one of those staging posts where history, in its various phases, has bifurcated, but where few traces remain of vanished passions and ancient struggles: one among sleepy little places such as are to be found in plenty on the African mainland. It is not, however, a matter of indifference to us that chance chose to endow it with an additional prestige, archaeological as well as historical. It is there that we find past and present richly and intimately mingled in the sea: it is there that an ancient wreck was located with a more than usually large crop of "finds."

The discovery would never have been made had not the quadrilateral of several sea miles lying off Mahdia continued to attract the sponge divers who for two thousand years have been drawn to the spot from always the same Greek villages. In the old days they went about their work naked, reaching the required depth by means of a stone attached to their feet. Nowadays they have been replaced by helmet divers. The boat they use is the local *sacolève*, which carries one enormous sail, and can be propelled with oars like the vessels of Homeric days. (The word is also written "sacolève," "sakolève," and even "sacolère." Its tradition is less ancient than that of the Greek divers, and it is now rigged with a *livarde*, or spritsail.)

In the neighborhood of Cape Ifrika, which gave its name to the continent, the coast is flat and the water relatively shallow. At close on five thousand yards offshore, the depth is no more than twenty fathoms. One might swim around the whole of Africa and at no point find such another long, shelving formation covered by a thin layer of mud in which marine animal life flourishes. For the most part the continental land mass ends in a sharp escarpment from which deep water is never very distant.

It is when the *sacolève* has left Mahdia and doubled the lighthouse of Sidi Jaber that the anchor is dropped overboard and the fishing begins. The diver enters the sea from the bow, while the boat rides the swell. Amidships is the pump, mounted low in the hull, with two assistants turning the wheels with a slow, continuous movement. Other divers, awaiting their turn, recline in the stern. As soon as one returns to the surface, another puts on his helmet and climbs overboard. Each evening the boat returns to the port of Mahdia with a sticky harvest smelling of ozone and a Brittany beach at low tide.

In the month of June, 1907, a diver belonging to one of these groups, working at some distance from the shore, noticed in the course of one of his descents a submarine "tell" or mound projecting from the general level of the mudbed. When he returned to the surface he reported that he had seen something that "looked like a lot of big guns." A more attentive examination of the site revealed fragments of bronze corroded by the sea, and a deal of broken earthenware. These remains were duly handed over to the local authorities, and the find was officially catalogued.

The Director of Tunisian Antiquities, who at that time was

Alfred Merlin, realized the interest attaching to this discovery. He at once organized a quick underwater survey and devoted all his efforts to recovering from this particular site everything of archaeological and instructional value. The enterprise was, at this time, one of especial daring, and he managed to enlist the interest of the Maritime Prefect of Bizerta, Admiral Jean Baëhme, as well as of several distinguished patrons of the arts: the Duc de Loubat, James Hazen Hyde, and Edouard de Billy. He obtained financial aid from the Government of Tunis, from the Ministry of Public Instruction, from the French Institute, and from the Académie des Inscriptions. His action makes it clear that the first duty of an archaeologist is to obtain sufficient monetary support to enable him to carry out his task. This is a lesson which we should do well to remember. (Alfred Merlin later became Curator in Chief of the Greek and Roman Antiquities at the Louvre. He has been kind enough to give me the benefit of his great experience, not only in this matter of the Mahdia hoard, but of all the other sites of which I shall speak later.)

Five exploratory expeditions were undertaken in 1908, 1909, 1910, 1911, and 1913. Greek divers were employed, because at that time they were almost the only men capable of working at a depth of twenty fathoms. They were joined by a Turk, whose ambition it was to obtain from the Bey of Tunis, the Nicham Iftikhar, a distinction which was conferred upon him in recognition of the services he rendered, and of the high degree of professional devotion which he had shown in the matter.

The Navy helped by sending the tug *Cyclope*, commanded by Enseigne de vaisseau Tavera. To this the Ponts et Chaussées added the whaler *Eugène Resal*. These vessels, however, were not always available, and most of the work had to be entrusted to *sacolèves*. With a favorable wind these boats took about an hour to reach the site, three miles out from Mahdia Point. It was necessary, too, to reckon with the vagaries of a sea which Sallust, in his own day, had described as "terrible." It quite often happened that sudden storms carried away, in the course of a single night, the buoys which had been set to mark the limits of the area to be searched, and whenever this happened, the whole laborious task of sounding had to begin over again.

The main scene lay at a depth of just under twenty fathoms.

Its central feature consisted of some sixty or so columns. They were lying side by side in six rows, one behind the other, from north to south. The space thus covered was about thirty-three to thirty-five yards long. The rows contained an unequal number of columns varying in size.

All around lay a mass of marble fragments piled up in no sort of order —capitals and bases, carefully squared blocks, architectural elements of many different types. Mixed with these objects, and especially towards the northern end of the site, was a profusion of broken earthenware, all that remained of the pottery which had been on board— amphorae, very few of which were intact, vases of many kinds used for the carrying of oil, wine, water, foodstuffs, and ingredients needed by the crew during the voyage. . . . Further columns, marble blocks, amphorae, and anchors were found under a deep layer of mud from which they stuck out in a confused mass. Before any results could be achieved, it was necessary to move the various obstructions, and to dig into and clear away the enveloping slime. A. Merlin: "Les fouilles sous-marines de Mahdia"; *Revue Tunisienne*, 1911, pp. 113 ff.

Most of the column shafts were rather more than twelve feet in height, and about twenty-five inches in diameter. Such massive objects were very difficult to move. As soon as they were disturbed, the water in their immediate neighborhood became dark and opaque. The diver worked with his hands, kneeling on the sea bed, feeling his way forward, now contriving a small tunnel through which a hawser could be passed, now scooping out a trench by which he might reach something which, by the feel of it, promised to be interesting. So strong was the current at this depth that the men had to keep up a continuous struggle. From time to time one of them would return to the surface in an exhausted condition, and not a few of the operations ended in tragedy. It was impossible to work under water for more than thirty or forty minutes on end, and quite often the state of the sea or the strength of the current made it necessary to suspend all diving for a while.

When the men managed to dig under such of the columns as could be separated—or to work their way between them [wrote Merlin] they very soon came on a layer of timber, about eight inches thick, and in a condition, more or less, of decomposition. Penetration of this protective envelope brought to light objects of a more delicate type: bronze statuettes of fine workmanship, fragments of beautifully ornamented furniture. It seems clear that when the vessel foundered, she plunged straight to the bottom without breaking up, having sustained a certain amount of damage, but not turning turtle. The rotting timber had once been the ship's deck. The columns and some of the less fragile objects had rested upon it, the columns having been laid sufficiently far apart to make movement between them possible, and so as not to interfere with the handling of the vessel. The bales containing the smaller and more precious portions of the cargo were stowed between decks. The hold was filled with works of art in metal or marble. Two large openings, one forward, the other aft, and so arranged as to correspond with the gaps in the stowing of the columns, gave access to the interior of the ship.

The principal articles contained in this cargo and saved from the sea in the manner I have described now fill six rooms in the Bardo Museum at Tunis. The main items are as follows: An Eros as a Victorious Archer, a bronze of rather less than fifty inches in height: a Hermes of Dionysos, signed "Boethos" (Picard is of the opinion that these two bronzes form part of a single group). The Eros would then be interpreted as a personification of Ἀγῶν [Competition, or Conflict]. He places Boethos in the third century B.C., though previously he was held to have worked in the second); two large cornices, which were almost certainly figureheads taken from a votive monument; eight large statuettes, three of which were grotesques and represented dwarfs playing at knucklebones, and a clown; numerous decorative motifs, and fragments of a number of beds, urns, and candelabra.

The works in marble are no less numerous and no less beautiful: a bust of Aphrodite, a Pan, a Niobe, two Niobids, two Satyrs, one male, one female, and a Youth. In addition to these fragments of full-sized statues, there are two torsos of youths, several statuettes, and some fine decorative pieces—candelabra and bowls in the Neo-Attic style.

This mere listing has something of the dryness of a catalogue. It can give no idea of the thrilling reality. That could be conveyed only if each separate dive were described, and each hour of the time spent waiting on the suface of a sea being thus forced to yield up its secrets. Gods emerged from the water, covered with shellfish, unrecognizable, and many of them mutilated. The operation went on, and suddenly a piece of bronze released from the mud would turn out to be a missing part of the Eros, one that completed the pose and restored the sense of life of what, till then, had been a dead object. The boat lay rolling on the swell. Twenty fathoms down, in a sea so muddy that no eye could penetrate it, a man was busy searching for the past, hard on the track of yet further masterpieces. His only means of communication was the safety line. If he signaled that he wanted to be pulled up, the reason was that he was bringing with him yet another portion of the drowned treasure. A row of faces lining the gunwale watched while he was slowly hoisted to the surface, bearing in his arms another god dripping water and draped in seaweed. It is easy to imagine the globular brass helmet, the shining rubber suit, the lump of corroded bronze, and the outstretched arms of the watchers, as eager to grasp it as rescuers in some dramatic lifesaving adventure.

There were, too, long hours during which the wreck seemed to refuse all access to the searchers, when the sluggish, muddy water kept curiosity at bay, when the divers went overboard, one after the other, only to return exhausted, empty-handed, incapable of speech. Deep down, in the secret places of the sea, they were waging a struggle in which none could help them. It was a question of waiting until, under the pressure of their attack, something gave, a column consented to be moved, a sculptured limb to be torn free. This unrelenting battle went on in a world very different from ours, far from the sky, and in a fog of liquid mud. The crew of the *sacolève*, and the archaeologist in charge, kept their eyes riveted to the man on duty at the pump, who kept tight hold of the safety line and was the only one of those present who could make a guess at what was happening below. From time to time a murmur would escape him—"He's just moved forward," or, "He's onto something."

Anxious eyes were turned on the roughening sea. "In half an hour, perhaps less, we shall have to start back . . ." Far away, the coast of Africa showed as no more than a thin line on the horizon.

"It was," says Merlin, "the most exciting of all the operations in which I have been privileged to take part in the whole course of my career."

The divers could not find words strong enough to express their feelings about the mud which the smallest gesture set swirling. All the same, this mud it was that had protected most of the

works of art from the depredations of shellfish. "It may have
smothered everything, but it preserved everything," writes Merlin. It fulfilled, in fact, the same protective role as the desert
sands of Egypt. What it covered and buried was shielded from
the assault of rock-boring animals—*Pholas* and *Lithodomus.*
Mud had protected one of the faces of an Ionic capital; the
other was terribly worn away. Seeing so much clean, sharp defini-
tion neighbored, on the same piece of marble, by such terrible
scars, we felt as deeply moved as we might be at the sight of
some human loveliness horribly mutilated.

☙ ☙ ☙

GLAMOUR still surrounds the Mahdia adventure, even after forty
years, for it was the first triumph of undersea archaeology. It was
amazing luck that the first ancient wreck on which divers were
able to lay their hands should have been carrying a load of
masterpieces. It is as though the sea, wishing to make offering of
a vessel which had lain for two thousand years in the depths,
had chosen the richest.

"Nothing comparable has come to light," wrote Salomon
Reinach, "since Pompeii and Herculaneum."

The Mahdia incident showed archaeology in a very different
light from that expected by the layman. Its fascination derives
not merely from the hazardous nature of a twenty-fathom operation, but also from the fact that the object of search was neither
a palace nor a tomb, but a ship. Wherever and whenever a ship
goes to the bottom with all hands, there is drama. The only remains of the burning of Troy are fire-blackened stones, but the
sight of them has power to move us still, and how much more a
great hulk settled in the sand, a timber shell which has remained
for so long in one place, anchors which have not been shifted
since the day when they failed to bring safety to a storm-battered
vessel.

But that is not all. This particular wreck is, as it were, an in-
ventory, an epitome—than which none could be better—of
civilization as it existed at the moment of the disaster. Only on
board a ship could one hope to find assembled, in so small a
space, so great a weight of evidence—cooking pots and millstones,
lamps and foodstuffs, with, in addition, a cargo of the kind re-

covered at Mahdia. It is as though a whole segment of human life had gone, complete in every detail, to the bottom of the sea. The great aim of archaeology is to restore the warmth and the truth of life to dead objects. Even on the sea bed marbles and bronzes still retain the power to move us.

But not only had the sea hidden away a large Roman ship in a state of preservation better than we could ever have dared to hope, it had left sufficient testimony to make possible a plausible reconstruction of its story.

We know, as near as no matter, what sort of a vessel she was. Her over-all measurements were approximately a hundred and twenty feet from stem to stern, and thirty-six beam. In other words, she was a merchant craft, a "round" ship rigged for sailing, a *corbita*, certainly not a galley. The type has persisted in the Mediterranean for five or six centuries. It was not an outstanding design, and doubtless had deteriorated under Roman influence. With her square canvas and excessive superstructure, she was markedly inferior to her Greek and Phoenician forebears, but almost certainly her capacity was greater, though that in itself spelled danger.

Driven by a storm, and far too heavily laden with a deadweight of marble, this Mahdia ship sank rapidly, carrying with her at least one member of her crew, for a human fibula was recovered from the wreck. The animals on board also perished: there were bones of pigs and sheep scattered about the sea bed.

Whence was the shipwrecked vessel sailing? Thanks to the extremely competent observations carried out by Merlin, this point has been elucidated. "One of the most spectacular discoveries in connection with the Mahdia wreck," he writes, "was that of a number of inscribed Greek slabs. These were probably shipped as ballast. Alternatively, they may have been curiosities intended for the collectors' market. They are especially welcome as furnishing us with the most valuable evidence about the port from which the vessel had sailed."

Two of these texts engraved, one on a stele, the other on a small marble column, are decrees issued by the *paraloi*, those Athenian citizens who formed the crew of the trireme *Pasalos*, which was one of the two Sacred Ships. (The Athenians maintained at the Piraeus two triremes, the *Pasalos* and the *Salammia*, which were employed on missions of high importance. They

were always in readiness to sail at short notice, and fully equipped.
One of their duties was to fetch criminals to stand trial at
Athens. In wartime they served as flagships.) It seems certain,
therefore, that Athens was the port of registration. The works
of art and the building materials found in this particular ship
seem to have come from that city, and of some of them we can
say for certain that they were taken on board at her home port,
the Piraeus. Doubtless it was in the arsenal there that the monument in the form of a ship's prow stood, from which two cornices, adorned with the heads of Dionysos and Ariadne, had
been wrenched away.

Two heavy cornices of bronze (maximum height about eighteen
inches, minimum, an inch and a half) were obviously intended for use
as a pair. Their upper and lower edges are beveled, and in the lateral
channel there are holes for nails. They had been used to decorate an
ex-voto monument, a trophy in the form of a ship's prow, some sort of
pedestal, doubtless of the same general type as that on which the Victory of Samothrace is mounted. They capped the ends of the beams
which protruded on either side of the prow, serving as a protection for
the hull against the shock of collision. Rising from the corners are two
superb half-busts, facing one another, and crowned with ivy (about
one inch in height). That on the left represents Ariadne, dressed in a
light tunic suspended from the arms and shoulders; that on the right
shows an unclad Dionysos, his long, curling hair falling lightly about
his neck. Round his forehead there is a narrow fillet with a hint of
horns.*

It is from the Piraeus, too—we know that Asklepios had a
temple there—that an ex-voto comes with the figure of the god
reclining on a couch in front of a table laden with food, with
his daughter, Hygeia, seated in front of him, and attended by a
servingman and a number of worshippers. The white, heavily
veined marble, from which the columns, capitals, and statues
are cut, could have come only from Hymettus.
So much for the port of origin. It remains to establish the date.
One of the objects recovered from the sea provides invaluable
evidence on this point. It is a lamp with its charred wick still in

* Merlin and Poinssot: "Cratères et candélabres de marbre trouvés en
mer près de Mahdia," p. 6.

position. It seems certain that this formed part of the ship's furniture. Its characteristic shape shows that it was made at the end of the second century B.C. It must, therefore, have been in use during the early years of the first.

There is one historical event which seems to fit in with the evidence here described—the sacking of Athens by Sulla in 86 B.C. Not only does the date coincide with what we know, but we have textual proof that, at this period, the arsenal and storehouses of the Piraeus were looted and burned—which would explain the presence on the Mahdia ship of ex-voto figures from monuments in the Port of Athens.

This hypothesis is so plausible in the matter of the cargo as to seem almost certain. But the vessel's destination is more open to doubt. What was this consignment of Greek *objets d'art* doing in the Gulf of Gabes? Was it being taken to Rome? We must assume that it was unless we can find some other place to which, at that period, a cargo of this nature was likely to be sent. If Italy was, in fact, its destination, then we are forced to the conclusion—far from impossible—that a storm had driven the ship very far off its course. The direct route from Athens to Ostia would have passed between Italy and Sicily, through the Strait of Messina. It must have been after doubling Cape Malea that she was driven toward the African coast.

It does seem, however, that the gale which sent the ship southwards must have veered suddenly in a very odd manner and been blowing in a northerly direction, because the way in which the anchors were lying round the wreck leads us to suppose that the vessel was being forced *out to sea* when the catastrophe occurred. The evidence goes to show that five anchors in all were dropped, including the heaviest, the sheet anchor, which was used only in cases of extreme danger. Now, all were dropped in a straight line from the bows, along the side facing the coast. This, presumably, would have been done only if the ship had been making for Mahdia and wanted to avoid being blown out to sea. It seems that this is a case of a ship bound for Mahdia and trying to prevent itself from being blown out to sea rather than a ship blown toward the shore by the wind and letting go its anchors to avoid driving aground.

There is no doubt whatever that the ship was found lying on a general north-south axis, or that the anchors had been dropped on the south side, at some little distance from the wreck's final position. In a letter dated February 16, 1947, Poinssot wrote to l'Eprévier: "Since anchors, as a rule, are carried for'ard, there is every reason to suppose that when disaster struck the ship, her bows were facing south or, more accurately, southeast. The divers state that the wooden deck on which the cargo of columns lay terminates at the southern end of the seventh row, beyond which there is nothing but sand. It is worth noting that the anchors lie, not, like the rest of the cargo, in a mass of sludge which has gone black as the result of metallic decomposition, but in an area of clear sand. There is only a narrow fringe of blackish mud round each of them."

An opposite point of view is expressed in an account by Captain Taillez: "Two anchors were found lying on top of the sand a few yards from the columns. They must, therefore, have been stowed when the ship foundered." Merlin writes: "The position of the anchors, which lie quite definitely *outside* the area of the wreck . . ." Of the five anchors dropped overboard two thousand years ago, two were raised in the course of the salvaging operations carried out in 1909 and 1911. These are now in the Bardo Museum at Tunis. Two others were raised by the G.R.S. (Groupe d'Études de Recherches Sous-Marines), and one of them is on view in the Toulon Naval Museum. None of the four carried any inscription. The sheet anchor, which, to judge by the dimensions of the central opening, must have been twice the size of the others, is still, presumably, at the bottom of the sea.

The extremely unequal value of the cargo leads one to the conclusion that the ship was *not* carrying a load of booty to Rome on Sulla's orders, for, had that been the case, the objects would, one assumes, have been chosen with greater care. It seems more likely that we have to deal with a contractor's consignment rather than a collection of spoil from a conquered country. It is true that the Mahdia ship was carrying works of art of undoubted value, but these were in close juxtaposition with marble blocks which clearly had been newly worked and, in some cases, were unfinished. "The statues had been loaded in sections waiting to be assembled on arrival. The capitals, decorated with griffin heads, had their volutes supported on rough projections of solid marble. The candelabra and bowls, parts of which had not yet received their painted or gilded decoration, came, clearly, from workshops engaged in supplying goods for export. The drums of the columns are mere rough-hewn cylinders, without fluting or astragal, and must have been shipped straight from the quarry." All these things point to a commercial "order" rather than to a collection of war booty. "Surely," writes Merlin, "Athens could have supplied the all-powerful Sulla with more magnificent trophies than these examples of routine commercial exploitation all made from commonplace materials?"

Even terra-cotta tiles were found in the wreck, but these may well have formed part of the vessel's normal equipment. Similar objects have been noted in the case of other ancient wrecks, notably at Albenga (see below). They were doubtless used for the roofing of the wheelhouse. F. Benoît has assured me that ships in the Middle Ages, plying on the Rhône, carried a tiled construction called the "Timbanao," from the Latin word *tympanum.* The decks of the ships of Nemi were made of tiles.

Carcopino, on the other hand, takes the view that the hypothesis put forward originally by Salomon Reinach is the right one, that the cargo almost certainly represents Sulla's booty and may be taken as·exemplifying his artistic taste. Carcopino has produced convincing arguments in support of this opinion. He points out that Sulla had an especial liking for mimes and clowns, which would explain the bronze figurines. He stresses the fact that the presence on board of a Hermes and a Dionysos would accord with the title of "New Dionysos" with which the cities of Greece welcomed the conqueror of Mithridates. Finally, he gives proof that Italian taste was influenced by articles of furniture of the same general type as those found at Mahdia. This influence, according to Pliny, began to make itself felt after Sulla's return. It remains to explain the presence of the unfinished columns. It seems possible that these had been put in hand for use in the Olympeion at Athens, that not all the capitals which should have accompanied them were sunk off Mahdia, and that some, at least, got safely into port and were among the similar objects later recovered from the ruins of Pompeii. If these were not the actual capitals belonging to the Mahdia cargo, they were at least their younger brothers and had been copied from Greek originals.

It looks as though the return of the Roman dictator marked the beginnings of a renaissance and gave rise to a new fashion, if not a new style, in architecture and furnishings. Here is something to reconcile us to the rather light-fingered man who burned the Piraeus. *"Crimen deorum erat Sylla felix"* ("the Gods were guilty of Sulla's good fortune"). That, at least, is obvious. But was the looting for which he has been blamed any more reprehensible than the ransacking of the East by the Crusaders which enriched our churches with treasures and played its part in the flowering of Western art—or than the pillaging of Italy by Napoleon? Pillage or homage? There has always been an element of love in the theft by continental peoples of the artistic heritage of the seafaring nations. It was not altogether a bad idea on Sulla's part to show Rome what his new conquests could achieve. The Greece which educated Rome was not, to be sure, Greece in her prime, but it was through the one that Rome learned to respect the other. At the very heart of Athens, Sulla had declared that he would show mercy to the living out of respect for the dead. In the last analysis, therefore, it is difficult to know whether we should show more resentment than gratitude for the "pillaging" in which he indulged.

The case of Verres was by no means exceptional. Cicero was forever plaguing his friend Atticus with requests for Greek bronzes and marbles. We know that another ship, with just such a cargo of works of art, foundered, at a somewhat later date—round about 50 B.C.—off Anticythera. It was from this wreck that the famous bronze "Youth" was recovered. We know in what prodigalities of theft a Romanized Berber prince, Juba II, indulged in order to adorn Caesarea, his Mauretanian capital.

Merlin has, in fact, suggested that it may well have been this same Juba II for whom the Mahdia consignment was intended. This theory was put forward when the first finds were brought to the surface. Subsequent operations, however, by enabling us to give the first century B.C. as the date of the wreck, made it necessary to abandon a view which no longer fitted the chronological facts.

Perhaps there is still an element of uncertainty about the Mahdia cargo, its destination, and even the date of the disaster which overtook it. At the time when Sulla was busy looting Athens, Africa was still in the hands of the supporters of Marius. It would, therefore, be rather surprising to learn that the ship in question was making for an African port. On the other hand, if we put the date forward thirty-five years, making it contemporary with that of the Anticythera wreck, that particular argument falls to the ground.

Where history is silent, archaeology is sometimes inclined to be rather too talkative.

GENEROUS though the Mahdia wreck has been, there are reasons to suppose that the sum total of its secrets has not yet been revealed. That is why when, thirty-five years later, Merlin was informed that the Groupe de Recherches de Toulon was proposing to devote one of its routine dives to a further examination of the site, he welcomed the idea with enthusiasm.

A team of nine free-divers proceeded to the spot on board the sloop *Elie Monnier*. Harbor launch No. 8 was also pressed into service. Commandant Philippe Taillez and Commandant J. Y. Cousteau were in charge of the operations. They took with them the report drawn up by Ensign Tavera, who, in 1908, as commander of the tug *Cyclope* had discovered the exact location of the wreck. Unfortunately, the points of reference chosen at that time—an isolated tree, a thicket, a ruin—no longer existed. When she was five miles offshore, the *Elie Monnier* began to make a series of reconnaissance sweeps. All the members of the team leveled their glasses on the desperately flat coast line where, at wide intervals, a number of ruins, each indistinguishable from its fellows, was visible, alternating with similar isolated trees. For five days the divers carried out an exhausting search at a depth of twenty fathoms. An area of approximately nine acres of sea bed, which had been "squared" by means of submerged lines, was examined square yard by square yard, but all in vain. An all-over survey, carried out by a diver attached to a leaden weight and towed by launch No. 8, did at last reveal the whereabouts of the "big guns" on which so much depended. The wreck was found lying some 220 yards from the spot mentioned in Tavera's report.

Next day a preliminary examination was made. "The sight," wrote Philippe Taillez, "was a thrilling one. All that remained of the Mahdia 'Galley' after two thousand years, amounted to a collection of widely spaced lumps, with a number of columns arranged in four main rows. The general effect, in spite of the disturbance caused by the Greek divers, was overwhelmingly that of a ship, thirty-six feet wide by one hundred and twenty long, lying on a north-south axis. Fragments of the ribs of the hull, of the deck, and of the keel were visible beneath the columns, or in the intervals between them." *

Five days had been spent in finding the wreck, and very little time was left in which to carry out a serious investigation. The free-divers and the *Elie Monnier* were due to report back at Toulon for naval duties. In order to enlarge the breach made by the helmet divers in 1913, four columns, the heaviest of which weighed three tons, were secured by slings and hoisted onto the afterdeck of the *Elie Monnier*, whose derrick was hard put to it to lift them. Two anchors were also raised.

The columns were covered with marine flora and fauna which had burrowed almost to their centers. They emerged from the sea in a rich cascade of water and vivid colors. The anchors, brutally torn from their oozy bed, were hauled obliquely to the surface, leaving behind them a·wake of liquid mud. It took a lot of hard work to raise one of the capitals which had been deeply buried; the crust of sand in which it was encased was quickly scraped off and a block of pure marble came into view, an Ionic volute in a perfect state of preservation, with the marks of the chisel still clearly visible. The divers worked under the columns, using improvised dredges. These implements dug deeply into the mud, raising an infernal cloud of black ooze and bubbles. The men crawled forward flat on their stomachs through a sea of liquid sludge, churning it up with their bodies as they worked, fumbling about in it with their hands. Each time they touched a solid object their hearts gave a jump. A great shoal of fishes surrounded us, prodigiously interested in what we were doing, and turning to their own advantage the freshly opened furrows, like birds agog at sight of a peasant digging. The groupers in particular, weighing from twenty to forty pounds apiece, never stirred far from our "scrapers." Until the very end we were on the most friendly and trusting terms with the inhabitants of the sea-jungle.

In all, only about eleven hours of these exploratory labors were productive. The main object, which was to mark the position of the wreck and to carry out a preliminary reconnaissance, had

* "La 'Galère' de Mahdia"; *Revue Maritime*, May, 1949, pp. 574-585.

been achieved, and Merlin, in his comment on the operation, was able to say: "The first results obtained show that there is good reason to believe that the possibilities of the site have not been exhausted. It seems likely that important discoveries will be made when the search is resumed. It is certain that once the skeleton of the ship has been freed from the accumulated deposits of the sea much valuable information will be gained."

Several bronze rings which were found on board the wreck in 1908 and 1913, now in the Tunis Museum, have been identified by Jean Poujade as forming part of the running tackle of the ship. It has long been known, from the evidence of bas-reliefs, how this running tackle was composed, and it now seems probable that we have in our hands examples of the actual rings and of the fastenings by which they were attached to the mast. (See Jean Poujade: *La Route des Indes et ses Navires*, 1946, p. 132.)

The men who carried out the diving operations at Mahdia and who saw and touched the wreck share this opinion, but they know, too, that this type of search can be brought to a successful issue only if the men on the job—whether archaeologists or not— can be assured of a supply of efficient technical equipment. Unfortunately, what they chiefly need is powerful lifting apparatus, a dredger, and a vessel specifically designed, as was the *Elie Monnier*, for assisting an organized diving program. Such things are beyond the reach of our archaeological services with their limited financial resources. It must, however, be stressed that no attempt which cannot rely upon the necessary material means will succeed. Imperfect equipment will only break up still further what remains of the wreck, without any appreciable gain. (It should be put on record that the G.R.S. has in its keeping at the Toulon Arsenal a Greek Ionic capital of marble, with about three feet of the column attached, an anchor, and a small amphora, all belonging to the Mahdia hoard.)

᪥ ᪥ ᪥

IN connection with this last of the Mahdia expeditions, mention should be made of recent laboratory researches which are likely to prove of great interest to archaeologists. The divers of the G.R.S. succeeded in recovering from the Mahdia site one of the ship's nails. They had, on another occasion, and on another site, about which I shall have something to say later, at Anthéor, on the Côte d'Azur, found a similar nail. These two objects were entrusted to Madame A. R. Weill, one of the scientific staff of the Naval Laboratory, for purposes of analysis.—This is not the first time that physicists and chemists have come to the aid of archaeologists. There have been illustrious precedents. The great Berthelot did not disdain to write an *"Introduction à l'étude de la Chimie des Anciens"* (1887; second edition, 1938). A votive figurine, bearing the name Gudea, and found at Lagash, was declared by Berthelot to be made of pure copper. He also carried out analyses of a number of bronzes.

Madame A. R. Weill has been kind enough to show me the results of her work (published in the *Revue de la Metallurgie*, 1952). The essential facts are as follows. Ultraviolet analysis shows that the *chemical composition of both nails is the same:*

Copper: basic element
Silicum: approximately 0.5%
Magnesium: approximately 0.5%
Iron: approximately 0.5%
Silver: a few traces
Aluminum: very faint traces.

That the Mahdia and Anthéor nails should have the same composition is a remarkable fact. The archaeological evidence leads to the conclusion that the two wrecks were roughly contemporary. The lives of ships in the ancient world were short, and we can only suppose that those of Mahdia and Anthéor were of about the same age. It is to be assumed that the copper of which both the nails were made had the same origin.

The spectrographic analysis and the X-ray indications show that the metal content is 98.5 percent pure. "Now, the most carefully refined copper of our own day still contains as much as 10 percent impurity," writes Madame Weill. "We are faced, therefore, with the fact that ancient articles which are found to contain not more than 1 to 2 percent impurity were made from non-alloyed copper. It can be said for certain that we are dealing with no raw material, but with an ore which has been treated by skillful metallurgists."

Archaeologists have, as a rule, assumed that ships' nails in the

ancient world were made of bronze. This error is due chiefly to
the use of a Latin vocabulary which we have probably miscon-
strued. The English specialist R. J. Forbes, in *Metallurgy in
Antiquity*, has given much thought to this problem. He proposes
to distinguish clearly in ancient metallurgy the different varieties
of copper or pre-bronze, among which should be included the
earliest alloys of copper, lead, and antimony, refined copper, and
nonpurified copper.

The nails found in the ships of Nemi were also of pure copper.
When chemically analyzed and examined under the microscope,
they showed a degree of purity comparable to that of the copper
sold at the present day—approximately 99.60 to 99.71 percent
of copper, but with impurities differing from those revealed in
the copper of Mahdia and Anthéor: 0.03 to 0.06 percent lead;
0.18 to 0.25 percent iron. We are forced, therefore, to assume
that the refining of copper made considerable strides in the
course of a century (the date attributed to the Mahdia wreck is
86 B.C., and to the ships of Caligula at Nemi, 37-41 A.D.), and
that the copper used in each case had a different origin. That
used in the Nemi nails seems to have been an Italian chalcopy-
rite, while that of the Mahdia ship may have come from Spain,
a theory which is suggested by the presence of silver traces.

"If the metallic impurities in the nails of Mahdia and Anthéor
are identical," writes Madame Weill, "there is reason to suppose that the two objects came from the same source and were
probably treated in the same workshop, or at least with identical
charges. It is probable, therefore, that they are within twenty
years or so of the same age."

The two nails, however, suffered different fates. Whereas that
of Mahdia is intact, its Anthéor companion has become completely sulphurated. Madame Weill attributes this high degree
of transformation into pyrite to the presence in the sea off
Anthéor of sulphurous elements produced by the disintegration
of vegetable and animal matter. "It still remains a matter for
surprise, however, that the metal should have been attacked
throughout the whole extent of its mass."

We can only echo Madame Weill's hope that such analyses
will become more frequent. It would be interesting to know the
metallic composition of the nails in the ship of Albenga, which
seems to have been wrecked at a date anterior to those of Anthéor

and Mahdia. It may well be that this ship, which was carrying
Companian amphorae similar to those of Anthéor, came from
the same place and had the same type of nail.

ₓ   ₓ   ₓ

A SIMILAR analysis could be usefully applied to other metals,
especially to lead, which was widely used in the ancient world.
"Research of this kind is still so rare," writes Madame Weill in
conclusion, "that we are not yet in a position to classify antique
objects merely on the strength of laboratory examination. But
already that possibility has been envisaged. Forbes has traced the
whereabouts of various mineral deposits at different periods, and
we have only to add the results of chemical research to have at
our disposition a series of frames of reference into which the
observations which follow can be inserted."

There were several leaden ingots, or "pigs," on board the
Mahdia ship, with curved upper surfaces and flat under ones.
They measured roughly fifteen and a half inches in length, and
weighed between sixty-two and sixty-eight pounds. They were
stamped with Latin characters.

Did these form part of the cargo, or was the lead present on
board for the purpose of carrying out running repairs, such as
patching the outer sheathing of the hull? It was thought at first
that the lead came from the Laurium mines, but Besnier has
pointed out that "the Mahdia ingots resemble in every respect
those known to have come from a Spanish source." This is not
easy to explain if the lead formed part of a cargo sailing from
Greece, but offers no difficulty if it was part of the normal ship's
stores of a vessel fitted out in a Roman port. A sample which was
analyzed in the Tunis Chemical Laboratory yielded 98.60 percent lead and 0.95 percent copper. A pig of Spanish lead contained 99.55 percent lead and 0.42 percent copper.

3.   The Journeys of Dionysos

*Oneravi vinum, et tunc erat contra
aurum, misi Romam . . .*
  *Scitis, magna navis magnam for-
titudinem habet.*

                  Satyricon
                 PETRONIUS

Two wrecked ships belonging to the world of classical antiquity have recently been found in the Mediterranean. Both resemble the Mahdia specimen in that they were cargo vessels, and all three hulks would seem to date from approximately the same period, that is to say from the first century B.C. It seems likely that the time can be still further whittled down to the first half of that century.

The lading of the two recently discovered ships did not, however, consist of works of art. Both were carrying wine jars, or amphorae. They were, in fact, what in sailors' jargon would be called *pinardiers*, or "liquor tubs." One of them sank off the Côte d'Azur, in the neighborhood of Anthéor Point, the other near the small harbor of Albenga on the Ligurian Riviera, rather more than thirty-five miles from Genoa.

                🌾   🌾   🌾

WE owe the discovery of the Anthéor site to Henri Broussard and Dr. Denereaz, who visited it for the first time on August 8, 1948. A second examination was carried out on August 28 of the same year with the assistance of Chénevée, Souquet, and several members of the Club Alpin Sous-Marin. MacEvoy, who has since then met a tragic end, put his yacht at the disposition of the divers. A more complete survey was made, and a number of amphorae were brought to the surface. Some of the broken necks still contained stoppers marked with inscriptions.

It was far from obvious at the time that a wreck was in question. The proximity of the mainland led many specialists to think that the amphorae thus discovered might have been thrown into the sea in ancient days, as quite often happened in the vicinity of many harbors. For several centuries amphorae were the commonest form of containers used throughout the Mediterranean area. When their usefulness was at an end they appear to have been tiresome objects to get rid of. Their fragments were put to many different uses. Sometimes they served as material for tombs, sometimes they were merely jettisoned overboard, as was the case at Lyon and at Châlon-sur-Saône. At Sidon, pieces of amphorae were incorporated in the cement used in the building of quays. They were also employed in the construction of water pipes. At Châlon, between the years 1869-1870, tail ends of amphorae were found in the Saône, but nobody knows what became of them.

The underwater site of Anthéor offered, at the end of 1948, the following appearance. Westward of the Point, and at no very great distance from the shore (some thirty-three or forty yards) at a depth of rather more than ten fathoms, in the area contained between the beach and the rock on which the La Chrétienne light stands, there was a zone of broken pottery, in the middle of which were rows of bodies of amphorae, with a few undamaged examples. These, it seems, were almost certainly the remains of some deliberate pattern of arrangement. But the flourishing nature and size of the various marine plants which covered part of the bottom made any mass raising of these objects a matter of difficulty. A series of dives revealed the fact that the amphorae still lying side by side had become cemented together by calcareous algae and adhesive animal life. Biologists to whom I have submitted fragments of the pottery encrusted

with this marine concretion have succeeded in identifying the
various species. They are the perfectly ordinary enemies encountered in all undersea archaeology. The most formidable is
a weed growth known as *Lithotamnion*. This produces a colored
surface, thick in substance, mauve in shade, smooth and greasy.
Lithophyllum, which has a wavy and bloated surface, is less beautiful in color but more irregular and "decorative." A third form
of calcareous growth had closed up the spaces between the objects and solidly cemented together the various archaeological
exhibits. This was the *Tenarea tortuosa*, a great builder of the
Mediterranean "ledge," which forms a cream-tinted skin harder
than stone.

In order to free some of the layers of amphorae and to separate
the component jars it was necessary to work with picks in a considerable depth of water. This at first caused a great deal of un-
avoidable damage.

In 1949, the G.R.S., which had carried out at Mahdia the
experiments already described, arrived at Anthéor on the sloop
Elie Monnier. This group, which at that time was under the
command of our friend Philippe Taillez, carried out a number of
dives and took several underwater photographs. The superficial
crust was loosened, a layer of amphorae in good condition was
reached, and many of the objects composing it were brought to
the surface.

From August 21 to 25, 1950, the *Elie Monnier* paid a second
visit to Anthéor, and the group, now commanded by Capitaine
de Frégate Rossignol, attempted to carry out an "archaeological
reconnaissance" of the site in response to a request made by F.
Benoît.

On this occasion an improved technique was employed. The
work carried out at Mahdia had shown that some sort of dredging
was imperative in this type of examination. A special machine
was built to specifications supplied by the group. It can be
worked on the sea bed by a single free-diver, and has made it
possible to reveal the material details of sunken ships—the oak
ribs, and the pinewood interior of the hulls.

In this way proof was supplied that the Anthéor wreck, like
the Mahdia ship and the vessels of Albenga and Artemision, of
which I shall have something to say later, had a still recognizable
hull after two thousand years of immersion. That this fact could

be ascertained, slight though its value may be, is not without
interest.

To discover more we shall need the type of equipment which
our archaeological services are in no position to supply. If the
sea bed is to be cleared and the vegetation torn up, we must have
a powerful suction pump with which to get rid of the mud. We
can, it is true, depend upon the willing co-operation of all free-
divers, but only the Ponts et Chaussées, or great private enterprises, can supply the indispensable machinery. The Navy, I fear,
is growing somewhat tired of archaeology. The Groupe de
Recherches Sous-Marines of Toulon means to devote itself in
future only to such work as may be important to national de-
fense.

The merely visual exploration of the Anthéor site—the only
method of investigation now left to us—is bound to be disap-
pointing. The clusters of *Posidonia* seem to have increased in
number, perhaps because the uprooted plants have seeded themselves and produced ever denser growths. The area has been
enormously enlarged and has been shamelessly ransacked by
visitors. Too many divers have been to the place in search of undamaged trophies. Broken objects have been widely scattered,
with the result that the topography has become much confused.
Only two years ago, Commander Rossignol gave it as his opinion
that at least eight days of work would be needed to clear the site
of all this rubbish before the approximate outline of the wreck
could be established.

This disturbance of the area is much to be regretted. The
wreck lies at no great depth, and very near the shore. The sea
there is very much calmer than in the Gulf of Gabes. All the
conditions are better than at Mahdia, except, perhaps, the topography of the sea bed. Here there is no isolated "tell," or mound,
clearly emerging from the sandy plain. Rocks, vegetation, and
sherds combine to make a dreary landscape, the limits of which
are uncertain. Nor should it be forgotten that the Anthéor ship
can offer nothing of interest comparable to the cargo of works of
art which justified the very great efforts made at Mahdia. One
wonders, had this not been the case, what proportions the pillaging might not have assumed in view of the damage which has
been done to the site merely in order to get possession of a small
amount of pottery of no very great value.

What a change has come over the place since our last visit! There is nothing to be seen now but a waste of broken amphora necks and bodies. You may seek in vain among this desert of broken pottery for so much as a scrap of lead, a nail, a piece of wood, anything, in fact, that might indicate that you were in the presence of a ship and not of a public refuse dump. Clumsily, aimlessly, one swims over this mass of smashed pottery, occasionally and half skeptically picking out some fragment rather larger than the rest, only to let it drop again in a swirl of mud. It is impossible now to find the rows of amphorae which once showed how the cargo had been arranged, impossible to determine the precise position of the wreck. What was its length, what its breadth? You may move the body of a jar, lacking its neck, and then, when the mud has settled, find nothing but a litter of sherds. You may scoop out the interior with your hands and see nothing but a fragment with the clear mark of a recent break.

The sea has the blue color of fountain-pen ink. The depth is not worth talking about. Fish flicker beneath the iridescence of the surface which is their sky. What point is there in hanging about this underwater area which looks like nothing so much as a bombed site on the morning after? Who will ever take the trouble to raise this mass of pottery just in order to solve some hypothetical secret of naval archaeology? Year by year, since 1948, the spoliation has gone on, until now any hope of doing useful work has been destroyed. I know of one yacht which hung about here for a whole week loading amphorae.

Here is the rock beyond which, two years ago, Broussard found the fragments of an amphora of a somewhat different shape from the normal. (Chénevée and Souquet found, close to the same site, an intact amphora with an unusually wide body which can be classified as belonging to yet a third archaeological variety— Dressel type 3—which may have come from a ship wrecked at a later date.) On this escarpment once stood the beacon seamark. On its other side the bed slopes gently downwards into the blue depths. Nothing for it but to return to the surface.

And that once gained, there is matter still for wonder—a small miracle. Just before piercing the mirror beyond which lies the air of mortal men, I saw in my hand the glitter of a scrap of pottery. It gave off a sheen of mauve and rose; "sea squirts" had spread a coat of brilliant red upon the fainter color of the weedy incrustations. The part of it protected by the mud showed russet, like the crust of a loaf.

What I had brought back was a tiny scrap of life, not of the life of the past, but of the life of the sea, rather fatty, rather sticky. The light with which it had shone was dying out. Something had gleamed at that dividing line of sea and sky, something that I had held out toward the boat. On my way back this small piece of life had dried in the sun. The pottery had faded just as it was returning to the very earth from which it had originally come.

These brilliant tints which flash so brightly on the water's surface are an epitome of all submarine archaeology. They define its object. They declare its limitations. Deep down in the mud one is scarcely conscious of them, and no sooner are they brought to the upper air than they begin to fade. Our science, if science it be, belongs to the frontier of two worlds, and clings to a fugitive brilliance.

I take stock of the trophies with which I have loaded myself. The body of an amphora, divorced from its neck, lies against the white paint of the *pointu,* or local fishing smack, rolling idly to the swell. Its surface is a mass of concretions. It is already beginning to smell. A moment ago it was a thick and brilliant mauve. Now it is turning pink. Tomorrow it will be white all over.

One finds on objects recovered from the Mediterranean, in addition to the calcareous growths already mentioned, a deal of animal life. Most of the clinging parasites are annelids, that is to say, worms, and polychaetes, the most common of which are the serpulids—small, round tubes which lie on the surface of pottery like noodles on a plate. *Spirorbis* is smaller and has a sandy color. *Pomatoceros* is recognizable from the triangular section of its tube. The small red points so often visible on trophies of this kind are not, as is often thought, the first sign of growing coral, but the work of a foraminifera—*Polytrema miniaceum.*

It remains to sum up the results of the Anthéor venture.

It was clear from the first that the amphorae brought to the surface were all of the same general type, wine jars of the pattern classified by Dressel as type 1, and dating from the last years of the Republic and the first of the Empire. (See Appendix B. At the base of the neck of one of these amphorae I found a mark twice repeated. It has not yet been deciphered. The characters appear to be Oscan.) Tiresome though it may be that divers have made "souvenirs" of these ancient relics, the loss to our museums is not, it must be admitted, great, since they already contain many examples. These have been found in considerable numbers in the *oppida* of Gaul. Their presence under the sea is proof of the importance of the flow of trade between Gaul and Italy during the first century B.C. It is the ransacking of the site rather than the dispersion of these amphorae that is most to be regretted.

Perhaps the only matter for surprise is the great quantity of them collected in a single place. Commander Rossignol estimated the finds at over two thousand. We shall see that this was the normal capacity of a cargo ship in the ancient world.

Perhaps the greatest documentary interest—so far as Anthéor is concerned—attaches to the "corks" which were found still in the necks of many of the amphorae. These I have already mentioned. The word "corks" is not altogether accurate. One of the stoppers was, in fact, made of cork, but it was covered by a disk on which letters had been stamped, and these had remained undamaged by immersion. This disk was made of pozzolana, and not, as was at first supposed, from fat-lime. Pozzolana can stand up against prolonged burial in water without deteriorating, and the Romans used it in the cement with which they built their harbor works. Its volcanic nature goes far to show where the wine, if not the ship, came from. It is to be hoped that the inscription stamped on this stopper will, when read, throw more light on the matter.

In 1947, S. Gagnière found on the shore at Les Saintes-Maries-de-Mar, a collection of amphora necks, all of the same general type, and all of them dating from the same period. They resemble the Anthéor jars in one further particular: they have cork stoppers with a disk on top. One of these disks was found intact by Gagnière. The letters stamped on it were easily legible. They formed the name, twice repeated, of a merchant. His place of business may have been Pozzuoli, where there is evidence that somebody of the same name was, in fact, carrying on trade: L[ucius] Pompon[ius], combined with the letters M and P. The disks found at Les Saintes-Maries and at Anthéor were similar in shape and size. Both had a central boss, and the name on each was similarly repeated. It was therefore clear that we had to do with some traditional form of trademark connected with the marketing of wine.

It is not impossible that this tradition may have a very long history behind it. The custom may, indeed, date back to the Aegean civilization. There was, even fifteen hundred years before Christ, an active trade in wine throughout the Mediterranean area. According to Glota, "The consignments were carried by sea under excellent conditions. Methods had been devised for keeping the commodity safe from deterioration, and for protecting it against fraudulent practices. The jars were closed with stoppers of terra-cotta, covered with vine leaves, and daubed with clay. They were kept in position with twine. To the protective surface, while still in a soft state, and at the point where the bindings crossed, the producer set his mark with a seal." Methods changed little in the course of fifteen centuries, almost the only difference being that clay was replaced by pozzolana. The raised boss still recalls the "crossed bindings" of the Aegean jars. (This classic method of closing the jars accounts for the special Latin vocabulary used in this connection. For "corking," the Romans used the word *oblinere*—to daub, or *gypsare*—to plaster. "Uncorking" was expressed by the verbs *deradere*—to scrape, or *relinere*—to break. The finds at Les Saintes-Maries and at Anthéor throw much light on these linguistic uses.)

Fernand Benoît, Directeur de la XIIe Circonscription Archéologique, obtained possession of one of the Anthéor stoppers. For a long time the reading of the inscription presented great difficulties, and many interpretations were put forward. (This particular example was unfortunately in a poor state of preservation. Many others, with more clearly defined lettering, have since been found.) There was no getting away from the fact that the trademark affixed to the Italic jars and dating, apparently, from the first century B.C. employed, not, as might reasonably have been supposed, the letters of the Latin alphabet, but was inscribed in the Oscan tongue, which reads from right to left. To Jacques Heurgon belongs the credit of deciphering the names of a certain Marcus and a certain Caius Lassius, and for finding references to these names among the funerary inscriptions at Pompeii.

The memorial stone on which this name appears was set up by a Clodia Auli *filia* to commemorate herself and the members of her family (*sibi et suis*). Now, among the members of her family thus designated occurs the name of her mother, Lassia, who, as there is reason to suppose, may have been the daughter

of one of the two Lassii whose names are stamped on the Anthéor
stoppers. The husband of this Lassia served on three occasions as
duumvir. The Pompeii inscription gives the date of his last
magistracy as 2 A.D.

Scruples of conscience forbid me to say more, since, as I have
already pointed out, the merit of this discovery belongs to Monsieur Heurgon, and it is for him to describe the ingenious calculations and comparisons which led him to give for the Anthéor
wreck an approximate date somewhere around 80 B.C.

All the evidence goes to show that Campania was the place of
origin of the ship, of the amphorae which it was carrying, and of
the wine which they contained. (According to F. Lot, "The
'Italian' merchants whose traces are found all over Eastern Gaul
at the end of the period of the Roman Republic and during the
first years of the Empire were not inhabitants of Rome, but men
of Southern Italy.") These Lassii, who lived at Pompeii, had
contacts with a number of agricultural undertakings, as may be
seen from the fact that the funerary inscription already mentioned informs us that the women of the family served, in a
continuous line from mother to daughter, as priestesses of Ceres.

Clodii and Lassii, rich vine growers and export merchants, who
had much political power and religious influence, cultivated the
famous vineyards which covered the lower slopes of Vesuvius
and the hillsides of Sorrentum. The Lassii set their name upon
the pozzolana stoppers of their amphorae, and pozzolana was a
material which came also from Vesuvius.

The connection of these two families brings to mind those
Bordeaux marriages of our own day in which sound commercial
calculations and financial interests march side by side—sometimes
—with love.

❧   ❧   ❧

IT may seem surprising that as late as the first century B.C. the
Lassii should have been using Oscan characters on their stoppers.
It is extremely doubtful that this habit reflects a rustic boorish-
ness still unaffected by Roman influences. These great business
houses must have contained clerks who could write Latin, and
even Greek, correctly. The firm, therefore, could have given a
Roman coloring to its trademark had it seemed desirable to do so.

It seems fairly safe to say that political and historical reasons dictated this late use of Oscan. The Oscan confederation had won respect for its traditions and its language. The process of unification carried out by Rome elsewhere, often by rough and brutal methods, had moved slowly in this particular district of Campania. The "Nucerine" Confederation had won respect for its traditions because of its attitude of loyalty to Rome during the war against Hannibal. The strength of the bonds uniting it to Rome is proved by the fact that the cities which it had founded in North Africa managed to retain a high degree of independence. The linguistic unification of Italy was a later development which belongs to the period of the Social War.

The letters on the Anthéor stopper may, therefore, be regarded as a manifestation of local patriotism. Perhaps we are justified in assuming that this local patriotism was not without a certain publicity value. It may have served as an assurance to distant customers that the famous wine delivered to them was of the true, authentic vintage, much as the appearance of French names on the labels of champagnes and of Bordeaux wines is intended to reassure American consumers.

The reputation enjoyed in Gaul by the wines of the Mediterranean was of very long standing. It was in no way connected with the Roman penetration, and had nothing to do with the diffusion of Latin. It is even safe to say that the popularity of these wines was in inverse ratio to the Roman conquest. The wines of Greece and of Greater Greece long anticipated the advance of the legions. What amounts to a positive craze for them is known to have existed in Gaul as far back as the sixth century B.C. In a frequently quoted passage, Diodorus Siculus asserts that "the Gauls were prepared to pay for a jar of wine the price of the slave who served it." South Italian wines made their appearance in the fourth century simultaneously with the arrival of pottery from Campania. It is wrong to describe these wines as "Roman." According to Pliny, it was not until nearly 150 B.C. that Rome learned the technique of vine culture and wine making. It is obvious, therefore, that when the Romans founded Narbonne in 118, they were still newcomers to the craft of the grape. They may, however, have had more pressing reasons to acclimatize the vine in Gaul. The wrecks of Anthéor and Albenga show clearly that sea-borne trade was not without its risks. To install centers of production in close proximity to the local markets meant a saving on sinkings and on the cost of transport. But it is, perhaps, giving undeserved credit to the Romans to attribute to them the introduction of the vine into Gaul. We should remember that there had been two earlier stages, the one Greek, the other Campanian.

To some this distinction may seem oversubtle, since Campania became, in the long run, wholly Romanized. That is true: but the Anthéor wreck with its Oscan-inscribed stoppers is living proof that the flattening-out effects of historical classification do sometimes tend to conceal the existence of important and neglected nationalities.

The Lassii, therefore, may be regarded as possessing something of a symbolic value. Their chief merit is that they provide a link in the chain of commerce which stretches from the Phocaeans down to the *equites* and *negotiatores* who exercised such great power in the imperial age. The evidence of their broken amphorae in the sea off Anthéor shows that the Romans of Rome were not the first Italian people to establish contact with the Gauls, or to enter into competition with the Greeks of Massalia. Are we to assume, then, that these merchants of Campania were sailors and shipowners as well; that they possessed cargo fleets of their own? Or would it be truer to suppose that they relied on the captains and crews of Greater Greece who had long been familiar with the coast line of Provence? It is impossible to answer the question. The most we can say is that the Apennine folk who came down from their mountains and took possession of Etruscan Capua and Greek Cumae, thus laying the foundations of an Oscan State, did most certainly find in the coastal plain traditions of vine culture and seafaring which were not among the gifts showered by Providence on Rome at her birth.

The lesson is one that should not be forgotten. It shows that maritime activity is scarcely ever of spontaneous birth. It comes into being on the high seas, but when it reaches land it does not wither away but continues, even if the names of those responsible for that continuity change.

Thus, though the name may be Roman and the activity Campanian, it is the long memory of Greek colonization that lies behind.—I hope that I shall not be accused of harboring a Greek "obsession." I am well aware that other influences, notably that of Etruria, played a great part in awakening the barbarians of the West. But those influences moved along the land routes and over the Alpine passes, for which reason I have neglected them here, at the risk of falsifying the historical perspective. Can we, when we come to consider the actuality of Greek influence, say to what extent it made itself felt in the Gallic hinterland? "That," writes Grenier in *Les Gaulois*, "is a much-argued question, to which no satisfactory answer has, even now, been found."

It was as far back as the eighth century B.C. that the Greeks first established themselves in Southern Italy, notably at Cumae. They took with them, when they left their native cities, not only pottery, but cuttings from their vines, and the secret of wine making. But other things, too, they introduced into their new homes, things which had to do with the human mind and the human soul: the use of money and the worship of the gods. It was by way of the sea that, through the course of many centuries, wine was carried through the whole of the Mediterranean area. But in the wake of the wine ships followed arts, and crafts, and gods; the secrets of pottery making and navigation, but also the cult of Dionysos, Egyptian morality, and Ionian philosophy.

The amphorae which lie scattered along the length of this great sea route of the first century B.C. are all, save for minor differences, of the same general type. They are elongated and thick-walled, with handles springing from the shoulder and curving inwards to join the neck a little way below the lip. Of this type are the examples found at Anthéor, and of this type, as we shall see later, are those recovered from the Albenga ship. Others have been found at Carthage and in the small *oppida* around Marseille, at Vienne on the Rhône, at Fos-sur-Mer, at Ibiza, and at Bibracte. It was these amphorae which were at first dubbed Gallic because they turned up in such great abundance throughout Provence. Later, the name was changed to Roman. It would be truer to say that they are Campanian, made from volcanic earth taken from the slopes of Vesuvius, where flourished those terraced growths which have also been called Roman, though they were Greek by origin and owed their quality to the craft and cunning of the Oscans.

I want, now, to say something of the wine which these amphorae contained. Traces of it have remained in some of them—a blackish deposit which the sea has not washed away. It seems possible that the deposit is not of the wine itself, but of the resin with which the inside of the container was daubed. So far as I know, it has never yet been seriously analyzed.

We know approximately what these Greek wines were like, and their heirs, the wines of Campania. Small quantities have been found in sealed glass flasks deposited in tombs. Such analyses as have been carried out show that the wine of the ancients, so much appreciated by "our ancestors, the Gauls," had little in common with what we call wine today. The peoples of antiquity were constantly devising methods of blending, sweetening, and diluting, whereas what we most appreciate in wine is its purity. To say that wine has not been "adulterated" is, with us, to give it high praise. They, on the other hand, were particularly free-handed in the matter of adding sweet-scented substances in order to obtain a beverage with the consistency of syrup which, as a rule, even hardened drinkers could not swallow unless it was well watered. These "wines"—not unlike certain Greek wines of today —contained a great diversity of elements, including honey, aloes, thyme, berries of the sweet cicely, and sometimes—as in the wines of Ephesus and Clazomene—even sea water! The resultant mixture was stored, not in cellars, but in barns exposed to the sun's heat, whereas nowadays, in the Bordeaux country, wine is kept in buildings which face north, with no opening on the southern side, and so arranged as to maintain the temperature at from 54 to 57 degrees Fahrenheit.

These considerations may provide the answer to a puzzle which has long teased me. It is difficult to account for the fact that Gaul, which for so long had imported Greek and Italian wines, quite suddenly, about halfway through the first century A.D. became an exporter. Authors who mention this attribute the change over to the merits of the new growths introduced into Gaul by the Romans. They say little or nothing about the *processes* of wine making, though these were of a highly specialized nature, requiring a certain form of "manipulation" which would not, probably, have taken long to learn.

It seems logical to admit that the Greeks had already introduced the vine into Gaul, and perhaps even the art of vine dressing. But the presence of Greeks in Gaul never amounted to a full-scale occupation, which alone would have made the harvesting of grapes and the manufacturing of wine possible. Not until

the founding of Narbonne in 118 B.C. did any real occupation of
the country begin, and it was only after this that the Romans
began to see danger in Gallic viticulture and started to take the
first preventive measures designed at stopping the planting of
vines by the Gauls.

The introduction of new variants of the plant would seem to
have been decisive only at a relatively late date. Pliny says that
in the course of the ninety years after the death of Virgil, in
19 B.C., new and hitherto unknown varieties of grape were invented. These were remarkable by reason of the "exceptional
resistance which some could offer to cold and damp, others to
frost." These varieties were the Biturica, still, perhaps, known in
the Bordeaux region under the name of *bidure* or *vidure*, and the
Allobrogica, which produced at Vienne a wine of which the
Romans were especially fond.

It was about this period that the Gallic growers, having these
new species at their disposal, and strong in their possession of the
extremely Oriental recipes for blending wine with honey, resin,
and thyme, discovered that one thing, and one thing only, was
lacking for commercial success—an adequate container. The only
one native to them was the cask. It has been accounted a merit
to our ancestors that they should have invented it. But it was
boorish by nature, and seemed to lay under a suspicion of boor-
ishness the liquor contained within it. Four or five centuries
earlier, fine wines had been brought into Gaul by Greek and
Campanian ships. (R. Dion points out that "In the Middle Ages,
wines coming from the districts of Italy which had been col-
onized by the Greeks prior to the Roman conquests were still
known as 'Greek wines.' ") They had been carried in amphorae.
It takes time to accomplish so long a journey back into the commercial past. Nevertheless, the Narbonne growers managed to
get hold of a supply of the traditional wine-carrying vessels.
Whether these were imported from abroad or manufactured in
Gaul, we do not know. What is certain, however, is that there
did exist a local pottery industry. Sherds have been found (one of
them actually in Rome) bearing Gallic names. Thévenot has
pointed out that there lived at Lyon in the first century A.D. a
wine merchant who also carried on a business for the manufacture of pottery. The finds in the camp of the Praetorian Guard
at Rome, too, have made it clear that in the course of the first

century, wine from Béziers was exported in amphorae (Dressel types 2 and 3). Where were these made?

The numerous sherds discovered at Vienne have led scholars to the view that pottery was produced in the neighborhood. The fragments in question, however, were of oil jars which had come originally from Baetica. Similar finds have been made at Les Bolards, and at various other points up and down Gaul. Onward from the second century, most of the amphorae seem to have been of Spanish origin, and of the Dressel type 20: in other words, designed to contain oil.

¥   ¥   ¥

IN 92 A.D. Domitian gave orders that one half of the vines in the Empire should be rooted up. His object was to ensure a sufficient production of cereals for the Roman people. His instructions, however, were inefficiently carried out. They had little effect, and were ultimately rescinded by Probus in 276.

Petronius mentions a Falernian one hundred years old, and Pliny another, close on two hundred. Whether these figures be real or exaggerated, they do assume the existence of wines very different in composition from our present-day Bordeaux and Burgundies which, after that length of time, would definitely have perished or gone "sugary."

It would be a mistake, I think, to maintain that the Romans drank nothing but these old wines. We possess a good deal of evidence on this point, though most of it belongs to a later period. It is based upon a list of prices contained in an edict of Diocletian. Here are the figures as given in Tenney Frank's *Economic Survey of Ancient Rome*. A liter of ordinary wine sold for 8 denarii, or 18 cents. Second-quality "vintage" wine cost 30 denarii a liter, a first quality, 45 denarii. Great wines would fetch 60 denarii or more. The denarius under Diocletian should be reckoned as the equivalent of 2½ cents.

This scale of prices shows clearly that the consumption of wine was widespread in all classes of the community, and leads us to suppose that there was a considerable variety of types.

It was not until after the fall of the Empire, the barbarian invasions, and the crisis of the fifth century, that wine making entered upon its most important phase of evolution. It progressed as a result of the work done by innumerable nameless peasants.

If, to quote Roger Dion, "the French vineyard is one of the best preserved of all Roman monuments in our land," it has come down to us, like the Latin language and the system of Roman law, with the marks upon it of profound changes wrought by the native genius. Nor should we forget the large part played, in its early stages, by the Greeks.

The barbarian invasions, the economic troubles, and, later still, the Norman incursions and the Arab domination of the Mediterranean, by cutting off the western wine-growing regions from the Italian market, had a profound effect in substituting "continental" wine for its Greek forebear. No longer were spices used in blending, because they were difficult to obtain, and extremely expensive. But its less obvious, less crude quality derived from "bouquet" rather than from a mixture of different ingredients.

The Church played its part in this evolution by using wine in its liturgy. Communion in both kinds, which persisted until the twelfth century, encouraged the growing of the vine even in very northern districts. Local viticulture was, indeed, the only answer to the difficult problem of communications, even though its products might be mediocre.

In the long run, the care given to the vine by peasant communities—the extent of which it is impossible to calculate—imparted to French wine a flavor very different from that of any growth in the ancient world. Thus it was that our true Burgundies, our true wines of Bordeaux, came to birth ten or more centuries after the earliest successes achieved by the juice of the grape in the Roman world.

$$\text{\ding{43}} \qquad \text{\ding{43}} \qquad \text{\ding{43}}$$

It is matter for rejoicing that the presence off the Provençal coast of a vessel sunk some two thousand years ago, and examined carefully, thanks to the most up-to-date methods of free-diving, should have led to the consideration of the ancient and humble truths of agricultural labor. Maybe we needed this underwater evidence in order to understand how a fusion of Mediterranean influences with local peculiarities came about within the framework of Western Europe and, more especially, on the soil of France. Between two types of wine, Western civilization finally

chose the one produced by the peasants of "Francia" as against
that lauded by Horace.

☙   ☙   ☙

AT Anthéor, as at Mahdia, the ship itself was as important as its
cargo. The same thing is true of the third wreck, the most recently
discovered of the group. It is situated off Albenga, on the Italian
coast, and I propose now to give an account of it.

Albenga is a small and ancient port on the Ligurian littoral. It
was once a lurking place of pirates. Relations between it and
Marseille were sometimes strained as a result of disputes connected with coral-fishing activities. As a rule, they were close
and friendly.

In 1925, a fisherman of Albenga brought up two amphorae in
his nets. Various other discoveries made at the same spot led to
the assumption that there was a wreck lying on the sea bed.
Professor Lamboglia, Director of the Institute of Ligurian Studies, succeeded in arousing the interest of Commandant Quaglia.
The name of this officer will be familiar to all who have any sort
of curiosity about underwater operations. Commandant Quaglia
is that daring shipowner of Genoa who has specialized in the
recovery of wrecks. He has perfected a type of diving equipment
which makes it possible to work at great depths. His most spectacular success occurred in 1921 when, after many dramatic
vicissitudes, he brought to the surface a cargo of treasure from
the *Egypt*, which had sunk in fifty fathoms off the Pointe du Raz.
He agreed to give his services for a few days to undersea archaeology, and his ship, *Artiglio II*, took up a position off Albenga,
where it remained from the eighth to the twentieth of February,
1950. The results of the enterprise might have been magnificent.
The wreck lay at no great depth—rather more than twenty fathoms—and was scarcely at all dismembered. Naval archaeology,
which up till then had been able to work only on the authority of
a few contradictory texts and a handful of identifiable remains,
was at last in a position to survey a ship of large dimensions, a
wreck, perhaps, but a wreck which could still speak to us.

The position of the foundered vessel was soon located, thanks
to the information provided by the fisherman who had first
brought the amphorae to the surface. A preliminary investigation

by helmet divers show
sisted of an accumula
marine fauna and lyir
objects covered an ar
tical with those estab

In order to attac
common with marir
the *Artiglio* had rec
more than once sh
the iron hulls of s
chamber. The gra
metal plates loo
wrenched to pie
chamber dealt
in a steel turret,
pressure, and watch throug...
grab. Being in telephonic communication w...
could control the great jaws and direct their movements.

Setting aside the ships of I
of misfortune, having been
from the water—we are r
ments, reproductions o
the walls of his Albe
of the Trading Co
Antiquarium at
from Ostia rep
relief from
Simmacus
three s
Tebe
last

The means employed would seem to have been somewhat excessive in dealing with a wreck which ought to have been approached with respect rather than with a show of force. It appears that, before having recourse to such heavy-handed methods, those responsible for the operation sent down divers, but not a single photograph was taken, nor was any program of work drawn up. The whole affair became one of steel jaws manipulated with unthinking enthusiasm. It is a pity that Professor Lamboglia should not have had at his disposal a few free-divers who might have given him valuable advice, both before the work started and during its progress. In the small, specialized museum set up at Albenga, one whole room has been devoted to "the state of our present knowledge of navigation in the ancient world." The information there recorded serves only to increase one's regret, and, doubtless, Professor Lamboglia's. Faced by the puny results so far attained, one is more than ever conscious of the invaluable evidence which might have been forthcoming had the Albenga ship been thoroughly examined *in situ*. Such an examination would have entailed months of diving, but what a harvest might have been garnered, what glory might have accrued to Italian archaeological science!

ake Nemi—which were the victims
destroyed by fire after their removal
duced to interpreting the known docu-
which Professor Lamboglia has hung on
nga Museum: the mosaics from the Square
mpanies at Ostia, the large mosaic from the
Rome, which also comes from Ostia, a bas-relief
resenting a ship with a cargo of amphorae, the bas-
he Cathedral of Salerno, the ship from the *stele* of
, the Copenhagen sarcophagus with its decoration of
ips, the bas-relief from the Narbonne Museum, the
sa ship with its oddly arranged load of amphorae, and,
y, the mosaic of Althiburus, the evidence of which—I shall
ever tire of repeating (following in this the lead given by Commandant Guilleux La Roërie)—is, in many points, open to doubt.
To these should, perhaps, be added the *graffiti* discovered by
Commander Carlini at Delos, all of them probably anterior in
date to 69, or maybe even 88, B.C.

J. Le Gall has drawn attention to the "model of a Roman
merchantship," of which so far little account has been taken,
though it has direct reference to the subject with which we are
concerned. The object to which he refers forms the base of a
small Ionic column and is now preserved in the Thermae Museum at Rome. It shows a round-bellied vessel, the proportions
of which appear to have been accurately rendered. The ratio of
fore and aft length to breadth of beam is 1.75, the same, that is,
as that of the ships chartered by St. Louis. There is a similar
marble in the Torlonia Museum. Both come originally from
Portus Augusti.

This collection, it must be admitted, is small indeed when
compared with the mass of archaeological documents on which
we can call when reconstructing other aspects of Roman life.
This makes it all the more important that we should, in the
future, be careful, even to excess, in the methods we employ in
the examination of ancient wrecks.

❦ ❦ ❦

THE greater part of the booty raised from the sea at Albenga,
consisted of an impressive quantity of amphorae—728 examples

intact or only slightly damaged. From divers' reports it seemed
that something like the same number still remained on the bottom. This would indicate—after making due allowance for
breakages—that the original cargo consisted of 1500 or 2000 containers. Professor Lamboglia puts the total at 3000.

These figures are approximately the same as those arrived at
for the Anthéor ship. The amphorae, as at Anthéor, are of
Dressel's type 1, which was current in the second and first centuries B.C. The lip, in the case of the Albenga hoard, is thicker than
in the Anthéor amphorae, and shows as vertical in section,
whereas that of the latter is oblique. The height of the Albenga
examples is three and three-quarter feet (inside measurement),
whereas that of the Anthéor jars is, in every case, less than three
feet. None of the amphorae bears any mark. There is a complete
absence of *graffiti* and inscriptions. The contents were kept from
escaping by the insertion in the necks of cork stoppers, perhaps
sealed with wax. No pozzolana disk of the kind recovered at
Anthéor was found. On the other hand, pine cones had been
forced into some of the necks and were still in place.

Did these amphorae contain wine? Such a supposition would
at least seem to be plausible. The whole cargo bears a strong
resemblance to that of the Anthéor ship, and the jars have the
appearance of being Campanian in origin. An analysis of the
earthenware might, perhaps, reveal the presence of characteristic
volcanic elements. The residue, however, remaining at the bottom of the jars has been analyzed, and mention has been made
of "Judaean bitumen."

The content of three of the amphorae has proved easier to
identify. It consists of hazelnuts which have, miraculously, remained intact.

The pottery on board was mostly of black ware, and this has
made it possible to fix the approximate date of the wreck. Campanian vessels of types A and C (150-100 B.C.), cups of imitation
Campanian ware of the same period, ollae, and urns, would seem
to set the event in the first half of the first century B.C.

A leaden horn, brought up by the grab, had belonged beyond
any doubt to the head of an animal used to decorate the prow.
Several leaden drain pipes were also recovered. They were of
large dimensions and resembled those found in the ships of Lake
Nemi. There were, too, some leaden plates which had originally

covered the ship's hull. One of the most interesting objects found was a stone crucible still showing the traces of molten lead. Not only, therefore, did we obtain proof that the hulls of Roman ships had a lead lining—a method of building which, after being completely forgotten for several centuries was reintroduced in the sixteenth, first by the Spaniards and later by the English; but there is reason for assuming that ships were so equipped as to enable their crews to carry out running repairs at sea—unless it is a question of material simply intended for repairing the lead piping which was so common on ships of this type.

One of the most curious pieces of naval equipment found at Albenga was a leaden wheel, twenty-three inches in diameter, and weighing rather over thirteen pounds. It seems to have contained four iron spokes, and to have been fitted with ropes, since a considerable quantity of hemp fiber was still discernible when the discovery was made. It has been assumed that this piece of machinery acted as some kind of counterweight, though of what precise nature we do not know. Its weight would seem to argue against its having had any connection with the tiller. It may have had something to do with the working of a *tormentum*, or in the raising of the sail. It was mounted on a wooden base by means of a tenon still visible on one side. The manner in which it was lifted from one end of the site, makes it impossible to say more.

A few fragments of oak and pine, and some nails, are the only relics of the actual ship now preserved in the Albenga Museum. The nails are said to be of "bronze." It is a pity that no analysis has been carried out which might have enabled us to compare them with the nails found at Mahdia and Anthéor which have been examined in this way. The latter, as has already been pointed out, were of pure copper. It seems probable that those of Albenga—which are contemporary—were also of copper, as were those found in the ships of Lake Nemi.

Finally, four tiles were recovered, belonging, no doubt, to an enclosed building on the deck. Some such construction has already been referred to in the account given of the Mahdia wreck.

More puzzling are the fragments of three helmets. They are of three different patterns, none of which bears any resemblance to the helmets used by Roman soldiers. There are many theories to account for their presence. Lamboglia is of the opinion that they may have formed part of some equipment destined for the army of Marius, but no evidence so far discovered would seem to justify us in adopting this view.

ᴍ   ᴍ   ᴍ

AND now I must sum up the lessons to be learned from the three operations carried out, at Mahdia, at Anthéor, and at Albenga.

The three wrecks seem, for all practical purposes, to have been contemporary. That is to say, they all occurred between 100 and 50 B.C. The Anticythera wreck seems also to date from round about 50 B.C. This may be a mere coincidence, but it is worth noting. The examination of the sea bed is still in its early stages, and it seems curious that the first wrecks to be encountered should all be of Roman vessels belonging to the same period. Is there any rational explanation of this fact? Greek ships sunk within three or four centuries of the same period might just as well have resisted the effects of immersion. The explanation may be that the Roman ships were less seaworthy, or more heavily laden, or that they were accustomed to sail close inshore.

What does seem obvious is that the ships concerned in these catastrophes were all of the same type—round-bellied craft, measuring about 120 feet fore and aft, and 36 beam. From the evidence of the objects found in them—amphorae, works of art, and columns—their cargo would seem to have been heavy, too heavy, perhaps, for safety. They were slow-moving vessels and, in their case, sailing so close inshore must have been imprudent. These facts may explain their presence at the bottom of the sea.

ᴍ   ᴍ   ᴍ

MY subject is not navigation in the ancient world, or, rather, navigation forms only part of my subject. The thread which I have set myself to follow all through this book is concerned with the link between man, his technical achievements, and his gods. An amphora recovered from the sea has given me an excuse for tracing the history—marine history, all of it—of the wine made and drunk by the ancients. Now for the god.

By a coincidence which one might go so far as to call miraculous, he appeared at a point midway between Anthéor and

Albenga, at the very foot of that rock of Monaco which must have been one of the landmarks on the course of the Roman wine-traders, in whichever direction they were sailing—from Italy to Gaul, and then back again from Gaul to Rome.

On July 9, 1949, within sight of the coast of Monaco, and beneath the sea in the neighborhood of the Rocher Saint-Nicolas, a diver of the name of Giordano came on a large bronze statuette of a panther (now housed in the National Museum of Antiquities at Saint-Germain).

This animal, a rare beast on the coasts of France, broke surface in the arms of its rescuer, muzzle raised and one paw lifted. It was, however, completely covered by a patina of green oxydization and marine parasites, which gave it a bloated appearance as though blistered by fire. By the time I saw it, it was smooth and glowing with life, its open jaw revealing a copper tongue glittering between its teeth. Injuries inflicted by the sea are sometimes beneficial, in spite of appearances. The sea sets its mark on man's handiwork, wrapping bronze and pottery in a covering of worms and weed. Marble is the only substance which it eats away.

This panther is the animal associated with Dionysos: the beast ridden by the god.

No one will deny the part played by chance in this Bacchic discovery. The diver might have brought up a Venus or a Hermes. The ancient ship might have foundered far from the Provençal coast. But, as things turned out, this "manifestation" of the god took place in an area which could not well have been more suitable, a few miles only from hoards of wine-carrying amphorae which are evidence of his might, even in the sea: Anthéor, Albenga, Port-Cros—Dionysos, so often represented as ship-borne, whose influence in Campania rivaled that of Demeter, had come to join the Campanian amphorae beneath the clear waters of a French cove.

The theme illustrated by this bronze is known to us through the medium of numerous works of art, raised bosses, terra-cotta statuettes, etc; but the age of this particular object restored to us by the sea takes us straight back to its earliest Asiatic version. When this bronze disappeared in a shipwreck off the coast of Provence, it already had a long past behind it. In the course of the centuries it had suffered many accidents, as may be seen from the repairs made to the upper jaw in ancient days. Lantier has established a connection between it and the great statue of Dionysos showing a child astride a panther, which was found at Memphis and dates back to the period of Ptolemy I (323-283 B.C.)

By restoring to us this panther, which Charles Picard has described as "the most interesting of all the finds so far made in the field of undersea archaeology," the Mediterranean has placed in our hands one of the oldest known examples of Hellenistic sculpture, and a link in the history of art, and even of religions. The popularity enjoyed, at least since the reign of Ptolemy I, by this representation so dear to the Hellenistic heart, explains its reappearance in Greek art in the fourth century, in which the animal is shown either seated or standing, with its left forepaw raised—an attitude which the influence of the Orient had first led sculptors to confine to animals of fantasy: the sphinx, the chimera, the griffin, though it was later transferred to actual beasts.

What date should be given for this shipwreck? A subsequent series of dives, carried out in 1950, led to the recovery of a number of other objects, notably of a bronze lantern, which furnished Lantier with a certain amount of chronological data. This lantern was a ship's navigation light. In shape it is a crenelated fortress flanked by six square towers, each having a door and two windows. A pattern representing stonework is incised on the walls. This characteristic object is to be found in many places of Provence, even in mosaics dating from the first century A.D.—at Auriol, at Orange, and at Nîmes. It was during this same period that the architectural motif of a tower was being used in lanterns made of pottery, and the fashion persisted for many hundred years in the Rhineland and the Danube region. The date of the lantern being thus fixed within the first century A.D., we can place the wreck which caused the loss of the ship roughly in the same period.

Car nosto Provenço es talamen
    bello
    Que se la rapello
    Tau que noun lou crèi:
Nous amourousi e nous descoun-
        soulo
    Levant de cassalo
    Li fiho di rèi.
                        Lis Isolo d'Or
                        MISTRAL

N<small>O ONE, I THINK, CAN REALLY UNDERSTAND</small> PROVENCE WHO
approaches it from the north. The land route gives a wrong impression. The country faces seaward. The firm-ribbed, muscular
hinterland can be seen in its full extent only by an observer situated offshore. Provence greets the visitor, and bares its heart,
only through the medium of its coves and creeks.

I shall never forget my first introduction to this country—the
revelation of that moment when I reached Marseille on board a
cargo ship after a crossing at a time when my life was that of an
eternal emigrant. I had had a long buffeting at the hands of
a spring sea which flung its spray high in the sunlight. And then
at last we reached a sharply indented line of cliffs. There was no
sign of a harbor. On one side lay Marseille-Veyre. On its sandy
bed was a mass of amphorae, anchors, and the relics of a long
marine past, undisturbed beneath the green water. On the other
side was the island of Maire and the smaller islet of Jarre, with,

64

beyond, Pomègue—which takes its name from Phoenicia—and Ratonneau. The tarred buoys bobbed, with their names painted in white. Instinctively I leaned over the rail, gazing with questing eye at the still choppy surface. Twenty fathoms down was the bottom, thickly studded with wrecks.

Suddenly, in the white cliff wall, a gap appeared leading to the habitations of men. No need for those making this landfall, looking westward toward La Joliette and its docks, to realize that the channel has not changed since the days of Protis, the fair Gypsis, and the arrival of the Phocaeans on the coast of Lacydon.

This, perhaps, is the place in which to recall the legend which surrounded the founding of Marseille. It has come down to us in the pages of Justin, who took it from Trogus Pompeius. It seems that Protis, the Phocaean, landed in the creek of Massalia on the selfsame day on which the chief of the Ligurian tribe, King Nann, was to marry his daughter with the full solemnity of local rites. The fair Gypsis, scorning her native suitors, offered the nuptial bowl to Protis. Thus did a foreigner become the son-in-law of the king. He settled in the country, and Massalia was born. It seems probable that this poetic anecdote enshrines a substratum of historical fact. Phocaea, an Ionian city on the coast of Asia Minor, grew in importance as a maritime power during the seventh century B.C. Her sailors had already explored the coasts of the western Mediterranean and, more especially, had penetrated into the delta of the Rhône, where before their time the Rhodians had traded. The site of Massalia, with its coastal islands, was to some extent reminiscent of the approaches to Phocaea. With the approval of the Delphic Oracle, and that of the Ephesian Artemis, both of them religious centers for the Ionians of Asia, the Phocaeans settled in the neighborhood of a harbor, the admirable features of which could scarcely have escaped the notice of such trained seamen. The marriage of the leader of the expedition with the king's daughter, long negotiated, and by no means due to a young woman's whim, set the seal on friendly relations with the local population. All this occurred probably round about the year 594. Later still, the capture of Phocaea by Harpagus, the lieutenant of Cyrus, in 540, by compelling the richer commercial families to emigrate, first to Corsica and then to the colony of Massalia, was the decisive factor in the prosperity of the trading station at the mouth of the Rhône.

The pottery found at Marseille, in the vicinity of the Vieux Port, confirms all this—the existence of a primitive native settlement, repeated visits over a period of fifty years by sailors and merchants from Ionia, concessions granted to the Phocaeans near Tourette and Anse—which latter place took the name, eventually, of Anse Saint-Jean—and, finally, a period of intense commercial activity.

Already, in those days, the coast made that lovely bend which conceals under the Pharos shoulder a quadrilateral of blue water sheltered from every wind. By choosing this spot for their landing, the newcomers could make themselves familiar with a mainland which holds back nothing from the curiosity of those approaching it from the sea.

The whole coast line abounds in creeks in which the secrets of Provence lie open to all who are prepared to study them with unremitting attention. Thanks to the sea and, in particular, to the exercise of diving, I have been made privy to many half-hidden truths. No longer were my senses deadened by the spectacle of cultivated fields, or lulled by the purr of a motor engine. I found that in the water age-old claims were being made upon them, and knew again that sharpening of the human spirit which refuses to submit to the deceptive evidence of appearances. Instead, I learned the essential verities. It is the sea that has revealed to me the ancient past of this land of Provence, a past which far exceeds in grandeur the conventional picture which so many people have of antiquity.

ƻ   ƻ   ƻ

THE traces left by the Romans in Provence no longer have the power much to excite me. The land route from Paris to Toulon, which, unfortunately, I have taken far oftener than the passage by sea, is thick with them. I greet without especial pleasure the triumphal arch at Orange which now serves no purpose except to provide a "roundabout" for motorists. I know all about its archaeological importance, and that from its reliefs we may learn of the fusion achieved between the Roman world and the "barbarians." That fusion was rather too quickly achieved, and sounded somewhat too loud a note of the "triumphal" to enlist my sympathy. The few maritime objects to be found among its sculptures are not sufficient to make me fond of it. If its purpose be to glorify Caesar's victory at Marseille, we should surely be ill-advised to honor the memory of a man who, according to Plutarch, killed a million men in Gaul and rounded up about the same number of slaves. By what right is this triumph commemorated here? What has it to do with us? What does this arch, set between a *gendarmerie* and a school, stand for? The little town, with its narrow streets, instinctively repudiates the foreigner's loud-mouthed emphasis, no matter how good that may be for the tourist trade.

Under its assumed Roman garb Provence remains a land more in love with a severe economy of line than rich in glory; a land where lie those dead of many races by whom I would gladly be accepted. The flagstones of the legionaries have not completely crushed the memories of Ligurian and Celt. They cling, those memories, to the volcanic rock like wild heath plants and, like them, are capable of living off next to nothing. Now and again, when the wind blows from the sea, a breath of Greece sighs in the fibrous vegetation.

Long before reaching Orange I became aware of a very ancient and rustic civilization. The visible signs of it lie spaced along the roads of the Midi, and mark for me those prehistoric staging posts of which I never grow tired. They form a curious prologue to our underwater ventures in exploration. Merely to look at those fields, merely to seek out memories of a meager past—the line of a road, the site of some dead village—is to set the mind in tune with the humble treasures of the sea, to accustom it to the task of questioning the flora of the deep, of discovering strange stones, not only hidden beneath the soil, but lurking in the thickets of wet weed.

I would advise anyone who is truly anxious to understand Fos or the harbor of Narbonne to visit all the ancient sites which line the road, but only the most modest of them, those that call for discrimination: the hills that greet one south of Avallon, crowned with nameless ruins of unmortared stone; the "End of the World" and its rock; the cliff at Solutré, over which the hunters drove the herds of horses to their death; La Roche Pot and its crudely fashioned masonry; a tiny stretch of scrub, a patch of that mysterious mark where, here and there, a flagstone still shows above the ground, a spring whose water was canalized long centuries ago. It is by looking at these things that the landsman can best prepare his mind for dealing with the sea.

Why should this inglorious past seem so much more exciting to me than the thought of Rome? Is it unconscious memory or the prestige attaching to things known but imperfectly? In the opening page of *La Cité antique*, Fustel de Coulange tells us that the past never dies, because it continues in men's hearts. "Men may forget it, but it still lives on within them. No matter what a man may be at any given period, he is but the epitome of all the periods which have preceded him. If he dives deep into himself he can recover and distinguish all those different epochs by reason of what each has left within him."

What name should we give to the echo which sounds to our inner ear when Provence speaks to us? I have referred to our ancestors in this countryside as Ligurians and Celts because I have no other name to give them.—The unlearned no longer know what to make of these "Ligurians." It seems now to be an established fact that the territory occupied by them was far smaller in extent than scholars were inclined to think fifty years ago. "The theory of panligurism has, to all seeming, been abandoned." Raoul Busquet, whose subject was the history of Marseille, is prepared to grant them all the land lying between the Rhône, the Alps, and Etruscan Italy, a domain delimited by F. Lot as comprising "the Departments of the Alpes-Maritimes, the Var, and the Bouches du Rhône, in all some 9375 square miles." Albert Grenier, on the other hand, maintains that the name "Ligurian" should not be used of any people living outside Liguria. "The word should stand only for the idea of a Gaul peopled from the Bronze Age (1500 years B.C.) onwards, by tribes whose language, traditions, and origin seem to be related closely to the Celts of the historic period." André Berthelot concludes that they have become completely effaced, leaving nothing behind them but a name—"an empty husk." There were Iberians to the West, Greeks at Marseille and all along the coastal strip. If our ignorance is great, the reason may be that our curiosity has not been great enough.

It needed the operations of war to reveal, in 1944, the full extent of the great Celts-Ligurian city of Entremont, some two

miles from Aix. It would be going too far to say that until then
we knew nothing of this ancient capital built by our ancestors
on the soil of Provence. Only specialists, however, have shown
any interest in this relic of the past. The general public still
knows practically nothing about it. Recent excavations have revealed the walls and houses once raised by these vanquished folk
and, in particular, the statues used in their worship.

Theirs was a religion based on the honoring of the dead. It is
worthy of a place in the history of art and the history of mankind, if only because it produced these slim-waisted warriors,
these archaic Greeks, seated in the posture of the Buddha. To
refer to them in such terms, however, is to minimize an original-
ity which ought, on the contrary, to be stressed. From the material evidence it seems clear that our ancestors were no whit
inferior in sensibility to the craftsmen of India and of seventh-
century Greece. There can, all the same, be no doubt that they
were directly influenced by neither. "The Celts," writes Picard,
"were most certainly the creators of an independent art of sculpture which owed nothing to the Mediterranean Pantheon, and
assuredly nothing to India"—I shall have something to say later
on about the contact of the ancient world with India. There
were Buddhists in Alexandria in the third century B.C., and in
Rome under the Empire. An ivory figure of Indian workmanship
(the Goddess Lakme) has been found at Pompeii. The traces
of Greece and Rome found in India are even more numerous.
It was as a result of Ionian influences that Buddha was given a
human form.

The evidence can be studied in the Aix Museum, where the
Entremont statues have been lodged. A pilgrimage there is well
worth while.

The same pre-Roman flavor hangs about the incised and
painted figures in the Gorges of Ollioules, to which no motorist
has ever paid the tribute of a visit.

¤   ¤   ¤

PROVENCE is a complex land, very different from the idea that
most people have of it. It is very ancient, disturbing rather than
smiling, and peopled by the ghosts of the nameless dead, of
civilizations that came to nothing, of throttled cities: ghosts too

frail to call for vengeance, yet ghosts who have made of us their heirs.

Le Camp, on the road from Toulon to Marseille, just where Mémé's bistro now stands, was where the territory belonging to the Salluvii of Entremont ended. The only fault of which they were guilty was that of keeping Massalia too continuously in a state of uneasiness, that Massalia with a Ligurian name, of which the Phocaeans had gained possession in a manner somewhat less idyllic than would appear from their own traditional version of the incident.

It was Ligurians—Oxybii and Deciates—who threatened Nice and Antibes, both of them "Massaliet" colonies. Against them Rome twice intervened at the request of the people of Marseille, first in 181, and again in 154.

A more serious situation developed in 125, when the Ligurians, the Salluvii, and the Vocontii, it seems, joined forces with the intention of attacking the Phocaean city, which once again called on Rome for aid. It took four years to get the better of the "barbarians." It was then that Entremont was razed to the ground and reduced to the state in which we see it today. The Consul, Sextus Calvinus, set up a fortified post in the plain to which he gave his own name—Aquae Sextiae—Aix. The Romans took root in Southern Gaul, their object being to control the Spanish Road, the road taken by those who sought to discover and conquer the West, the prehistoric track along which copper and tin had been carried; the great highway of the slave trade, of successful generals, and of the mass migrations of peoples; the itinerary of Hercules and Hannibal, of the Cimbri and the Teutones.

According to Greek legend, it was by this route that Herakles traveled when he returned from the Garden of the Hesperides, and his name is frequent all along its length, from Monaco to Toledo and Carthagena. A Greek colony in the delta of the Rhône was called Heraklea (identified, rather arbitrarily, with Saint-Gilles), and Heraklea Kakkabaria later became our own Cavalaire. Fernand Benoît has even discovered the figure of Hercules above the door of Saint-Trophime at Arles!

In fact, the great East-West artery is a double trafficway, for a sea route neighbors the road along the coast. Though it was through Crau that Hercules chose to journey, the Rhodians, and after them the Phocaeans, with their *penteconters*, reached Tartessos and founded Mainake and Hemeroskopion. While Hannibal was putting his elephants across the Rhône, Scipio arrived by sea and landed, but too late, at the mouth of the river. It was by land that the Cimbri threatened Italy, but by sea that Marius, their conqueror, thanks to the port of Fos, assured his communications. When Caesar came, it was the turn of the conqueror to cling to the land, for he was concerned to get his fingers on the wealth of Spain. The heavy weight of Rome's legitimacy made itself felt at Marseille in the shape of sea power.

The Romans never really felt safe until they had got control of both routes. Fréjus, Arles, and Narbonne were the complement of the Via Domitia, and they it was that crushed the life out of Marseille. Caesar compelled the Phocaean city to deliver up not only its engines of war, but its ships as well.

Southern Gaul was already an ancient land when the shadow of Rome fell suddenly upon it. At a time when Rome was still almost in its infancy, when invading Gauls pulled the Senators' beards, the peoples of the Provençal hinterland, secure behind their seaward fringe of Greek civilization, were already learning to appreciate the pottery of Ionia, as, later, they developed a taste for the wines of Sicily and Greater Greece.

Just because these "natives" were regarded by Rome as an uneasy menace on her frontiers, that does not mean—far from it —that our ancestors had made no contact with civilization before the coming of Caesar. By the time the Phocaeans came, they had had a long past of friendship with the Rhodians, and, still earlier, with the Phoenicians. A Cypriot dagger has been found at Auriol, near Marseille. But in history, it seems, latecomers have a way of effacing the traces of their predecessors. In Provence the ethnic pattern is unusually confused, and we may search in vain for a principle of unity in either geography or history.

Nevertheless, a unity there is. It is strong, and more obvious than in many a "natural" region. The sea has imposed it, and it is from the sea that I learned it, or rather from my dives under the sea.

From the rock of Monaco, where Herakles set foot, as far as Agde, whither the Greeks went in order to control the course of the Garonne as it flows toward the Atlantic, and further still, right on to the Pillars of Hercules, land and sea tell the same story. But it would be a mistake to listen to each separately. It is as much in the mud of the harbor mouths, and in the submerged rocks of the creeks, as along the route taken by Hercules that we should seek to follow the clues of the past.

On this coast—and on many others—it is the duty of the archaeologist and the historian to remain always half immersed. Perhaps it would be truer to say that they must become amphibious, floating above the deep places of the ocean, taking notes of wrecked ships, moving up the rivers, crossing the lagoons, ever ready to call a halt to catch the play of water on the solid earth, in one place to garner a puzzling name, in another to identify an *oppidum* or rescue an amphora, to read an inscription. It is commando work, but not to be avoided, since to the archaeologist the sea is as generous as the land.

To prove this we have only to tell the strung beads of the many underwater finds which have been made in the course of a few years, all the way from Monaco to Narbonne.

The series begins at the eastern end, with a work of Alexandrian origin, the bronze panther of the Rocher Saint-Nicolas, which I mentioned in the previous chapter. It is no bad thing that through the medium of this Hellenistic bronze the sea should remind us how obstinately Greece touched Gaul with its golden sunlight, even when it came under the domination of Rome. Alexander, it is said, had he not died so suddenly, would have pursued his ambition of Hellenizing the West. His ghost is everywhere along the seaboard of Provence. The route which Alexander never took is marked, as with buoys, by Hellenistic works preserved beneath the sea. To the panther of Monaco must be added the fragments of a sarcophagus fished up at Port de Bouc, and the ivory Aphrodite found in the mud at Fos-sur-Mer. These are but two items in an already long list.

Cicero speaks of the "Greek fringe that lies like a strip of embroidery along the limits of the Barbarian lands." This fine needlework, once so elegant and trim, has now vanished from the coast, wiped out by a swarm of villas and "Provençal-style" hotels.

The very names of the towns are deceptive, and their seeming Greek sound but a trap for the unwary. Monaco is not a Greek place name. The Phoenicians arrived upon the littoral before the Hellenes. No doubt they built a temple to their god, Melkart,

who became changed into Herakles Monoikos, with confusing
results. The Middle Ages took this Monacus to be a monk and
included him in the heraldic blazon of the town. The Renaissance, thinking itself closer to the truth, re-established the figure
of Herakles, with his added attribute to Monoikos—he who has
one home. Thus Hercules the wanderer became a rich man and
a landowner, ending his days in honorable retirement instead
of at the stake—a tale more pleasing than plausible. (There is a
connection between Monaco and the name of the Isle of Man
in England—Mona.)

Nor, so the scholars warn us, should we be taken in by Nikaia
—the Victorious Goddess—which is merely the Greek version of
an earlier name. No matter. Nice was Hellenized: Cimiez remained Ligurian. Today, Nice is the center of the undersea-gun
trade, and its antique shops sell amphorae recovered from the
sea. If its pebbly beach offers few attractions to the diver, he has
merely to go to Villefranche, where he will find wonderful spaces
of deep water set between rocks where the cuttlefish flourishes
and sheer cliffs plunge straight down into the deep sea. It is a
seascape which holds a foretaste of the Italian Liguria and brings
to mind the pirates who for long years offered defiance to Rome.
In 181 B.C., at the request of the people of Marseille, a punitive
expedition was led by the Consul Aemilius Paulus against the
pirates of Ventimiglia and Albenga, and their ships were eventually put to flight by a fleet under Caius Matienus.

Antibes—Antipolis, the city opposite—opposite Nice (another
case of linguistic imposture)—is a Massaliet colony settled on a
site which marked an original Phoenician trading station. The
cape has become rather too well known, and divers there are
too plentiful for safety. But how lovely and translucid the water
is with its population of *Gorgonia*! Off its eastern face was found
the most interesting of all the anchors which have so far come
to our knowledge.

The capital of the diving fraternity, Cannes, headquarters of
the Club Alpin Sous-Marin, is more Ligurian and Roman than
Greek. At first it was known as Aegitna, later as Castrum Marsel-
linum. But up to the time of the Middle Ages La Croisette was
a marsh, the home of mosquitoes and those ancient boatmen
who used inflated skins—*utricularia*.

Far out at sea lie the islands of Lérins, Sainte-Marguerite, and

Saint-Honorat, twice, thrice dear to our hearts. The Léro, who gave his name to them, was a Ligurian Hercules who Hellenized his name into Herakles, much as the pirates who haunted his sanctuary dwindled into watermen.

The loveliest of all the underwater seascapes yet discovered is there. It is off Léro (l'Ile Sainte-Marguerite) that the slope known as the Vengeur plunges to the bottom. The frequent visits of the Club Alpin Sous-Marin have made the place famous. Some thirty feet below the surface there is a ledge warmed by the sun, and there we drop anchor. This ledge falls sheer into cold, blue water. One has only to let oneself go down. The shadowy *Gorgonia* traces in the watery sky a pattern of winter branches. The sandy bed lies at a depth of just over twenty-two fathoms, and there Broussard gives the accolade to young divers. Its waters have become a sacred place of baptism.

But it is round the other island, the ancient Lérins, now Saint-Honorat, that historical memories have mostly collected, for it is a very old sanctuary where an inscription can still be seen invoking the name of Neptune. But it has been the home of other cults as well. Only last year the monks unearthed a Priapus still visibly potent. If this site of pagan cults was chosen for the building of a church, the reason was that those errant ghosts might be caught, as it were, on the wing, and kept from aimless wandering. But of all those fourth-century monks who were so eager to Christianize the altars of the heathen, Saint Honoratus himself is dearest to me. Impelled by the most laudable intentions, he sailed to that place. Saint Ambrose has told us what they were: "It was in these islands, scattered by God upon the waters like a chaplet of pearls, that those took refuge who wished to find an asylum from the delights of unruly pleasures, fleeing from the world. . . . The sea hides them as behind a veil, and gives them deep retreats for penitence. There every prospect breeds thoughts of austerity, and there is nothing to disturb man's peace. The mysterious murmur of the sea is mingled with the sound of hymns, and above the thunder of the waves breaking upon the beaches of these happy isles are heard rising to Heaven the peaceful voices of the choir of the elect."

Today those "peaceful voices" are mingled with the muted shouts of divers when they find upon the submerged foundations of the isle traces, not of God, but of the Roman navy—in the

form of ancient anchors. There was at one time a mooring between Antibes and Fréjus which is mentioned in the *Antonine
Itinerary*.

But I cannot take my leave of the monks of Saint-Honorat on
this note. They have devoted themselves to pious enterprises,
such as taking in orphans and giving them an education—in addition to which they discharge their principal task of praying for
a world which has much need of prayer. But they are somewhat
disturbed by the arrival of the midday boat. Convenient though
the little port may be, the abbot thought it necessary one year
to tar its flagstones so as to spare the community the spectacle
of summer visitors, who used it rather too publicly for the purpose of sunbathing. The words of St. Ambrose have a slightly
ironic sound—"The sea hides them as behind a veil, and gives
them deep retreats for penitence." That veil I have seen, and
those retreats, but at a depth of six or seven fathoms. It is there
that men may still flee the world and find God's peace. Will
somebody, I wonder, some day found an order of diving monks?

Such an idea would have shocked nobody between the fourth
and the eighteenth centuries. What a valuable contribution
might have been made toward the "humanization of the sea"
by a monastic community drawing from it all that the Cistercians
delved from the soil of the West!

To construct an agricultural civilization, and to conceive the
idea of a civilization based upon the sea, are linked endeavors
which demand patience, abnegation, and continuity. Certain
types of exacting and hazardous toil lead men into the ways of
mysticism. Those ways are, perhaps, not closed to the men of
the twentieth century. One of my friends, an Air France pilot,
has become a Trappist. How he came to adopt this unpredictable
vocation I shall never know. All I remember is his description
of those nights over the Atlantic when, seated in the cockpit
of his four-engined machine, he used to take his bearings by the
stars. The only element of mysticism that I could see in that
solitary task which sets men playing games with the heavenly
bodies in the silence of the night while flying above the ocean
was that it bore some resemblance to the hermit's toil. Whether
his home be in the air or in the waters, the hermit, as Nietzsche
says, "must be forever giving." Hermits at Lérins might give us

the sea. The Aegean religion, and its heir, the Greek, did no less at a time when divers were the equals of the gods.

ᕯ   ᕯ   ᕯ

IT is difficult to make a reckoning of all the ancient anchors which have been found during the past few years (see Appendix C). Those brought to the surface all have an identical form, or what remains of them, which is always the stock. This is either of lead or strongly constructed of timber with a leaden sheath. The two arms taper toward their extremities. In the middle there is a square hole crossed by a tenon, cast in one piece with this "box." Into this fits the shaft made of twin lengths of wood joined by a collar. The general pattern is the same as that of the anchors in the ships of Nemi which were found, undamaged, in the mud.

A stock of this type, rather more than six feet long, was fished up in 1880, off Carry-le-Rouet to the east of Port-de-Bouc. It is now in the Borély Museum at Marseille. Knuckle bones (symbols of protection) are carved on the top and bottom sides of the arms, at their extremities. The four different faces of the knuckle bones are shown, carrying the numbers 1, 3, 4, 6, in this order.

A smaller example was found and recovered in 1948 by Donnadieu and Broussard, at a point to the east of l'Ile Saint-Marguerite. It measures rather more than three feet in length and weighs approximately 151 pounds. Still more recently Girault has found, close to the Ilot de la Fourmigue, opposite Le Lavandou, an even smaller stock, four feet in length.

An object discovered in 1949 by Chénevée, on the shallow, submerged shelf of La Péquerolle, to the east of Cap d'Antibes, not far from the small island of la Grenille, is one of the most interesting of this type of find known to me. It is rather under six feet in length and weighs well over eight hundred pounds. It obviously formed part of an anchor belonging to a good-sized vessel, perhaps a *corbita*, of the same class as the wrecks brought to light at Mahdia, Albenga, and Anthéor. What is chiefly interesting about this heavy lump of lead is that it bears, at its extremities, three times repeated—and not four—a figure in relief. This has nothing to do with the "trademarks" which are found on the anchors submerged off the coast of Spain, but is clearly a protective talisman, a sign possessing magical powers, the oldest, perhaps, and the most deeply revered, of any in the Mediterranean area—the head of Medusa, the "Gorgoneion."

When Perseus, with the help of Athena, had rid the world of the Gorgon, Medusa, whose face turned all to stone who looked on her, he washed his hands in the sea after setting down the bleeding head upon the sandy shore. It was from this blood, when it ran into the sea, that coral was born. Such was the fable of classical Greece. Like other elements of Greek mythology, it had an Aegean origin. The severed head appears on a Cretan intaglio (Middle Minoan I) found at Mallia. There can be little doubt that it already possessed at that period protective powers which came from a still more distant past.

In the *Gigantomachy* it is Athena herself who cuts off the monster's head. She fixes the bleeding trophy to her shield, whence the dead gaze continues to produce fatal results.

The Greeks made many such efforts to poeticize the beliefs of an earlier age and to disguise a "cult" which shocked their sensibilities by its realism. They drew a veil over a magic power which they dared not challenge. They Hellenized it. A Gorgon's head was carved on the walls of the Acropolis at Athens. The myth of Perseus was given graphic expression on one of the temples of Selinunte. Gorgons formed part of the decoration on the breastplates of the Roman Emperors.

The Celts, the Iberians, and the Ligurians who lived on the Mediterranean coast took over this magic emblem. How this, one of the oldest symbols of the human race, reached them we do not know, nor whether they brought it with them when they settled. It is necessary only to leave the littoral and to travel into the interior of Provence, where so much is secretive and harsh, to find upon the walls of more than one isolated hilltop *oppidum* a severed head, sister to the Gorgon of the Acropolis—for instance, at Bringasses, close to Les Baux, and also in Spain, at Alariz.

But in Western hands the same emblem became something quite different. Poetry of a different sort touched it, a slightly morbid mysticism, a melancholy romanticism. On the soil of Gaul the severed head remained the image of a funerary cult, but shaped by men who were not Greek, it expressed a different thought. What had once been announced in terms of light was now explored in terms of shadow. And so it was that there came to birth those heads of Entremont and Roquepertuse over which there hangs an air of resignation which is quite foreign to the spirit of Hellenism.

Should we perhaps see in this a form of pre-Christian resignation, a foretaste of the religious sculpture of the twelfth and thirteenth centuries in France? However that may be, it is worth paying attention to the first note struck by an indigenous art which is wholly different from that of antiquity in its treatment of a similar theme. Celto-Ligurian and Hellenistic art each tried in its own way to purify this symbol which was common to both. Both repudiated the horrifying aspect of Athena's trophy. One touched it with sweetness, the other with nobility. The three Medusas of the anchor already express something of the Hellenistic change. Their elongated faces are peaceful and eloquent of a grave serenity. The serpents have become heavy ropes of falling hair. What they show is a repudiation of the horror implied by the very word "Gorgon" (γοργός in Greek means "terrible"; to give that name to the graceful, delicate creatures which we gather in the sea is to attach to them a terrifying character which they do not naturally possess). The sculptors of Entremont, in whom Celtic, Iberian, and Ligurian influences met, reached out, it seems to me, toward something lying behind that air of gravity, and expressed a sentiment which for us is wholly modern—the acceptance of death, the belief in survival. The sense of death that shows upon these faces seems to express only a tender sweetness. In this creation of our native art we should do well to see something of that Punic element which persisted with such vitality all along the Iberian coast, an element in which "the oriental character made common cause with the Ionian." Medusa becomes the sign of a different type of victory, a victory over the beyond. There is a resemblance between the spirit of these mixed populations and those Provençal sanctuaries which mark the beginnings of new roads and are the prolongation of the old roads of humanity.

If we seek further evidence of that unity of Provence which the sea reveals, it is to be found in two bronze appliqué reliefs adorned with this same type of the "lovely and tranquil" Medusa, which were recovered at Saint-Gervais, close to Fos, on a

site about the wealth of which I shall have something to say
later. (Now in the Museum of National Antiquities at Saint-
Germain.)

🚩   🚩   🚩

CORAL, emanation of the Gorgoneion, formed from the dried
blood of Medusa dripping on the sand, possessed the same protective powers as the head itself. Whence it comes that coral, too,
is one of those links which, defying space and time and, to some
extent, our understanding, bind men to the sea. It is impossible
to deny that, since the earliest periods of prehistory, its fragile
fronds—sacred objects rather than adornments—spread by way
of the Greeks, all through Europe from south to north, all
through India, from west to east.

There is cause for wonder in the fact that the Gorgon anchors,
with their symbolism which is so closely connected with the
gathering and the cult of coral, should have fallen into the hands
of twentieth century divers at so little distance from those sea
grottoes where the living coral hangs in tiny stalactites. Only the
free-diver can visit those recesses which hold the throb of silent
life—recesses which the ancients would not have hesitated to call
sacred. Only with the help of flash-lamps producing thousands of
volts, and of all the latest improvements in photography, can
their colors be seen.

What could those Celtic warriors have known of the sea and
its marvels, those rough men of the European continent, with
their sense of the mysterious, who bought, at the price of blood,
flowers which had the color of blood? They treasured them as
potent charms against death by violence.

A tumulus in the district of Baden, belonging to the Hallstatt
culture, was found to contain a necklace composed of small sticks
of coral. These had been pierced lengthwise, threaded, and arranged in nine rows, alternating with strips of ivory. It appears
that, during the La Tène period, great quantities of coral were
imported into Champagne from the Stoechades Islands, that is
to say from the islands of Hyères. (We have reason to believe that
in the ancient world the name Stoechades was given indifferently
to the islands of Hyères and to those of Lérins. My own view is
that coral came from Lérins. It is found there in abundance, but

I have never found it either at Porquerolles or at Port Cros. Perhaps I did not look hard enough.) There already existed in prehistoric times a great artery of traffic which, branching from the route of Herakles, drove northwards by way of the Rhône and Seine valleys. It might well be called the "Coral Road," just as that other prehistoric route, which in the Bronze Age, and even the Neolithic, linked the distant coasts of the Baltic with the head of the Adriatic Gulf, was long known as the "Amber Road." Both have their starting point in the sea, and in the earliest beliefs of mankind. (Yellow amber, a fossilized resin, came from the Frisian Islands, from the estuaries of the Weser and the Elbe, and probably, in later times, from the southern coast of the Baltic.)

Pliny tells us that the coral fishers neglected their Western customers in favor of the Indian market, to which they sent the major portion of their catches. This change in trading habit belongs to the fourth century, after the death of Alexander. It was the precise point in time when the Celts must have begun using a substitute product for the adornment of their shields and helmets—enamel. Wonder has sometimes been expressed that the Gallic craftsmen, in other ways so highly skilled, never used any other color than red. The answer is simple. Only red enamel could be regarded as a suitable substitute for coral.

It was long a custom with the Moslems of North Africa to bury a few branches of coral with their dead. It lasted into the nineteenth century.

A vast amount of religious, warlike, commercial, and naval activity had as its cause these branches with retractile mouths, these scraps of animal flesh grafted on tiny pieces of red-colored limestone. Though centuries have passed, coral still retains its prestige. There are still many people to be found who regard it with devotion and even with superstition. Women divers are never weary of gathering it with maniac intensity for the sole pleasure of putting it away in jewel cases which they are afraid to show to others.

If I write here of the living coral and its open "flowers," all these ghosts of the past which I am trying to evoke will fade and vanish into the darkness. Ancient verities so very real to our predecessors on this coast have now to be gathered from the pages of books as well as from the deep places of the sea. How different does this effort seem from that which went into our days of diving, and how guilty I feel toward them!

Only free-divers will understand what I mean when I say that most of our "searches" were scarcely ever planned and had no purpose beyond the satisfying of a desire to know the nature of deep water. The sea alone unites and justifies us, and not at all a deliberate intention to tear loose its historical secrets. The past lying beneath the sea's surface shows as part of it, as an added shimmer.

The stretch from Monaco to Narbonne is less a hunting ground to be exploited than a festival hall opening before our eyes. The attraction lies in the sea itself, not in the amphorae or the leaden anchors which we may find there.

Sometimes, at high noon in full summer, a shadow will creep across it. Laughing and limpid as a running stream, it seems, and we never know why, in one place to look like a winter sky, and in another an endless spring. Often, standing upon the shore, I have seen the movement of the seasons reflected in the lazy sway of knobbly weed—hot hours of summer when one plunges as into the welcome mouth of some cool cellar, winter noons when one hesitates to cross the frontier of the cold and stares too long at the jade-green streak, with its color of washed-out paint, made by some sandy spit far down in the black waters.

In the sea one has a feeling of relief, of lightness and irresponsibility. The free-diver is no longer anything but a vague hope. Nor am I sure that the hope is entirely related to archaeology. What point is there in searching if one is not poised above a site which is already known and has been surveyed! Sea life, seaweed, sea mud quickly cover up the traces of the human visitor. One needs to have a wild enthusiasm, a vocation for self-sacrifice, to spend one's days in this incessant search, surrendering all else to its pursuit. Since its foundation, the Club Alpin Sous-Marin has registered 7000 dives between Cannes and the islands of Lérins, but, even so, has but a partial knowledge of the depths, so vast is the sea.

More often than not, our only trophies are treasured scraps of animal life which we carry before us in cupped hands, only to see their colors fade as we approach the light of day. The boat is far off; the air in our cylinders is giving out, but we swim with our legs alone rather than risk the loss of such jewels. We come to

the surface with a piece of "Neptune's Lace"—it is always the
loveliest specimen we have found—only to find that somebody
has sat upon it in the boat that takes us to the shore. And then,
when evening comes, we fall asleep with our arms flung out upon
the table, exhausted as a result of too much blue water, relaxed,
and with finger tips as wrinkled as those of any washerwoman.

※ ※ ※

I MUST still say something more of this parallelism between the
life we lead and that of the past. I have not yet done with the
Cannes-Antibes sector. In the heyday of the ancient world it was
the center of a maritime activity which must have left more traces
on the sea bed than we have found. In addition to coral fishing
there was the making of garum, which took on such proportions
at Antibes and in the region round Fréjus that it became a local
industry. It gave employment to a population of active fishermen,
and it needed an outlet. For the most part its product must have
been carried by sea. Tunny in oil, a specialty of Antibes, was
much appreciated. Martial speaks of it: "*Antipolitani, fateor,
sum filia thynni.*" Garum, which the Romans called an *irritamen-
tum gulae,* a "stimulus to appetite," came originally from Spain,
but so great was the demand for it throughout the ancient world
in the imperial age that centers multiplied far and wide for its
preparation. I have been shown in North Africa the ruins of a
fish-preserving factory, where garum most certainly was made (at
Saint-Leu—excavated by Dr. Vincent). The fittings are all there
still, the vats, the washing installation, the jars. Enormous quantities of fish refuse have been found nearby, bones that must go
back at least 1800 years.

Preserving stations existed also on the west side of the Étang de
Vaccarès, and at the Étang de Lion, not far from Marignane,
where remains of them have been found, rectilinear cisterns into
which the mullet, so plentiful in those standing waters, were put
to soak in brine. There was no lack of salt in the neighborhood.
There were similar concerns in Baetica and in the South of Portugal, not far from Villaricos.

"Garum," says Grenier, "was a highly spiced and aromatic
relish made from the insides of small fishes, which were salted
and left for some days exposed to the sun. The liquid which they

exuded was 'garum.' Other small fishes were mixed with it whole,
anchovies and sardines in particular, but also oysters and shrimps.
This much prized sauce was used with many different articles of
food. It was very expensive: two *congii* (about 1½ English gallons) of the finest quality sold for a thousand sesterces, but the
enormous demand for it all over the Roman world must have led
to the production of cheaper varieties."

The *muria*, which perhaps even more than garum was a specialty of Antibes, consisted of pickled tuna. Its name, derived
from the Greek word meaning sea water, indicates that, like
garum, it was a product of Hellenic culinary tradition. It is possible, though far from certain, that the Greeks drew their knowledge of it from India, where *mam* and *soy* are still popular. On
the other hand, it is no less possible that India learned about it
from the Greeks.

This Provençal food-preserving industry stimulated the growth
of a local shipping organization, of the kind known to have
existed at Narbonne, Arles, and Lyon. It took the form of a
corporation of *utriculares*, a name derived from the inflated skins
used to give buoyancy to their flat-bottomed rafts. An inscription
at Antibes and another on the island of Saint-Honorat gives evidence that these craft were known in both places. Though I am
prepared to believe that these inflated skins may have been of
some use on the standing waters behind the coast, or on such
slow-flowing streams as the Var and the Loup, I very much doubt
whether, starting from Antibes, or even from the mouth of the
Var, with a cargo on board, these craft could have established
regular communication with the islands·of Lérins, except in the
calmest of calm weather, or even have maintained a coastal service. Still, it is never safe to be dogmatic about matters of which
one has had no experience. It might be well worth while to build
a model of one of these craft and test its seagoing qualities. The
trouble is that we do not really know how they were made. The
skins were animal hides filled with air, similar to the African
"guerba," but how were they fixed to the body of the boat, and
where?

I am inclined to think that the word *utriculares* referred to the
watermen (in contradistinction to sailors) who made use of these
vessels in certain places, or had made use of them, more from
reasons of economy than convenience. Small flat-bottomed boats

would probably have been far easier to handle on the Loup or the Argens—which has a swift current—than one of these bladder-supported coracles. It seems certain that the Croisette at Cannes was a marsh up to the time of the Middle Ages. It still remains to be proved that a coracle riding on inflated skin bags would be less liable to sink into water-logged ground than a flat-bottomed boat. We know of the existence of Scapharii, Lintiarii, of Betis, Guadalquivir; of Ratiarii (Lake of Tunis). But is it certain that these different words really refer to different types of craft. May they not merely be dialect variants?

It would not surprise me to find that this is yet another case in which the Herakles tradition was still strong. There are in existence mirrors, vases, and engraved stones on which the hero is shown crossing the sea on inflated skins. A long time after his day, in the seventeenth century, a Jesuit father named Montigny was still to be seen negotiating the Rhône on a form of boat similarly supported.

For many centuries, a large coastal traffic continued to ply from the mouths of the Loup and the Var, and as far off as the anchorage of Hyères. There was also much movement of ocean-going ships. I would go so far as to say that, for the ancients, this stretch of sea was much what the western approaches to the Channel are for the people of our own day. If any proof of this be needed, it will be found on the sea bed. It is within that area that the bulk of our collections of anchors and amphorae have been found: it is within that area that the Anthéor wreck occurred. It was through that area that the main route from Marseille to Narbonne ran.

ッ   ッ   ッ

IT is impossible to make an accurate statement about the number of amphorae brought to the surface during the last few years, even if we restrict our calculations to this one short stretch of coast. The richest and the best known deposit is that of Anthéor, just by the La Chrétienne buoy, where a good thousand amphorae of the same general type still lie embedded in the mud. They come from the wreck of which I spoke in Chapter 3. I have already pointed out that the presence of others, belonging to a later period, indicates the existence of yet other wrecks.

What a lot of divers have brought amphorae to the surface, whether openly or in secret!—at Port Cros, where a rounder-bellied example was found than at Anthéor, at Porquerolles, at Le Drammond, at Fos-sur-Mer.

An amphora of a rather more unusual design, slim and pointed, was found at Sanary, and is now in the Borély Museum at Marseille (it was recovered by Pihan de la Forêt, and Sérénon). The Saint-Germain Museum possesses another very much like it. It may have been used to contain *liquamen*—one of those juices or sauces so much beloved of the Romans, but different from garum.

A line of trading stations set up by the merchants of Massalia continues all along the coast. There was one at Athenopolis (Saint-Tropez), where we discovered nothing but Roman relics, enormous marble columns—about which I shall have something to say later—into which clumps of date-mussels had bored as deeply as do the spines of sea-urchins into human flesh. One day of last September, these columns emerged all dripping from the water. A glittering mosaic of marine plants and animals lay thick upon their wounds. They were all that remained of a wreck belonging to the second century.

ᴎ   ᴎ   ᴎ

AT the head of the Gulf of Giens, quite close to Hyères, at a place known as l'Almanare (an Arab word meaning "fire"—the lighthouse) excavations have been carried out on the site of yet another Massaliet colony—Olbia, a name which signifies "the happy," as Nikaia, Nice, means "the victorious." But it would be dangerous to let ourselves be caught in the trap of place names. The fact that many towns on the seaboard have Greek names should not be held to imply that they were not in existence before the coming of the Phocaeans. Beneath its Hellenic vocables Olbia reveals a "Ligurian" root which is to be found also in Léoube.

Olbia, which must have been founded from Marseille at some time between the fifth and third centuries B.C., is one of the few Greek colonies in the West to have been excavated. Jacques Coupry found traces of the ancient defensive wall on the seaward side. He later took charge of two underwater surveys which were carried out on the 21st and 28th August, 1949, by members of the Club Alpin Sous-Marin. The Roman influence, however, had successfully obliterated all Greek traces beneath the surface. The divers recovered nothing but a few door fittings dating, apparently, to a period later than that of Greek activity in these parts, and the remains of a construction which had nothing to do with the sea—a hypocaust. The Roman station of Pomponia (the naval station of Pomponiana which is marked on the *Antonine Itinerary*) has wiped out Olbia, The Happy.

This is an instance of the disappointment that still lies in wait for undersea archaeologists who find that Roman building has triumphed over earlier Greek traces. Others are Cherchel, Tyre, and Sidon.

Beyond Toulon lie Le Brusc, Sanary, and the underwater areas particularly associated with Frederic Dumas, J. Y. Cousteau, and Georges Bertrand. None of these free-divers has as yet produced any conclusive evidence which would establish the precise position of Tauroentum. Was it the port of Sanary, as Jullian believed, or was it Le Brusc? Tauroentum is one of those names in which a native root is recognizable under a Greek disguise. *Taur* means height. Boyancé duly carried out a course of excavations on the plateau of Le Brusc. He found traces of a citadel and recovered a certain amount of Campanian, Arettine, and la Graufesenque pottery, as well as coins bearing the emblems of Marseille and Rome. Is this really the site of Tauroentum, and if so, where was the port?

Did it face onto the islets of Embiers, where we carried out a dive and found nothing but some dead coral and a disdainful grouper? There is just an underwater labyrinth, where the rock which carries the Tour des Magnons is completely pierced. This was the studio in which J. Y. Cousteau made his first submarine film with the help of a watertight box designed by Vèche, and without using a diving helmet. A friend on the surface, standing at the foot of the tower, dropped his right arm. Cousteau dived and took up a position with his camera focused on one of the openings of the tunnel. A second later, the same friend dropped his left arm. Dumas dived, in his turn, reached the other entrance of the passageway, took aim at a grouper, fired, and then remained as long as possible within the camera's field of vision.

LAST of all comes La Ciotat, where one day we paid a visit to the sea depths in which Cousteau, Taillez, and Dumas have made part of another film: *Paysage de Silence*.

La Ciotat was, in ancient days, called Kitharista—"The Woman playing on the Cithara." Camille Jullian has always maintained that the shape of the nearby hills gave the idea of this cithara, the valley, the gulf, the indentation of the coast line appearing to him to combine into the shape of a lyre. Dauzat, however, who is careful not to let himself be browbeaten by what is Greek in Provence, has revealed beneath the seemingly Hellenic dress the existence of a name native to the locality— which occurs at Céreste (Basses-Alpes), between Forcalquier and Manosque.

However open to argument the lyre may be from a purely linguistic point of view, it certainly proved as beneficent to us as the instrument with which Arion charmed the dolphins. In cool, clear water we reached what must be one of the most smiling of the world's seascapes, a bottom on which pink gorgonias, studded with mauve and scarlet polyps, lay like colored hangings on the rocky walls.

And now I have a terrible confession to make. However admirable the companions of my diving exploits, however fearless their conduct and staunch their friendship, they always, to some extent, put a check upon my pleasure. I love nothing so much as setting out, dressed in an old sweater, and diving when and where I will. My chief enjoyment is to move slowly through the water, or to stand stock-still with leisure enough on my hands to mutter over to myself down there, beneath the surface, all the words that have become so mightily enriched by their sea associations, that I may compare them with the dream that memory distorts. Is this just one of those vices so frequently to be found in the literary gent, or is it the effect of age? I am rapidly becoming an old and rather grumpy gentleman, a veteran of the diving community who, as he sits taking the air in some public park, hates to be disturbed by children's balls bumping against his legs and by dogs nosing about for stones between his feet. I have reached a stage when, during my moments in the sea, I am conscious of a "tetchy" intolerance.

IN the neighborhood of Marseille, Georges Beuchat has found amphorae almost everywhere and brought many to the surface. They are Roman. Dry-land archaeologists are certainly one up on him, for they have recently discovered what remains of the Greek port. Distasteful though the admission may be, they owe their success to the destruction carried out by the Germans, who, when they blew up many of the buildings in the district of the Vieux Port, opened the way for excavations which have brought to light the stakes belonging to the sixth-century Greek breakwater. Whether or not we like the circumstances which made this discovery possible, it was thrilling in the extreme. There, on the sand, lay the great balks of unseasoned pine and holm oak. Two thousand five hundred years of wars and struggles and toings and froings have failed to wipe out the traces of the ancient quay and the plank road up which men long ago had pulled the ships coming from Ionia.

At the water's edge, in a confusion of masonry, and badly damaged by the waves, one of the most precious relics imaginable was brought to light, a mutilated Ionic capital dating quite certainly from before the fourth century and perhaps as old even as the sixth. Set in one of the volutes was a piece of marble, undoubtedly of Greek origin, a reminder of Hellas beneath barbarian skies. This "oculus," so firmly, so carefully wedged into position, will undoubtedly be the occasion for much learned wrangling. Let me fire the first salvo of words by reminding those who will later move in to the attack that many marble eyes, "large enough to have been mounted on a trireme," have been found in the port of Mounychie, at the Piraeus. May there not well be some connection between these eyes and the "oculus" found on the Marseille capital?

In its original state this capital measured close on six feet in width. It is safe to assume that it adorned the façade of one of the temples of Massalia—that of Apollo, perhaps, or of Athena, both of which faced the sea and would catch the attention of approaching mariners while they were still far out. The temple of Artemis, on the other hand, built on the hill where the General Hospital now stands, faced inland, toward the barbarians. It was probably Caesar who, after the defeat of Massalia in 49, ordered the demolition of the city's temples and used their stones as rubble for the quays of the Roman harbor. The particular

fragment of which I am speaking is now in the Borély Museum.
It is the only piece of Greek architecture which has ever been
found in Gaul and therefore an archaeological "document" of
quite exceptional importance.

It was my good fortune to be allowed, last spring, to put in
some work with a pickaxe on a patch of waste ground in the rue
Négrel, where a good deal of Ionian and Attic pottery has already
been found: fragments of vases with black figures on a red
ground, showing galloping horses, a frieze of lions and swans, and
battles between warriors wearing crested Corinthian helmets—all
dating from the first half of the sixth century.

From the rue Négrel one can see right over the Vieux Port.
Here was the site of the Greek defensive wall. The ground is
thick with sherds, their flecks of mica glittering in the sun. The
whole of this area has been earmarked for rebuilding, and the
preliminary work of leveling is now being carried out. While a
mechanical excavator, making an infernal din, was busy disem-
boweling ground which is all a clutter of history, we managed to
recover an earthenware disk which had been used to weight the
net of some fisherman who died some two thousand five hundred
years ago.

                          𝕳   𝕳   𝕳

IT has been the custom to maintain that the Romans had a
great respect for, even a love of, Hellenism. It was certainly mani-
fested in a very unequal fashion. Sulla looted, Caesar destroyed:
nor did the one activity always exclude the other. Did Rome leave
on the soil of Gaul anything comparable to what she smashed?
She built with a heavy hand, and hers are the last traces in the
sea before our own Ponts et Chaussées got to work. Rome, too,
carried out the last overhaul of place names: Forum Julii—Fréjus;
Fossae Marianae—Fos-sur-Mer; Narbo Martius (Narbo seems to
have been a pre-Indo-European name).

Forum Julii, a late and artificial inland harbor, was already
silted up in the second century A.D. The port to which Octavius
sent the ships of Actium is now a market garden, and the Lantern
of Augustus has become a storehouse for flowerpots. The railway
line crosses the dock where galleys once were moored under the
protection of Venus. We shall see in the next chapter that

the harbor of the elder Marius, Fossae Marianae, has left in the
water and the mud relics of a more strictly naval type.

Narbonne shares with Arles and Ostia the distinction of being
a prototype of the Roman port—an entirely new conception, a
center of commerce rather than of ships, the invention of a race
of middlemen in whose minds there stirred old memories of
Latium. There had been throughout the Mediterranean many
harbors built on the Aegean, Phoenician, Punic, and Greek
model. All these were sited in places blessed with natural conditions which favored their function—in creeks more or less improved by human labor, or in some heaven-sent place like Marseille, or on some island which it was only necessary to link with
the mainland by a causeway in order to ensure two safe anchorages. But the Romans, when they became masters of the Mediterranean, had no seafaring tradition behind them. What they
looked for was not the natural harbor, the sheltered inlet, but the
land center where highroads crossed. Their coastal stations are
not so much ports as drainage and pumping centers. Arles, Fos,
and Narbonne are, from the sailor's point of view, detestable.
But Arles and Narbonne do at least have the advantage of a
system of lagoons and navigable waterways. Both were already
situated at the meeting point of continental arteries before the
date of their official founding.

At Arles, whither the Greeks had come, calling it Theline (the
Saluvii destroyed this first settlement before the end of the sixth
century), the great north-south highway, which drove straight
down the valleys of the Rhône and Saône, by Lyon and Châlon,
met the east-west road running from the Durance to Nîmes.
Narbonne was even better placed. It was the meeting point of
two prehistoric routes—one leading from Spain into Italy, the
line along which Herakles had journeyed, the Via Domitia, running lengthwise through the city; the other coming from the
Ocean and terminating at the Mediterranean. Both are very
ancient tracks, but what is really important is that each served
for the carriage of one of the two different metals which together
produce bronze. The road from Spain was the "Copper Road"
which led to the mineral deposits in the valleys of the Orb and
the Bogne. The ocean road was the "Tin Road."

At the Palm Door of the Cathedral of Cordova stand two
milestones. The inscriptions upon them prove that the Romans

had completed the road from Rome which led across Gaul and
Spain, *"usque ad Oceanum."*

In the region of Narbonne and Béziers, on the edge of the
Étang de Vendres, what most strikes the observer is not so much
the influence of Rome as the evidence, there apparent, of a
strange and brilliant local culture. Montlaurès and Ensérune
were twin cities to which, from the sixth until the end of the
second century B.C., the finest Greek vases and objects of Campanian pottery were brought by sea. The wealth and activity of
that part of the coast were bound up with certain ports which
have not yet yielded up their secrets. It is there, no doubt, that
we must hope to find decisive information about Greek influence
in Gaul and about the vine-growing industry. There are a number
of wrecks off the coast.

Numerous points of resemblance between Arles and Narbonne
exist which have not always been sufficiently stressed. Both are
cities built on rivers; both are trading centers rather than ports.
Arles and Fos, linked by the Canal of Marius, correspond to
Narbonne and Capelle, which are joined by the Roubine. Both
had direct access only to an inconvenient stretch of sea which
was always exposed to the danger of silting. Both were confronted by the same difficulty of keeping a navigable channel
open. There is a similar resemblance between the old centers of
local habitation. Montlaurès is another Entremont. The same
sort of traces, whether on land or in the sea, exist in both regions.
Rouzaud has found on the site of Capelle, the oldest of the
Narbonne harbors, pottery of precisely the same type as that discovered by Beaucaire at Fos—Campanian wine amphorae and
Italic and la Graufesenque sherds.

The inconveniences of the Roman system are so obvious that
they must have been accepted deliberately: on the edge of the
sea, improvements barely sufficient to serve their purpose, ancient
local traditions adapted to later needs; further inland, a town
protected by solid walls to provide a safe place in which wealth
might be concentrated. There are two possible explanations of
this strange arrangement. It may have been due to the failure of
landsmen with little knowledge of the requirements of sea-borne
trade, to adapt themselves to novel conditions, or it may have
been produced by the age-old suspicion of the peasant whose
only concern is to set up his barns beyond reach of danger. What-

ever the reasons for the choice may have been, Rome did, in fact, choose this particular "layout." Up to the time of Claudius, and even of Trajan, Ostia was woefully lacking in technical equipment. It was in Rome that sea and river traffic became concentrated, and the same is true of Arles and Narbonne.

❦ ❦ ❦

THERE is still much work to be done in tracing the remains of antiquity all along this coast and as far as Spain. A few relics have been recovered at Agde,—Aγιθη Τυχη, or "Good Fortune"— a name which is merely a Greek disguise. The whole of the sea route is densely sown with amphorae—as at Collioure, where Lieutenant Dupas has brought a few samples to the surface, and also at Port Vendres.—"The people of Massalia maintained commercial relations with the rich city of Pyrene, in the territory of the Sordones, which was later destroyed by the Iberian invasion. Some have identified this place with Elne, others with Port Vendres. They ventured still further, and made contact with the Phocaean colonies on the Eastern coast of Spain." * Rhoda, Kallipolis, Hemeroskopion, the Iberian Cape Artemision, Almeria, Abdera, and Mainake are, all of them, places crying aloud for underwater examination. So far as I know only the approaches of Carthagena have so far been prospected. Several anchors and amphorae were found there, off the Island of Escombreras, where once there stood a temple of Hercules—we never seem to get away from him! The head of Hercules figured on coins struck at Gadès, and, according to Pliny, the Garden of the Hesperides was situated on the Atlantic coast of Africa, in the estuary of the Loukkos, on the site of Lixus, in the vicinity of the present-day Larache—which is the only natural harbor on that coast.

❦ ❦ ❦

IT is something of a gamble to attempt to follow two tracks at one and the same time, that of the sea and that of the land; to move in the wake of the free-diver, and in the footsteps of the archaeologist.

* R. Busquet: *Hist. du Commerce de Marseille*, p. 29.

The attempt, however, will not have been valueless if it has
succeeded in convincing the reader that the evidence still hidden
under the sea is not to be despised. These watery fringes of the
past may seem to be less clear-cut, more confused, than the Roman masonry of Provence. It remains to be seen whether this submerged mirror of truth may not prove to have more meaning for
us than the firmer contours of the land. For us, the underwater
aspects of antiquity have a glamor which nothing else can equal.
They show us, side by side, real coral and the carved face of the
Gorgon. "The crimson shroud in which the dead gods slumber"
is, for us, this sunlit sea where the depths are as rich in flowers as
is a Persian garden.

Only what is hidden is a fit field
for scientific enquiry.
                    GASTON BACHELARD

THE MOMENT HAS COME TO CALL A HALT, TO STAY FOR A WHILE
on one section of this coast, and there to describe in more leisure-
ly fashion a single underwater site—perhaps the richest and the
most instructive which I have so far come across. In it is summed
up the whole life of Provence as seen from the sea and beneath
it. I refer to Fos-sur-Mer. There, as in the tabulated synopsis of a
textbook, the various influences are exposed, one above the other,
and we can see in the mud the economic and religious currents
in superimposed layers.

I have known the place in all weathers. I have always found it,
in many different ways, heartbreaking, but, in the long run, have
come to have feelings of affection for it. In its marshy setting,
under the rain and winds of winter, it is a desolate spot—little
more, indeed, than a seashore, with bits of old iron sticking up
through the shingle against a background of *bastidons,* or country
cottages.

94

On Summer Saturdays, Marseille families swarm at Fos. The
air resounds to the shrill cries of timid bathers, and the gray sand
provides a scene for idylls. In spite of the blows dealt it by the
Germans, the beach is by no means dead. The whole of this corner of Provence was heavily dynamited in one of those last-
minute spasms of destruction which were carried out less in a
spirit of ferocity than from sheer stupidity. In any case, it was
utterly useless, and now the process of rebirth is continuing slowly
and, I fear, without much air of gaiety. Between what remains of
disemboweled gun emplacements, villas are rising, but the material used in them is of poor quality. There is no vegetation, not a
mimosa, not an aloe, not even a cactus, to give a touch of color
to this dreary shore. Inland from it lie the waste lands of La Crau
—Campus Cravus—where grows in its simplest and most eloquent
form that famous root known as "car," which dates from the pre-
Indo-European past, a word which mankind, for thousands of
years, has used to express all that is stony, incapable of cultivation, and hostile.

At Fos we are still upon the road of Herakles. Aeschylus provides the evidence of this, for he mentions the very place when
he gives the hero pebbles of Crau to use as missiles. "You will
come in the course of your journeying," says Prometheus to
Herakles, "upon the intrepid army of the Ligurians . . . but
Zeus will have compassion on you. He will cover the ground with
a mass of rounded stones, and you, making of them your weapons, will easily scatter the Ligurian warriors." The Ligurians have
vanished, but the stones remain. As to Herakles, he is far away.
A religion not his own has taken root in this unfertile soil. On the
beach where now there lies the roof-tile rubble of prewar Fos,
rests the lid of an Early-Christian sarcophagus. Others show
above the surface of the sea close inshore. This playground of
young people from Marseille is a cemetery: a cemetery without
crosses or gravestones, only of great monolithic troughs and heavy
lids with projecting ornaments cast up on days of storm—a
necropolis of monolithic tombs of the same kind as those at
Alyscamps.

To find out more we should have to dig in the sand, both above
and below high-water mark, and perhaps bring to a full stop the
building of the Casino which is going forward with so much dash,
for, like Herakles, the Casino has returned from the country of

the dead. We should be better advised, I think, to turn our backs upon the beach at Fos and go a little way beyond the cove of Saint-Gervais, where the villas have matured into small houses, all freshly blooming. Here some ancient traces, which neither war nor the passage of the centuries can efface, still cling to the sea: fishing boats drawn up on the shore, brown-meshed nets hung on poles to dry, a ruined quay, and a few pieces of masonry half hidden in the water. Saint-Gervais is a rocky inlet or a sandy coast. Though harsh and very small, it has long served as a shelter for fishermen. Through a narrow channel cut in the rock, a lagoon discharges its superfluity of muddy water. Whether this lagoon is natural or a harborage contrived by men it is hard to tell. When I saw it for the first time, I could not help being reminded of a similar site which I once visited in North Africa, at Port-aux-Poules, not far from Arzew. I record the impression for what it is worth, because nobody has ever found any evidence at Fos which would justify the theory that it is an artificial harbor constructed after the Punic manner.

To get a closer view of the rocky seaside, one has to work one's way through a barrier of small houses. Hard by the canal which joins the lagoon to the sea there is nothing to catch the eye but bathing huts and a few slots and holes cut with the pickaxe. These, doubtless, are the remains of "improvements" made long ago. The place must have served, too, as a quarry, for one can see there a great block of stone half cut through but never moved —a job left unfinished as the result of who can say what weariness, what drama. Once more it is of North Africa that I am reminded, and especially of Tipasa, where, at sea level, there stands a quarry of that shell-blotched limestone out of which the town was constructed.

A crumbling jetty juts into the sea. For the diver the site continues under water. Beyond the mole, at a depth of two and a half fathoms, are great blocks of fashioned masonry and weed-covered columns which may be the remains of an archway or of a building with doors. (It was found possible to raise one of these columns. It is of quarried stone and of a very old molded design. It has an impost intended to carry the springing of an arch or the lintel of a door. It is of the same general type as the examples found at Volubilis and Palmyra.) The sea here, however, is never clear, even in summer, but dirty. The shallow bot-

tom is of mud. In the cove of Saint-Gervais the Rhône silt has
been tirelessly deposited through many centuries.

Those who carry out in this spot one of those underwater per-
ambulations which are the peculiar prerogatives of the free-diver
stand little chance of making any sensational discovery. All
around is gray weed and ooze. Between the rather too slimy cliff
walls, among the scattered masonry and in the murky water, one
seeks in vain to fix a fruitful thought, to find any sharp excres-
cence to which the intelligence may hold, or any evidence that
life in these surroundings has ever shown a touch of brilliance.
This abandoned harbor is a wreck, swathed in weed, a drowned
corpse from which the mud forever swirls up to the surface. One
cannot even say that the past has been effaced. The truth is worse
than that. The past has been stirred into nothingness.

It may be just possible to fish up the fragments of an amphora
which has escaped the vigilance of earlier searchers. But there
are many such mixed with the pebbles on the beach. There the
past crunches beneath one's feet. After days of storm a flood of
red and black sherds rises to the surface from the tormented sea
bed, the separate pieces showing a network of bristle worms and
serpulids, all tangled together like centuries-old spaghetti.

The seashore, accommodating and deceptive, supplies only
fragments, scraps, though, if asked, it would furnish a cartful. By
merely bending down one can follow the spoor of five or six centuries of history. Moving with head bent, like a sleepwalker, one
forgets the repellent setting, the charmless sea, the suburban
architecture. Sometimes, in the course of a single hour, I have
garnered an exciting, shabby harvest of the kind I used to collect
at Cherchel and at Arzew: a crazy knapsack load of Italic sedi-
ment, scraps of Graufesenque ware, the mutilated form of a god
on some fragment of red pottery, amphora handles, and the
necks of vases—a squalid collection of objects which had ap-
pealed to me by reason of a dab of some unusual color or an odd
shape, but which, on the morrow, I should throw away.

It is there, in a restricted area not far from the shore, that the
most sensational discoveries have been made. Each year, since
1948, Beaucaire has been carrying out excavations which have
turned out to be no less productive than they deserved. In a space
measuring anything from ten to five hundred yards, in a depth
of water varying from three to fifteen feet, he and his team of

voluntary workers have accomplished a tedious task. They found, among other things, a Roman villa and exposed its walls. Step by step they followed the clues in the water and the flooded sand. The alluvial deposits of the Rhône had left the smallest objects just as they were, and preserved them. The searchers, after first lifting a top layer of sand, and next a deposit of thin sticky clay, close on thirty inches deep reached the archaeological level. From then on, there was no lack of finds.

It is difficult to imagine what this work entailed. For four years they kept at it, sometimes working with picks below the water line. It was a terrific task, since it meant the shifting of great quantities of sand, pebbles, and, above all, mud—thick, sticky mud. Many cubic yards of soil had to be sieved so that nothing should be missed.

Today, the results of all that labor are on view in the small museum which was set up by a local society working under the inspiration of Beaucaire, a society called Les Amis du Vieil Istres.

꙰   ꙰   ꙰

As I have had occasion to say elsewhere, there is good reason to consider Fos-sur-Mer to be the very model of a well-conducted undersea archaeological operation. By great good fortune, all the necessary factors were present in the right place and at the right time: skill and willingness, a rich site not too far from the mainland, shallow water, courage which no amount of hard work could daunt, and finally, the creation of a local museum in which the finds were immediately housed, protected from weather and accident, identified, catalogued, and shown to the public.

If Dr. Beaucaire and his friends have been able to grapple successfully with a task which does them honor, as much by reason of the methods employed as of the results achieved, the reason is that, with them, archaeology was not a matter of sudden whim or of sluggish pursuit. Their discoveries were not made by divers on a lightning visit, who come to a site, are quick to grasp its possibilities or lack of them, and then clear off to pluck easier laurels elsewhere. Their success at Fos was the result of a series of researches carried out in one given area and according to a well-thought-out program of work.

The underwater explorers who were responsible for this triumph had been trained on land in the hardest of all archaeological schools—that of prehistory. They had already carried out the methodical opening up of the Abri Cornille, close to Istres, which has now been classified as a historical monument. The Abri Cornille is of interest because it shows traces of uninterrupted occupation from the Palaeolithic to the Bronze Age. It provides evidence of much that occurred in this one district in the earliest times.

I know only too well what work of this kind means: lying on one's stomach and scrabbling away with bare hands which still, after ten thousand years, are the best of all tools; exposing, one after the other, all the superimposed archaeological levels; getting rid of the rubbish, and collecting every scrap that may be of importance, even though quite often it is no more than dust.

How hard that school can be may be seen from the fact that many of those who worked on the Abri Cornille, young and vigorous men, quite often fainted from heat and exhaustion. All the same, it is the best of all schools, for it produces hardened and meticulous archaeologists, men skillful in collecting the tiniest scraps of evidence, in love with the humble but important labors of their calling, champions of teamwork and anonymous victories.

A day came when these many virtues found employment not only on land, but in the sea. This was the result neither of chance nor of vainglory, but of a logical process. What these men were concerned to do was to let nothing escape which might serve to reconstruct the past of the region in which they were working. And so it came about that the Société des Amis du Vieil Istres turned from the mountain to the seashore and set about examining the beach of Saint-Gervais.

What they achieved can be seen in that small house at Istres, standing at the corner of a medieval street, which has now been turned into a museum. What thrills the visitor is not only the wealth of rare and precious objects, but the diversity as well as the unity of this underwater conquest—its weight of human associations. There can be found all the influences to which this corner of the earth has been subjected, the conditions in which successive generations of its inhabitants lived, exhibited not only in masterpieces of art, but in the products of humble lives—a cheese mold cheek by jowl with an ivory head, kitchen pottery and precious vases.

The impression is much the same as one gets from a visit to the Musée des Antiquités Nationales de Saint-Germain, but on a reduced scale. Before our eyes we have the history of one section of our native soil, set against the background of the sea, and freed from the haunting ghosts of Caesar, of Alesia, of Napoleon III. Here are no weapons, no swords, no helmets, but wine jars, drinking cups, and lamps: *instrumentum domesticum*.

☙ ☙ ☙

WHO were these folk of Fos? Since when had they been settled round their little creek between the sea and the lagoon?

Tradition gives to Marius the credit for having built the port and dug the canal which, by avoiding the silt brought down by the Rhône, linked the sea with the great river harbor of Arles which served the whole region. There is no lack of texts relating to the subject: Strabo, Pomponius Mela, Pliny the Elder; but they are texts only. Before the researches carried out by Beaucaire, no archaeological evidence existed which could confirm them. But now from the sea have come examples of Campanian pottery of types A and B and dishes of black Arretine ware which enable us to say with certainty that on this spot there existed a town in touch with Italy at the time of Marius, the conqueror of the Cimbri and the Teutones.

The Fossae Marianae are the fosses, or ditches, of Marius, the memory of which is preserved in our own Fos. Their purpose was to form a canal by which the Roman army could be supplied. It was near Aix that Marius crushed the Barbarians (102 B.C.), and thereby saved Narbonne, Marseille, and Rome. After his victory the canal was given to the people of Marseille in token of friendship. They did not particularly want it, and contented themselves with drawing a considerable profit by levying dues on all ships moving along it in either direction. This was also a convenient way of making more costly a traffic artery which did not use their own port and, in the long run, took what should have been their own proper trade away from them.

If we are to believe the Roman historians, this port shot up like a mushroom, at the word of Marius, in that region of the

barren Crau where no port had existed previously. I see no reason
for believing this. There was already a small anchorage there.
That it dated from before Marius is proved by traces of local
pottery dating from the fifth century B.C. At Fos itself, a heeled
axe belonging to a period subsequent to Bronze Age II has been
found. Earthenware has been fished from the sea bearing a strong
resemblance to that of La Tène, examples of local Phocaean
pottery of pale, micaceous clay, and fragments of "Iberian" ware.
Should we ever succeed in reconstructing a picture of the activities carried on in this region during the great periods of prehistory, the results may well be surprising. Not only was there a
settled community in these parts before the coming of Marius,
the name of which is lost, but it is quite possible that it had
already established contact with the interior by means of a chain
of lagoons and inlets which the famous canal merely improved
under Roman direction. It was too quickly constructed to have
started from nothing. Nor is that all, for discoveries in the neighborhood have confirmed the existence of a considerable amount
of activity in pre-Roman days. These inland waterways, these
lagoons, must assuredly have provided communication with the
sea for a number of very ancient sites. Whether they were Greek,
Celtic, or Iberian, whether they succeeded, for the most part, in
retaining their autonomy—like the ancient Fos—in spite of the
nearness of Marseille, we cannot say for certain. All we do know
is that traffic continued up to the time of the Middle Ages. The
Rhône delta still holds surprises in store for us. The salt pans,
the fish-infested lagoons, the waterways, attracted and maintained, from the great periods of the prehistoric cultures, a considerable number of mixed populations.

For some years now Henri Rolland has been carrying out excavations at Saint-Blaise, on the rocky spur which separates the
lagoons of Lavalduc and Citis, a site which apparently goes back
to the sixth century B.C. The *oppidum* occupied the tip of the
spur and was defended on the land side by a wall which has been
entirely uncovered. The stones of this *enceinte*, which archaeologists attribute to the sixth century, show marks of "Graeco-
Punic" workmanship, and of incised characters having to do with
some sort of numbering. (Only one Ionian fragment was found
at Fos.) "Such parts of the parapet as have been unearthed are
of the rounded type common in Sicily, at Eryx and Motya." Is

it too much to assume that Fos, in the sixth century, was the
Graeco-Punic port of the Saint-Blaise *oppidum*, which some have
identified with Mastrabala? They are only two and a half miles
apart, and there is more than one lagoon in the intervening area.
At the period in question the Rhodians frequently visited the
delta before they were driven from it by the Phocaeans of Marseille. The very name Rhône recalls their presence, and Rhoda-
nousia may well have been at Beaucaire, where there is still a
quarter known as Rouanesse.

It is pointless to dwell too long over so confused a "pedigree."
It would be of far greater interest to show that, under the very
shadow of Marseille, Fos long retained its native flavor. But is
this possible? The misfortunes of Marseille are better known than
the glory of Fos. The fact that no Ionian pottery has been found
at the latter place (actually one piece *was* found), but only later
deposits of Campanian amphorae similar to those at Anthéor,
would seem to prove a certain degree of economic independence
and the existence of lines of communication which did not pass
through Marseille.

It was about this time that there arrived at Fos a small piece of
ivory which has since been recovered from the mud: a tiny
Hellenistic masterpiece which is undoubtedly a head of Aphrodite and may well rank as one of the most exquisite of all the
objects discovered there. It dates from the first century B.C.

Miscalculation began to produce its dire effects at Marseille
shortly before the beginning of the Christian era. Forced to
choose between Pompey and Caesar, the people of that city,
whose clearness of vision may have been misted by middle-class
prosperity, opted for the established power as against the climber,
for Pompey the sailor as against Caesar the discontented general.
They opened their harbor to the squadron commanded by Domi-
tius Aenobarbus, who had been named by the Senate as Pro-
consul of the two Gauls.

Caesar refused to let himself be halted at the gates of Marseille, but left his lieutenant, Trebonius, there, giving orders that
twelve ships should be built and equipped at Arles. These he
entrusted to Decimus Brutus, while he himself marched westward. He had an eye for the essential and wished to seize the
key of what has been called the Eldorado of the Ancient World,
namely Spain and its riches. That key was the Route of Hercules.

With his twelve ships Brutus won two victories. He defeated
the fleet of Marseille in the waters of Le Frioul, and another
which hastened to its support under one of Pompey's lieutenants,
off Tauroentum. Where could Brutus's naval base have been
situated if not at Fos? Caesar had his ships built at Arles, the
reason being that its outlet to the sea, that is to say, Fos, was free,
and not controlled by the forces of Marseille.

Marseille was conquered. Its maritime activity and its commercial prosperity were finished for a long time to come. Pre-
eminence passed to Arles and its seaport, Fos. Marseille dwindled
to the status of a university town where the sons of troublesome
families, and exiles, were sent.

Marseille, wedged between Arles and Narbonne, was not the
new type of harbor demanded by the Romans. The rising masters
of the Roman world were businessmen. The naval potentialities
of a town mattered little to them. What they wanted was access
to land routes and inland waterways. Arles, from this point of
view, was ideally situated. It stood at the last crossing point of
the Rhône above the delta and commanded northward the road
to Lyon, eastward the line of communication with the Durance,
and westward the great arteries leading to Nîmes, the Cevennes,
and the Auvergne. What did it matter if access to the coast
presented a problem, if Fos was less satisfactory as a harbor than
Marseille? Henceforward, all traffic was to pass through Fos.

And this traffic was very heavy. The remains show that clearly
enough. It was at this time that fragments of Italian verra sigil-
lata became thickly embedded in the mud of the Saint-Gervais
cove; at this time, too, that some rich shipmaster, some new-
comer to the district, some recently Romanized provincial, doubtless built the villa, the submerged walls of which our divers have
examined, and from which they have salved an altar still surrounded with lamps.

It is probably to the same period that one of our finest prizes
belongs—the fragment of an Italic vase with a green lead glaze
on the outside and a yellow glaze on the interior, in imitation of
the silver vessels of Asia Minor.

One of the lamps ought to be given a full-length commentary.
It shows a fisherman and a siren—that mythical creature closely
connected with the cult of the dead which reappears in the

twelfth century on the capitals of our Romanesque churches. It is to be seen on the façade of Saint-Sernin at Toulouse.

For the sake of my fellow divers let me here say something about these sirens with whose name they make so free. The siren is not, as they think, half woman and half fish. In the purest tradition of the antique, the siren has the head and the bust of a woman, with a bird's body and claws. The Greeks never represented sirens in any other way. They derived the conception from Egypt, where this hybrid signified the soul separated from the body. It is thus that the sirens are shown on a mosaic-encrusted cistern now in the Cherchel Museum, their slim claws and multicolored feathers framing a ship and a shoal of leaping dolphins. I find this motif endlessly fascinating. The fishtail is due to a confusion, dating from the sixth century A.D., between sirens and female Tritons, and it was to female Tritons, not to sirens, that Horace's famous lines referred:

> . . . *Ut turpiter atrum*
> *Dessinat in piscem mulier formosa superne*

—a not very flattering description of the ladies who come diving with us.

ꚜ   ꚜ   ꚜ

Toward the middle of the first century, the inhabitants of Fossae Marianae, who, like the whole of the Latin world, had formerly imported much Italic pottery, began to be flooded with Gallic ware. From the first century onwards, and especially in the second, this Gallic variety began to oust the foreign article and, in its turn, spread through the whole civilized world. The center of its production was a place close to Millau, La Graufesenque, whence it traveled into Italy, Germany, and Britain. At Pompeii, a packing case newly arrived, and which the recipient had not had time to open before the catastrophe of 79, has been found to contain bowls and lamps of La Graufesenque ware.

The main loading port for Italy was Narbonne, but many of the consignments traveled also down the Rhône, by way of Lyon. It should cause little surprise, therefore, that numerous examples, many of them of superb quality, should have turned up at Fos. Several of the smaller vases have been found intact, while innu-

merable fragments of dishes and decorated and carinated cups
have been collected. These pieces belong to many different periods. (The following are among the makers' stamps which have
been found on the examples of La Graufesenque pottery discovered at Fos: Carinus, Niger, Primus, Aufinus, Irmo, Cartus,
Macer, Via, Mommo, Bassus, Vitalis, Germanus, Albanus, Pas-
seus, Sulpicius, Cocus, Cosius, Rufus.)

The wealth and activity of Fos seem to have been firmly established by this period. The many scraps of glass, and the quantities of fused glass "paste," the intact miniature amphorae (some
of which may have been used merely as stoppers for the larger
amphorae), the innumerable decorated lamps, the profusion and
the quality of the pottery concentrated in this one small area
indicates the existence of a prosperous town, of a level of civilization not greatly, if at all, inferior to that of the Greek and Italian
cities of the same epoch. It is impossible, after seeing these
remains, to doubt that Fos was a maritime center.

This role she was to play for some considerable time. A road
map of the Roman Empire, the *Peutinger Map*, still survives, on
which the Fossae Marianae are marked. (The *Peutinger Map* is
a unique copy of an ancient map now in the Library of Vienna.
It was found at Worms in the fifteenth century, and given in
1508 to Conrad Peutinger of Augsburg. It seems to have been
copied from an official document put in hand by Caracalla in
the early years of the third century. But this document was itself
a copy of an earlier map constructed at the orders of Agrippa,
which Augustus caused to be painted on the wall of the Porticus
Vipsania.) Their position is indicated by a small design showing
docks arranged in a semicircle. It would, however, be a mistake
to conclude that any installation of this precise form existed at
Fos. The drawing is merely a conventional sign used in the map
to indicate harbor works, just as turrets and gables in Michelin
are used to show the different categories of hotels. Exactly the
same design is used for Fos as for Ostia, though the latter has,
in addition, a lighthouse. What *is* significant is that neither the
conventional sign nor the lighthouse is given to Marseille.

The *Antonine Itinerary*—which is less accurate than the *Peutinger Map*, and almost certainly dates from the reign of Diocletian (284-305)—and a text which accompanies it, *Sea-routes
from Rome to Arles*, shows Incaro—Carry le Rouet—as a *positio*,

that is to say, an anchorage or natural harbor, and Fossae Marianae as a *portus*, or artificial installation.

Fos, then, was the outlet for all Central Gaul, since it served
Arles, which was the official port of the Annona, the government
corn supply district. Marseille no longer played even a subsidiary
part in the commercial activities of the second and third centuries. The cargo fleets making for Ostia were assembled at Arles
and reached the open sea at Fos.

Arles was better suited to serve as a trading center than to
exploit the agricultural resources of the region.

Its shipowners had their warehouse under the portico at Ostia.
It was adorned with a mosaic representing the bridge of boats
over the Rhône, and the three mouths of the river. They also had
an establishment at Beyrouth, the metropolis of all the caravans
from the East and the Far East.

There can be no doubt that the lead seals used in commerce
which were found in the Saône at Lyon came from cargoes handled by them and passing through Fos. Some of these seals are
those used by Tyre and Alexandria. Scraps of hemp or flax are still
visible on a number of them. The Tyre seal is attached to a
twist of reddish-brown silk which must once have been crimson.
This humble witness to a long voyage made in the second century
of our era sets one dreaming. For all we know it may have formed
part of one of the earliest consignments of silk to reach Lyon.

A collection of 167 coins was found at Fos on the beach, within ·
reach of the breaking waves and among other archaeological
deposits. A considerable number of them were of bronze and
bore the emblem of a bull with lowered horns. There were also
several pieces of silver-washed bronze with the superscriptions of
Gordian, Julia Pia, Gallienus, and Maximin, as well as solid silver
coins of Vespasian and Trajan. There was one gold piece which
is now in the Cavaillon Museum. Several coins which an Italian
workman claimed to have found at Fos are held to be "suspect."

The specimens with the bull with lowered horns, found at Fos
by Beaucaire, are of Marseille issue. But Arles, too, had adopted
the same emblem. We are here in the presence of one of those
iconographical coincidences which are the lifeblood of history. It
is perhaps worth while to point this out. It seems unlikely that
the bull of Marseille and his fellow of Arles had the same origin.
Arles owed hers to Caesar. The bull with lowered horns was the

"crest" of the Julian *gens* to which Caesar belonged. He gave it as an insignia to the Sixth Legion, the founders of Roman Arles, and the city had it carved upon its walls and stamped on its coins. It referred, not to the herds of black bulls of the Camargue, but to the conqueror of Gaul.

The entrance to the harbor at Fos-sur-Mer was, however, always deplorable. Strabo bears witness to the fact. It seems that many attempts were made to improve it. The trouble was that it was always silting up. The enemy was sand.

It has often been stated that ocean-going vessels could reach the quayside at Arles without transshipping their cargo. Such a thing was by no means impossible. The canal was sixteen miles long and seems to have joined the Rhône, not by way of the present main channel, but at a point some four or five miles further west, where there was an extension of the Redon lagoon. It was somewhere about here that the Gradus Massalitanorum was situated, the entrance to the port of Arles, at least at the end of the first century A.D. In the absence of conclusive archaeological evidence it is difficult to be sure whether the ships were warped up the canal and the Rhône, or whether, as the abundant remains of amphorae at several points seem to indicate, transshipment did, in fact, take place. Conditions must have altered according to the state of the weather, and the silting up of the sand probably necessitated a good deal of maneuvering. Much work has gone into trying to find the course of Marius's canal, and this has now been traced along almost the whole of its length. Desjardins firmly believed that he had found its banks under two mounds of pebbles known locally as Les Coudoulières. Clerc, however, and the engineers of the Ponts et Chaussées are of the opinion that these form part of a coastal deposit of recent date. Beaucaire, who excavated them and found nothing but Christian remains, thinks that they have no connection with the objects recovered from the sea in the Saint-Gervais cove, but that they are the debris of a nearby settlement belonging to a much later period.

Les Amis du Vieil Istres, who are striving to establish the ancient topography of the whole delta region, have no easy task before them. Not only have the mouths of the rivers changed their course, but there have been land subsidences, and a general rise in the sea level. (See Appendix A.) It seems probable that some part of the remains found in the sea at Fos were formerly situated on dry land and that what Dr. Beaucaire and his friends have recovered from the water originally belonged to houses standing on the shore.

¥   ¥   ¥

At Les Saintes-Maries-de-la-Mer, too, the Mediterranean has encroached upon the land. The level of possible finds, now scarcely below the surface, has been surveyed. A thin-walled vase, and the head of a statue—in a bad state of mutilation—recovered by Beaucaire, have provided proof of what was long contested, that this site is a very ancient one.

It is most unlikely that there was ever a port here. The lesser arm of the Rhône came into existence at a relatively recent period, and the flat and rectilinear nature of the coast affords no shelter. The objects found must have come from a villa which today is partially submerged. It is true that, in his *Ora maritime*, F. Avienus mentions a harbor which was probably that of the *oppidum* known as Priscum Ra. If this identification is correct, then we are forced to the conclusion that the configuration of the coast line has greatly changed.

There can, however, be no doubt that there was much seagoing activity here in ancient days. A wreck has been found lying under more than twenty feet of mud at the entrance to the Port de Bouc. It was carrying a cargo of works of art. A Ponts et Chaussées dredger brought to the surface, quite by chance, not only some of the ship's ribs and an anchor, but also a Corinthian capital and part of a marble Hellenistic sarcophagus (now in the Istres Museum). It is to be hoped that somebody will recover what still remains of it.

¥   ¥   ¥

The discoveries at Fos constituted something of an event in the history of archaeological science. It was the first time that sea and dry land were both investigated simultaneously, not in a haphazard fashion, but in accordance with a well-thought-out plan and in successive stages. The underwater site brought as much satisfaction to the searchers as did the land excavations in the same region—and more. It has provided evidence, confirmation of texts, and chronological data such as the land failed to supply, especially in connection with the constructional work initiated by Marius at the end of the second century B.C.

The life of a port which has been neglected by history, forgotten and lost, can now be in part reconstituted, thanks to what the sea has rendered up. That life was a short one. By the time of the Middle Ages, all that remained of its former glory was a fishing harbor, and perhaps not even that. (The pottery fragments stop short, chronologically, at the fourth and fifth centuries. So far no traces of the Visigoth occupation have come to light.) The movement of trade had passed to Port de Bouc and, even more markedly, to Marseille. Its resurrection is still incomplete, and much remains to be done. The method, in any case, has shown itself to be effective. It is well worth applying it to the whole of the Rhône delta, and to other sites as well.

6.   Carrara Marble at Saint-Tropez

The marbles of Carrara and
Pentelicus are better suited than
bronze for the depicting of young
and nude immortals.

THÉOPHILE GAUTIER

IN THE COURSE OF THESE UNDERSEA EXCURSIONS ON THE COAST OF Provence, I have so far allowed myself to be caught in the snare of very small things—sherds of Campanian pottery and fragments of La Graufesenque ware, as at Fos, or the broken amphorae of Anthéor. Now I propose to offer, in the interest of those who are susceptible to the appeal of quantity, examples of the enormous, the colossal: in fact no less than tons of marble still lying in the sea.

The length of their sojourn there is not open to doubt. The marble of which I am about to speak has been burrowed into by the creatures of the sea, perforated and bored as were the capitals found in the Mahdia ship. Such a work must have taken centuries to accomplish. It is, indeed, extremely probable that the blocks in question went to the bottom 1800 years ago, at the entrance to the port of Saint-Tropez, the name of which, perhaps, was then Athenopolis—"The City of Athena."

110

They had long been known to be there. Fishermen have an intuitive knowledge of the sea bed which often surpasses that of many divers. They have the advantage, too, of local traditions which go back a long way. It is always foolish to neglect such things. At Saint-Tropez, however, tradition was wrong. It had decided that these ancient remains were millstones thrown into the sea in ancient days. In any case, the fishermen who saw them did not, I imagine, show much interest, for this corner of the Mediterranean was for a long time plentifully stocked with fish, and to the fisherman it is fish that matter. The bream, who love rock passages open at either end, and a geography complicated, cramped, luminous, but at no great depth, had annexed this Roman marble without bothering overmuch about what it was doing there.

The site is close to the shore. To reach it one has only to get away from the summer bustle of the jetties, reach the Bar de la Ponche, and the little fishing port where one of the liveliest of the branch establishments of Saint-Germain-des-Près is situated. A little farther on, off the cemetery, and about two or three hundred yards from the shore, one's eye was caught, not so very long ago, by fourteen large blocks of weed-encrusted stone, which did not look so very different from ordinary rocks.

It was possible to examine them without the aid of a diving helmet: goggles were quite sufficient. Through them one could see that the group was firmly embedded in the bottom, which at that point lay at a depth of anything between nine and twenty-one fathoms.

The Club Alpin Sous-Marin came from Cannes to have a look, drawn there by some archaeological premonition. Somewhat later, on the 10th and 12th September, 1950, its members undertook a detailed examination, equipped with tape measures, map boards, pencils, chisels, hammers, and cameras. The "rocks" were duly counted, measured, photographed, and drawn. They turned out to consist of nine fragments from enormous columns, three pieces of which were thought to be Doric capitals, and one very big architrave measuring about fifteen feet in length. The weight of this object was calculated at something in the neighborhood of thirty-eight metric tons.

Samples were taken, and these proved to be of fine Carrara marble. The natural conclusion was that these remains—obviously of a very considerable age—had formed part of the cargo of a ship which had sunk off Saint-Tropez. But once again the sea which had preserved these vestiges of antiquity could give no indication of date. Was an ancient wreck really the explanation of their presence? The importance of the objects threw doubt on the theory. The assumed disaster might belong to a much more recent period. Napoleon, for instance, had shifted a great many objects of marble, most of which were landed at Toulon. But there was no written record of any such wreck during the nineteenth century. As against the Napoleon explanation one fact carried great weight. Clumps of date-mussels had eaten deep into the marble, and this piece of evidence was difficult to ignore. The most plausible conclusion was that the voyage in question, and the subsequent foundering, belonged to the Roman period. But if that were so, for what possible monument could architectural elements of such a size have been intended? There is in France no ancient building which could conceivably have required blocks of these dimensions, and what is more important still, none constructed of Carrara marble.

It is not difficult to understand that F. Benoît, who was in charge of the archaeological district to which Saint-Tropez belongs, should have waxed enthusiastic over this discovery. These blocks of masonry, lying in shallow water so near to the coast, became something of an obsession with all of us. But there seemed to be little hope of moving them. The least heavy must have weighed almost four metric tons.

But fortune smiled upon the devotees of undersea archaeology. It so happened that an extremely powerful crane had been brought into the Bay of Saint-Tropez to carry out some work having to do with the Navy. Since it was already on the scene, we had only to enlist its help and that of a few kindly sympathizers. Friends of ours at the Arsenal of Toulon were only too glad to put in a word for us with the Dodin Company who owned the floating crane which was so necessary to us. (The success of our operations was more particularly due to Monsieur Mullois, the Managing Director, who superintended the work in person.) The crane, one of the most powerful pieces of lifting apparatus anywhere in France, was on three separate occasions put at the disposal of the archaeological services, without a penny of expense falling upon the Ministry of Fine Arts.

The first urgency was to carry out the preliminary task of passing "slings" under the blocks, thus making it possible to raise them. This was strictly speaking a job for a helmet diver, but to have employed one would have cost a great deal of money, and the work, in his hands, would have taken time. Consequently, the Club Alpin Sous-Marin undertook the task—needless to say, without payment. A team of free-divers, consisting of two men under the direction of Henri Broussard, took lessons from a professional helmet diver, who admitted after the first of them that there was not much he could teach the amateurs.

He had never taken part in any comparable aquatic frolic, and was surrounded, photographed, and courted. There is one picture showing his feet in their enormous boots, taken just as they were sinking below the surface. The great copper bowl of his helmet became the central feature of a regular ballet of divers, both male and female. Somewhat disturbed by these circling buzz-flies, he turned his attention to his duties. All his demands were anticipated. Three swimmers fought to supply him with pliers and hammers, while, overhead, a "tritoness" schemed to deprive him of the leaden heart which he wore on his chest as part of his equipment.

He smiled indulgently behind the glass pane of his "porthole," like some paternal and friendly sea god in a group of half-naked immortals. But when he noticed that one of the ladies of the group was preparing to pass to him one of the slings, which tear the hands and break the nails, a reproving bubble escaped from his helmet, and it was clear from the faces he pulled that he thought this no work for women.

It is worth stressing the friendly atmosphere which prevailed in this little Saint-Tropez band. Many different types were engaged—engineers in charge of the crane, sailors from the tug which had brought the free-divers to the spot, and a naval technician. For all these men one thing alone counted—the success of an enterprise which may well rank as the most important undersea operation ever conducted in France.

There was reason to fear that the self-contained equipment that makes free-divers almost as light as air when in the water might prove unsuited to the hard physical labor involved. This fitting of slings to great blocks of masonry had already been carried out at Mahdia; but the men of the *Elie Monnier* had all been highly trained, and there was no knowing what efforts they had had to make, since it is not the habit of the members of the Groupe des Recherches Sous-Marines to talk about their difficulties. It might well turn out that, as soon as a man lost his weight, he might find it impossible to do work which demanded a high degree of physical strength. The experience gained at Saint-Tropez, however, has shown that this is far from being the case, and that the weight of the cables handled by the divers provides sufficient stability. It must not be forgotten, though, that the work was done at no very great depth.

Any sort of generalization in this matter would be foolish, and it is clear that there are certain types of operation in which the helmet diver with his head covering and breathing tube has an advantage over the free-diver floating just below the surface. This is true—but here I am expressing only a personal opinion—of all jobs involving the use of a hammer, especially where the depth is considerable. No matter how vigorously one may try to manipulate it, a hammer can become a diabolical instrument a few yards down. I am not thinking about the way one may hit one's own fingers. What really disappoints is the too obvious disproportion between the effort made and the results achieved. It is worth mentioning the very odd effect produced by a too violent movement, which may result in throwing the diver's "glorified body" off balance, with the result that he misses the object aimed at by several inches. There is often something highly comic about such attempts, and the other divers, who are merely spectators, are quick to see the joke.

᭙   ᭙   ᭙

It needed only two working days, with a week in between, to bring half the number of blocks to the surface. But then, bad weather put a temporary stop to the operation.

I had occasion to revisit Saint-Tropez in October. A strong east wind was whipping the sea to fury, and the powerful crane, condemned to remain in harbor, was passing the time by shifting pebbles near the jetty. I showed my disappointment so openly that my friends, to make up, took me on board the tug—which was pitching as badly as though we had been off the Breton coast —to have a look at the blocks that were still submerged. The waves were violent and made themselves felt in the shallow water under which the blocks were lying still undisturbed. But their effect was to make the outer surface of marine fauna show as washed and polished and more brilliantly colored than ever.

I can still see us there in the churned-up water all clouded by the suspended particles of mud, unable to take our eyes off the mosaic of living creatures which covered the stones like a garment, but would inevitably fade as soon as the reprieve occasioned by the storm had ended. The wonderful thing about this multicolored surface was its smoothness and the closeness of its texture. The words "precious stones" or "tapestry" are useless to convey the impression. Ordinary, earthy comparisons are not of any value. This marble, conquered and subdued by the sea, had about it the brilliance of twelfth-century stained glass. The monk Theophilus, who in his *Diversarum artium schedula* has left us the formula for the making of glass, explains that the paste or mixture must be left to "cook" for a long while in order that it may assume the color of flesh. For the production of other colors he says that small cubes of glass, taken from old mosaics, should be crushed to powder. The only idea I can give of the sight that met our eyes is to say that it was as though the stone had been spread with just such a medium, but so lightly as to give the impression produced by the flowered background of that series of tapestries known as *The Lady with the Unicorn*. To these patches of color a velvety quality had been imparted by the living insects, and by the faint, scarcely perceptible movement of the sea. A growth of weed no bigger than a man's hand had the swollen look of an octopus, and displayed the same white and reddish markings, the same ringed, brownish spots, that one sees on the skin of a snake. What it is impossible to describe in words is the consistency, the rather fleshy richness which is the prerogative of good painting and of marine life.

Just to stand and look, without having to put ourselves to the trouble of looping this wonder with cables and dragging it to land, was a marvelous experience.

🙪   🙪   🙪

IT was not possible to finish the work until January 1952. All the blocks except one have now been reassembled on one of the Saint-

Tropez jetties, just beyond the Chapel of the Annunciation, where they stand neighbored by old rusty cables and boat-building yards. Their colors have gone dead, and through the rags and tatters of dried weed can be seen the deep scars made by the molluscs. Even today they must give off that odor familiar on the coast of Brittany at low tide, but which seems very strange at Saint-Tropez. Careful hands have polished a few square inches of one of them, and the white marble gleams in the sun. These huge masses, looking as though they had been piled by a giant's hands, give the impression of having been rolled haphazardly into their present position, with their bases washed by the black water of the harbor. The Ministry of Fine Arts plans to re-erect the columns and to crown them with the architrave. I cannot help hoping that this portico will not be trapped in the higgledy-piggledy of its surroundings. Its only background should be the sea. If the work is done properly, then Saint-Tropez will be graced by a monument, unusual, to be sure, but no more strange than the Obelisk in the Place de la Concorde.

The first lesson that emerges from this successful operation is that undersea archaeology must be able to call upon powerful technical equipment and an unlimited amount of keenness. The presence of both at Saint-Tropez made the task relatively simple. This new field of archaeological endeavor demands means which the Ministry of Fine Arts has neither the money nor the manpower to supply. Even admitting that a day may come when a special team of free-divers can be trained by the G.R.S., the various departments of archaeology will never have at their disposal the necessary pieces of lifting apparatus which are essential in underwater operations of this type. Without the assistance given by the Navy, without the co-operation of the Ponts et Chaussées, without the help of the Club Alpin Sous-Marin, the work done at Saint-Tropez would have been utterly impossible. What happened there merely confirmed the experience gained at Mahdia, and that experience will certainly be repeated in all similar cases. Nearly always the right sort of combination of human effort and mechanical means will have to be contrived. If that is impossible, then it will be far better to do nothing than to run the risk of damaging a site without any compensating gain to the cause of science.

Another point: no matter how careful the drawings made on

the sea bed may be, no matter how good the photographs, they must always be treated with the greatest caution. As a result of the survey made in 1950 by the Club Alpin Sous-Marin, everybody was convinced that the objects found were Doric capitals, whereas in fact they were the bases of columns.

These spectral "capitals" were for a long time an embarrassment to Fernand Benoît in his efforts to identify the remains. Apparently there had never existed in Gaul more than one building of marble which could have involved elements of such a size, and that was the Temple at Narbonne, which had been rebuilt in the reign of Antoninus. But the capitals in that case were Corinthian. When the blocks were lifted from the water it was established beyond a doubt that the so-called "capitals" were in reality the bases of columns. Archaeological probability, and an hypothesis established on dry land as the result of sheer scholarship, prevailed over the evidence of the divers and their photographs. It is to be hoped that nobody will ever lose sight of that lesson. The diver can no more claim to do without the erudition of the archaeologist in identifying and establishing the value of his finds than the archaeologist can do without the diver and the powerful lifting apparatus.

If Fernand Benoît is right and the discoveries at Saint-Tropez are really parts of the Narbonne Temple which were being transported by sea at some time in the second century A.D., and perished in a wreck off the harbor mouth, then it follows that we have in our possession elements of a building, now vanished, which belong to a type of monumental architecture of which no other example exists in Gaul. Even at Narbonne itself, there are only three pieces of a temple which was once universally admired. These were brought to light during the construction of a *lycée* at the end of last century. They consist of the remnants of one Corinthian capital, half of one drum of a grooved column, and a fragment of the cornice. Their dimensions are slightly less than those of the Saint-Tropez marbles, which is only to be expected, since these prefabricated portions were sent in an unfinished state. They had been merely roughed out, and the flutes had not been cut.

The size of these remains are reminiscent of a type of Roman art unknown in France. They are closely related to the most grandiose buildings of Italy in the imperial age—to the Temple of

Mars Ultor in Rome, for instance. Anything like the edifice to which they must have belonged would be hard to find anywhere, except, perhaps, at Leptis Magna in Tripolitania.

Nothing, I suppose, would have seemed too large or too magnificent for a temple intended to do honor to Rome, and especially not for one put up by a rich freedman. It so happens that we know the name of the man who erected this one, and the name of his family. He was called Fadius Musa, was an Imperial freedman, a shipowner and a merchant. We can say with certainty that he was vain. When the Temple of Narbonne was destroyed in 149 by a fire which laid waste the city, it was he who undertook its reconstruction and paid for it. Such generosity entitled him to be its *flamen*, or priest, and we know from an inscription that this honor was actually bestowed upon him. He thoroughly deserved the appointment, judging by the expenses he shouldered, for he gave to Narbonne the finest temple in the whole of Gaul, and the only one built of marble. Ausonius, for whom all marble was Parian, wrote of it in somewhat doggerel verses in his *Ordo Urbium Nobilium*:

> Quodque tibi Pario quondam de marmore templum
> Tantae molis erat quantum non sperneret olim
> Tarquinius, Catulusque iterum postremo et ille
> Rursus qui statuit Capitoli culmina Caesar.

Fadius was guilty, I think, of a certain amount of ostentation. The marble of Carrara was, at that time, the noblest to be found anywhere. That of the Pyrenees was not exploited until the third century. The dimensions decided upon were exceptional for any provincial building. But this was not just *any* building. Fadius Musa had chosen the object of his munificence with great care—the more so since the reign of Antoninus was marked by a great wave of religious restoration. Antoninus himself came of a Narbonnese family. The importance of this Narbonne sanctuary was as great for Rome as it was for Gaul. It was the seat of a cult of federation which, even more than the altar at the confluence at Lyon, signified the uniting of the people of Gaul in one act of submission to one devotion: the cult of the divine Augustus and the City of Rome. That religion may not have been of a particularly exalted type, the humbug which it embodied may have been somewhat crude, but it is impossible to deny that it played a great part in unifying the different parts of the Empire. In that common cult Gaul had affirmed her solidarity. She managed to have the best of two worlds by putting up a mild resistance to her Proconsuls and, at the same time, enjoying a considerable measure of prosperity.

In undertaking to restore a monument which, more than any other, symbolized the harmony between Gaul and Rome, Fadius Musa showed his cleverness. As a shipowner he could carry the marble in his own bottoms. This enriched freedman was not ungrateful. By becoming the first citizen of Narbonne he served the interests both of Rome and of the province. As a leading man of business and one of the "pillars of the state," as a *navicularius*, or, as he would have been called locally, a *nauclarius*, he could aspire to play a part in politics.

The word *nauclarius* is derived from Greek ναυκληρος, but the occupation which it denoted had become by a process of evolution markedly Roman. Not only is the borrowing of this word significant, but a comparison between the Greek and Latin vocabularies in all matters having to do with the sea will be found to speak volumes. The Latin words are poor and made up of Greek and even Gallic borrowings. Seasickness plays a great part in the sailor language of the Romans: *nausea, nausio, nauseola, nauseus.* To express the same thing—my sympathies do not go to the length of denying that the Greeks knew nothing of seasickness—the Greek language has one verb, one substantive, and one adjective— ναυτιάω, ναυτία, ναυτιώδης. On the other hand, what a wealth of words it contains for every subtlety and shade of meaning with reference to maritime activities, from ναυλοχέως, which means "to ride at anchor for the purpose of keeping an eye on enemy ships, or to take them by surprise," to ναυμαχησείω, "to want to engage in a naval battle." Admittedly, "pirate" is a word of Greek origin, but it derives from πειράω, which signifies only the attempting, or the temptation, to engage in piracy.

The *nauclarius,* or *nauclericus,* is the captain who actually sails the ship and takes the risks: the *navicularius* is the shipowner, who shows little desire to face the dangers of the storm, stays in harbor, speculates on the market, and engages in a little casual banking. During the second century, when provincial prosperity was at its height, the fortunes amassed by these business tycoons very soon led to municipal honors. Rome encouraged men of this sort. She needed citizens of staunch loyalty who would ensure her food supplies. This loyalty was not only the kind that the provinces swore to the Emperor in their temples, but also the more active kind displayed over the Annona, or government corn supply. In order to be able to deliver the corn of Languedoc to Ostia, the Procurator of the Annona in the district of Narbonne made a yearly contract with the shipowners of that city. These agreements cannot have been unprofitable, as may be seen from the fact that there is no lack of monuments and inscriptions set up by shipowners anxious to express their gratitude to the Food Ministry officials.

These functionaries chose their men with care, and favored such shipowners as had shown themselves to be fairly enterprising, and those, too, who had given pledges of their loyalty. Many of these shipowners served as municipal magistrates, not only in the provinces, but also in Italy and Sicily.

Such political employments in no way excluded the enjoyment of the benefits of trade, and the powerful Corporation of Shipowners was at great pains to improve its technical equipment. There still exists at Ostia, behind the Theater, a huge portico where businessmen and shipowners from all over the Empire had their agency, which, no doubt, combined the functions of information center, clearing house, insurance office, and commercial bank. It was more than a meeting place: it was a primitive form of Lloyd's. On the mosaic floor of the Great Hall appear the names of the shipowners of Narbonne: "Narbonenses." Above these a piece of machinery is represented, consisting of a funnel through which two sacks are emptying corn directly into a ship's hold. The merchants of Narbonne must have been very proud of this object of harbor installation to have had it shown, for publicity purposes, in the Portico of Ostia. Rome, as we know well, was always waiting impatiently for the delivery of cereals from the provinces, and any device that would lead to a saving of time would be much appreciated. The men of Narbonne certainly did not fail to point out how admirably their equipment served the end in view.

The generosity of Fadius Musa was inspired by business, no less than by political considerations. His firm was a powerful one. The Imperial freedman had founded a family, and left de-

scendants who carried on his business, and remained staunchly
attached to their founder's Roman loyalties. Among the broken
amphorae of the Monte Testaccio (see Appendix B—amphorae)
are numerous fragments bearing the name of Sextus Fadius
Secundus Musa, who was not only a shipowner, but also a patron
of the Fabri Subaediani, or shopkeepers, of Narbonne. Five other
pieces, dating from 149, carry the mark of Sex. Fadius Anicetus,
who may have been his son. The stamp "Fadiorum" has also
been found. The freedmen of the Fadius family living at Ostia
enjoyed a high reputation, which they owed to the importance
of the firm of which they were the representatives. The trademark
of these Fadii has been found at Aix-en-Savoie and in many other
parts of Gaul. A certain M. Fadius styles himself *mercator cordu-
bensis*—"Merchant of Cordova."

♨   ♨   ♨

It would seem that Fadius Musa, in spite of his great experience,
was guilty of rashness in allowing one of his ships to be so heavily
laden. If the vessel which went to the bottom in the Bay of Saint-
Tropez was indeed one of his fleet, it must have been carrying
something like two hundred and fifty tons of cargo. It needed
only a strong east wind to drive it ashore before it could find shelter in the harbor, the entrance to which is still difficult to negoti-
ate when heavy seas are running, as many a yachtsman has found
to his cost.

How comes it that no traces of the ship have been found? My
friends of the Club Alpin Sous-Marin have looked for it in vain.
Its disappearance can be easily explained in view of the shallow
depth of the water at this point. The ships of Mahdia and
Albenga, both of which were found almost intact, had sunk in
twenty-two and a half fathoms. As far down as that, the surface
swell is imperceptible. The Anthéor wreck, at a little over ten
fathoms, was found to be in a far more battered condition. But
at Saint-Tropez, in three and a half fathoms, the effects of even
the mildest storm would have been strongly felt, and the waves
which buffeted Broussard and me, so that the taking of photographs became almost impossible, must long ago have broken up
the vessel belonging to Fadius Musa. All the same, it is decidedly
odd that literally nothing was found—not a nail, not an anchor.

(Unless we may associate with this wreck the stock of a leaden anchor, six feet long, which is said to have been landed by Timacheft and Chénevée.) There is some mystery here which has not yet been solved. No doubt the sea will keep the secret as long as it can do so.

7. The Port of Cherchel

*Vita populi romani per incerta
maris et tempestatum quotidie vol-
vitur.*

Annals
TACITUS

The following pages must not be regarded as furnishing an
archaeological study of the underwater site at Cherchel. They
make no such claim. At best they are the record of a reconnaissance. Work in this place was initiated by Pierre Averseng, and
he has, throughout, given it every sort of encouragement. The
leading parts in this particular enterprise were played by Madame
Monsenergue, to whom we owe a set of magnificent photographs,
and by Captain Olivier de Tonnac. I, myself, was able to spend
only a week at Cherchel, and during that time the weather was
so bad that, for the most part, diving was impossible. Anything
approaching a full-dress survey, here as elsewhere, would need a
far longer stay and the use of much heavier equipment than has
so far been available.

Particular thanks are due to Monsieur Leschi, Director of Algerian Antiquities, who did everything he could to encourage the
enterprise. Algeria, where aerial surveys of archaeological sites

123

have been of the utmost importance, thanks to the fine work carried out by Colonel Baradez, has now embarked upon a program of underwater activities. The Department of Antiquities now has its own diving equipment.

A SINGLE DAY'S HASTY VISIT, MY CHIEF MEMORY OF WHICH WAS a shady square in which antique columns alternated with gnarled tree trunks, had left me with feelings of regret that my first introduction to Cherchel should have been so hasty. I could still see in my mind's eye a flat blue sea neatly confined within a beautifully shaped bay. I recalled, too, a museum where the galleries, which opened onto a garden, were crisscrossed by the thin cries of swallows. . . .

So I went back. The reality did not disappoint me. Charged though I was with a load of memories and regrets, I found that Cherchel was, in fact, even more charming than I had remembered it. The sea, however, on the occasion of my second visit, was neither flat nor blue. Lashed by an unpleasant wind from the west, it showed as an expanse of white horses. An edging of surf surrounded the tiny island on which the beacon light stood, and set a white border about every piece of half-submerged masonry, as though intent on laying down, for my benefit, the lines of a diagram which I did not begin to understand.

It was not, this time, the sea that I found welcoming, but the public garden which was saved by massed roses and geraniums from looking like its ordinary provincial brethren. A central fountain, adorned with casts of four antique heads, gave proof that people of taste, some sixty years ago, knew how to achieve a design which was free from all taint of the academic or of official ostentation, in which memories of Rome should be happily combined with a living air of gaiety. The church was another example of the same thing. It is probably the only one in the whole of Algeria for which the inhabitants have no cause to blush. All the others seem to me appallingly ugly. This one, however, with its blind façade, its pediment, and its engaged pilasters, has the austere simplicity of an ageless monument. I see no objection whatever to putting historical remains to such a use. It is far better than offending the eyes of generations to come with a higgledy-piggledy of bricks and cement blocks, which is what the last hundred years have produced in most of the towns of North Africa.

🐦   🐦   🐦

At dawn next day, restless with impatience, I looked at the sea. The keen wind of a bad spring was churning it into ugly waves. The water was cold, muddy, and hostile.

All I asked was that for a short time it should show a little kindliness. I knew where the Roman jetties lay concealed beneath the surface. I knew just where they joined the shore. I had only to follow a well-marked course. I had spent weeks bending over maps. I had learned the sea bed by heart. But on that particular morning my efforts to explore the eastern end of the bay had brought me nothing more than an occasional glimpse, between the rollers, of shapeless blocks smothered in white foam. How in that race of waters could I hope to distinguish rocks from Roman masonry?

Sick of being driven hither and thither between the shore and the outer reefs, I gave up the attempt. Not on a morning like this could I hope to succeed in raising from the dead a doubtful jetty to which we had given the name of the Quémard Mole. I emerged from the water shivering with cold, to snatch a brief interval of sunbathing in some spot more sheltered from the edged wind. That is what African spring is like.

I decided to take a chance farther westwards, close to the mainland, where I might flounder among the sea-urchins and dive into the inhospitable waters. A ridiculous occupation, and, as it turned out, wholly without glory. Little by little I drifted close to the outlet of the town drains. Nasty, rusty, treacherous cables set a trap for my feet. Once again I gave up the attempt.

I wandered along the beach where the waves were nuzzling broken amphorae and pounding odds and ends of pottery. Fragments of history, or rather, history in fragments. This ragpicker's ramble was my only success of the day, for it brought me a scrap of marble with the carving of a torch upon it, a few sherds glittering with mica, and part of a Roman lamp.

I went home when darkness fell, my pockets weighed down by a mixed collection of objects smelling of mud. I crossed the square with its columns, where, under the newly lit lamps, a Franco-Moslem crowd was playing at *boules*. This, thought I, is an African Toulon, but never far from the shadow of Rome.

I felt inclined to sit down on the thick roots of a Belombra and listen absent-mindedly to the players' naïve discussions. But one by one the smacks were homing for the night, the red nets hanging from their masts. The light on the islet of Joinville was glimmering under a windy sky which was now swept clean and changing from gray-blue to the blue of the night. Already I had shaken off the weariness that comes when one has been bathing for the first time and has stayed too long in the water. I knew that I must escape from the moment's lethargy and return to the hotel, there to turn the pages of *Gsell's Atlas*, and pore over the *Dictionary of Antiquities*.

What I had felt that day at Cherchel I find it hard to say. It should be clear, however, from this brief confession, that it was not the exaltation bred of a facile evocation of the past. That I did not regret. The past, by hiding itself from my eyes, forced me to see more clearly the unchanging life of Africa. When the seven o'clock bus arrived at Algiers it would unload the subjects of King Juba II.

♥ ♥ ♥

UNDERSEA archaeology is full of strange twists and turns. I had started out with the intention of embarking on a simple and wholly material enterprise, that of measuring a few submerged quays and the remains of jetties. What had actually risen before my eyes were great chunks of African history which seemed more massive than any sea wall. Whether I wanted to or not, I felt compelled to come to grips with them, at the risk, if I did not do so, of failing entirely to understand what I might later discover beneath the sea. What, in theory, I should be engaged upon would be a search among blocks of cement marking the precise limits of the ancient harbor. But, even in the early stages, I knew that I was no longer sufficiently master of myself to confine my curiosity within the bounds set by a simple problem in undersea geometry.

There, then, I sat in my hotel bedroom, with Cagnat's fat volume before me. "From time to time," says Marc Bloch, "it is necessary to take the reader into a laboratory." Well, that was where I was. I regard Cagnat as one of my revered masters, as a man who knew more than most scholars about Roman antiquity. He spent ten years in examining the ruins of Africa with an appraising eye, in collecting inscriptions, in comparing written texts with actual places. His book *L'Armée romaine d'Afrique* is a monument of erudition, of sagacity, of prudent argument. It was the result of immense labor. Chance so ordained it that I, though unworthy, should come upon the scene and try to go one better than my masters. But Colonel Baradez, from his post of observation in the skies, has perceived more truths than ever Stephen Gsell saw upon the earth. I wish that I could quote here the whole of the preface which Leschi contributed to that remarkable work, *Fossatum Africae*, for it says all that needed saying on the subject—

For more than a century the scientific exploration of what was once Roman Africa has been proceeding. After so much investigation of detail, after so great a task of synthesis—the mere cataloguing of which would fill many pages—it is but natural to think that the last word has been spoken on all the main aspects of that country as it existed in the ancient world. Nevertheless, even Gsell did not consider his *Atlas archéologique de l'Algérie* to be a final and exhaustive publication. After him, after Réne Cagnat's *l'Armée romaine d'Afrique*, it has been found possible to tear from a part of the world which is stuffed full with history this *Fossatum Africae*. It marks what may well be a decisive stage in the examination of the North African past.

Whether diving can produce anything like such valuable results in this field as the airplane, I do not know. But the attempt is worth making, and at Cherchel more certainly than elsewhere. The dimensions attributed by archaeologists to this port in the periods of antiquity are surprisingly small, but so far nobody has troubled to question their improbability. Cagnat, who proved, thanks to an inscription, that Caesarea was the naval base of a Roman battle fleet, and, in fact, the only port that could be so used between Carthage and the Pillars of Hercules, was not prepared, on the strength of such remains as were visible above the surface, to allow that it had ever provided more than a very modest anchorage in the shelter of the islet of Joinville, though even that would, in fact, have covered rather less space than the

present-day harbor. According to his calculations the fleet at
Caesarea could never have counted more than thirteen *liburnae*,
that being the maximum number which could be accommodated
in so small a roadstead. (The *liburna* had a length of 72 feet and
a beam of 12. It was a lightly built, swift-moving galley, carrying
two banks of oars. The Romans had taken the model from
Illyria, where they were called *lembi*. The Liburnians were settled
on both sides of the Adriatic.) This would have been a totally
inadequate number of vessels, seeing that the fleet had to be
prepared to do battle with a pirate force which was solidly established in the West—in the neighborhood of the Rif—as well as to
police the Mediterranean from end to end, and to protect the
Italian convoys.

Was the harbor, then, larger than has been generally supposed?
Were there, perhaps, ships stationed along the African coast and
based on a number of other small anchorages? To these questions
the sea might well provide an answer. I had before me air photographs of the bay in which each sunken block of masonry, each
reef, showed a fringe of white foam, and the masses appeared
black beneath the transparent water. To get a clear view of the
whole pattern one would have to exchange the bird's-eye for the
fish's-eye approach.

In spite of the help given to the investigator by modern technical contrivances, he still feels curiously inadequate when confronted by the past. In the last analysis it is the human spirit and
its instruments that matter far more than any mechanical equipment, helpful though that may be—brain, eye, and hand. It still
remained to interpret the air photographs, as it would still remain
to interpret their underwater counterparts with which I should
be furnishing myself within the next twenty-four hours. The only
thing that would tell in the long run would be the first-hand
visual impression. Only by staring and touching can men recognize beyond any doubt the handiwork of man.

ᛘ   ᛘ   ᛘ

AND next day I did recognize it, deep down in a sea which had
become suddenly calm. The red light of dawn awakened me.
Creeping through the deserted hotel, I went out onto the terrace
to look at the sea. I saw before me a stretch of flat, blue water on

which the early light was playing. All I needed for breakfast was a few of the oily fritters known as *sfenj* which were sizzling in a frying pan in a nearby native café.

With my hands in my pockets, and sandals on my feet, I sloped down to the harbor. A fisherman took me out to the small island on which the harbor light stood. Was he really a fisherman, this Taïeb, whose acquaintance I had made for the first time that morning? Whenever I saw him he was always busy about some mysterious job on board his boat at the quayside, or frankly enjoying the delights of a midday siesta. He was a thin, smiling fellow, with very white teeth, and bright eyes showing from beneath an American soldier's khaki cap. He had something in common with a little urchin from El Golea who had firmly attached himself to our party. I never tire of the discoveries which one is always making in the marvelous land of Africa. Taïeb, like most of his companions, was quite convinced that he was an Arab. Could one have disentangled the confused web of his heredity, one would probably have found an instructive mixture of Berber, Maltese, Marseillais, Levantine, and Turk. If, indeed, there was a drop of Arab in his blood, there may well have been a drop, too, of Roman, and another of Byzantine!

He rowed with short, easy strokes, and we made an unhurried journey to the islet, leaving in our wake two broad ripples which wrinkled the placid surface and died away on the beach. I was impatient to set foot upon the rock ahead of us, to touch the Roman arch, the shape of which, seen from the shore, obsessed my mind, to slip into the cool sea without disturbing the marine life of its depths. All this was pure delight, stimulated by something of the archaeologist's fever. Bream were twisting and turning in the clear water. Above my head, mullet were pushing their noses through the surface. I came first on a patch of weed, then to a mass of concrete in which large stones were embedded. On the sandy bottom were a few blocks of hewn masonry.

The circuit of the islet's base was quickly made. A line of submerged rock joined it to the mainland. It was this ridge that the Romans had used as the foundation for their main breakwater.

Then, suddenly, I came on something more interesting. On my way round the islet, and at no very great depth, I noticed first one, then two, then three, and finally seven round and very clearly defined holes cut in the rock. I measured them. One of them was six feet in diameter and penetrated rather more than six feet into the solid mass of the islet. All were situated between six and twelve feet below the surface. (No plausible hypothesis has yet been advanced to account for them.)

When at last I emerged, a wind had got up, and the sea was marked with flecks of white. There was nothing for it but to go back. I should be more comfortable, I felt, in the water than in the boat, so I swam home, taking an oblique course across the bay which must once have been an ancient mercantile harbor. Below the modern breakwater the ancient jetty diverged slightly to the east. I found some rather light-weight concrete and a few squared stones which must have formed the parapet of a quay. My goggles were quite sufficient for this visit. The maximum depth was six feet, precisely that of the modern masonry, the top of which was flush with the surface. Once past the last block on the landward side, however, I found a complete change of scene; I was swimming over a huge area of stones and weed. Each of the stones ought to have been raised and carefully examined. It was more than likely that the sea bed on which they lay would have been found to hold many surprises. If only, like Colonel Baradez, I could have photographed the whole site! But the photographs would have had to be both aerial and submarine. Mere flying would not have been enough. What I needed was that this liquid sky should be as pure and cloudless as the true sky above it.

☙   ☙   ☙

THERE would be no point in elaborating my narrative indefinitely. What I have written is intended merely to indicate how slow and inglorious this kind of survey can be. The positive results were minute. If I were to record all the dives that I made in the course of that week, I should soon exhaust the reader's patience. I could offer him nothing but a succession of details which only a specialist would find interesting. All they added up to was an enumeration of finds made in the course of my undersea excursions at a number of different points with the object of verifying a hypothesis, or of identifying some object which had been battered by the waves, and so making sure whether, in fact, it was a rock or a slab of concrete. More often than not those excursions produced nothing because the sea was hostile and the water thick with mud.

Reports of this kind, useful though they may be in providing information about some given spot, can be really valuable only if they are accompanied by a map and a great quantity of pin-pointed underwater photographs. The only reward one has at the moment is the somewhat simple-minded excitement at making a discovery when one dives, and the illusory belief that one has understood its significance when one returns to the surface.

I shall concern myself here only with the essential points.

First of all the general layout of the Roman harbor.

It was my belief that I had found traces of four separate harbors, though it might well be that they were not contemporary.

The first of these, working from east to west, was protected by a jetty. Its existence was revealed in 1932, by Commandant Quémard, who sent a helmet diver down to report. (It was on this occasion that Quémard, on board the naval survey vessel *Beautemps Beaupré*, worked out a chart of the coast and amassed a deal of very valuable information.) It has been challenged, and is, indeed, open to doubt. In most of the area the water is relatively shallow, and an anchorage there could have enjoyed very little shelter from the prevailing westerly winds. The reason for the lack of depth is that the bottom is much encumbered with masonry and the rubble of every sort of building material. Such examination as I have made can give no positive evidence of date, though my own belief is that these remains belong to the periods of antiquity. The mere fact of their presence proves that there was "something" here. This is borne out by the fact that several concrete blocks are visible on the cliffs skirting the coast at this point. As to the jetty itself, I am as convinced as was the helmet diver of 1932 that I found its remains—if, that is, the mass of concrete which I came upon a hundred or so yards from the shore was really the foundation of a harbor work. It seemed to me, judging by a line of submerged material, that this work made an almost right-angled turn, thus providing the needed protection to the west. Account should also be taken of the fact that the direction of the main jetty, which starts from the headland known as Marabout Point, is not the same as that of the modern construction, but quite clearly diverges in an easterly direction. Finally, the breakwaters at the outer limits of the harbor, of which I shall have something to say later, provided an advanced protective cover. If this were so, then the nature of the basic problem becomes changed.

Admittedly, the exact position of this first and most easterly of the basins is far from certain. The area is too rich in remains of every type, most of which may well have come from the mainland, since the cliffs just here are very close to the beach. (It is quite possible that some of these submerged ruins are post-Roman, as, too, are many of the remains found on the shore.) I find it hard to believe that it forms the site of the mercantile harbor of Roman days, as Commandant Quémard and, following him, Marcel Hérubel, maintained. There may have been a fishing port here, a seaside pier, perhaps, carrying a range of buildings, which would account for the amount of masonry in the water. If a section of the bottom were cleared—and this could very easily be done—the results might be informative. It is by no means improbable that a certain amount of sculpture might be found.

᭼   ᭼   ᭼

In the center of the bay, at Marabout Point, a jetty projects into the sea. At the shore end it is very broad, but diminishes in width up to the point where it ends at the lighthouse. This jetty, which I have followed along the whole of its course, is broken about midway. I cannot say whether this breach belongs to the post-Roman period or whether a passage was contrived when the causeway was first built. The quantities of masonry—very considerable on the western side and near the shore—would seem to bear out the assumption that it supported a number of buildings. On Marabout Point itself, traces have been found of a storage tank and of a building which the construction of an emplacement during the 1940 war completely destroyed. That would be the logical position for the ancient port, since it is much closer to the town and within easy reach of the storage tank and of the stream which still runs across the beach. It is the exact spot where, no doubt, according to tradition, the Phoenician, Greek, and Punic ships were drawn up on shore, long before the days of the Romans.—It was here that I found micaceous pottery in the water.

It is beyond this basin, going westwards, that the real difficulties begin. The whole of the area containing the islet of Joinville and its immediate neighborhood was profoundly modified by French engineers employed by the Ponts et Chaussées in the nineteenth century, and even later. This is the nodal point of the whole harbor system of Cherchel. The channel which gives access to this section of the bay is closed to the east by the Joinville rock, and to the west by the modern jetty. Its orientation has been completely changed, and no matter what anyone may say, the new jetty is quite different in shape from the ancient one which was situated farther to the north and must have formed a concave bend. Furthermore, traces of submerged concrete have been found in front of the Joinville rock, and these may well be the remains of a vast breakwater protecting the seaward approaches.

Lying behind this bastion, the islet of Joinville had not originally the massive appearance which distinguishes it today, or not, at least, on the landward side. Beyond the breach referred to earlier, an advanced basin, partially filled in by the Ponts et Chaussées, has been found. It extends behind the ancient jetty, which, as I have already pointed out, makes a greater sweep than does its modern counterpart. Was this, perhaps, an outlying anchorage used for loading wheat, or was it an annex to the military harbor, a graving dock, or a naval station? I will not presume to answer these questions. All I can say is that remains abound in the whole of this area—stones, blocks of masonry, lintels, and even one large column, with the marks made in hoisting still visible. In the breach itself, at the very foot of the jetty, there lies one section of a monolithic arch which appears to me to be more than usually large.

Whatever may have been the purpose of this advanced basin, its size is far from negligible if we consider the general outlet of the Joinville islet, and can reconstruct in imagination, beneath all the modern "improvements," the indentations of the Roman port which doubtless followed an earlier layout.

The modern installations have caused the disappearance of the channel leading from the advanced basin to the naval anchorage, which stood, it is to be assumed, where the harbor is today. But even there the general lines are not the same. The ancient access to this basin, and the one now used, do not coincide. (Contrary to what has been thought and written, they could not do so, since the northern wall of the present harbor is formed by the earth platform constructed by the Ponts et Chaussées to the east of the Joinville islet. The ancient channel must have run under the lee of this platform. The Turkish occupation made a complete mess of the whole site.) The earlier approach can be traced, not *inside* the present too much scraped and tidied harbor, but under the eastern side, where I believe that I have found the line of the ancient wall which, for ten yards or so, follows an oblique line which gives it a more open angle.

If, after going beyond the modern harbor and crossing the wall which protects it on the west, one enters the sea just where the sewage is discharged and all the Franco-Moslem filth of Cherchel accumulates, one will be rewarded for this deed of courage by coming on what must—or may—have been a fourth harbor. It was, no doubt, covered on its north side by a breakwater linking up with its fellow covering the islet of Joinville. I could not get definite evidence that this was so, owing to the state of the sea and to the shortness of the time at my disposal. There are still visible on this western side of the islet several remains of buildings and storage tanks—the presence of which can be explained only if ships could tie up at a quay somewhere hereabouts.

I did, on the other hand, survey and precisely locate, halfway between the assumed breakwater and the shore, a series of submerged concrete blocks which seemed to me to be what Vitruvius calls *structurae*, huge affairs designed to carry a jetty on a series of arches, a form of construction the classic example of which is to be found at Pozzuoli.

Jetties were usually, and especially in the Roman period, built on foundations of masonry (*structurae*). There were several different methods to suit several sets of different requirements, all of which Vitruvius describes in detail. When adequate supplies of pozzolana were available, a form of concrete was used which hardened in water. Two parts of pozzolana to one of lime produced a cement with which very small fragments of tufa were mixed. Hollow molds of timber (*arcae*) were set up side by side in the sea, care being taken to make sure that their bottoms were clean and level, and into these the liquid cement was poured. The remains of such harbor works as still exist in various parts of Italy afford conclusive proof, in spite of Vitruvius's silence on the subject, that the Romans almost always built their jetties, not solid, but in this discontinuous manner. They were composed of pillars erected at intervals and supporting a line of arches. This method was imposed upon the builders by the danger of silting. The waves, with their load of sand, could wash through into the basin. In order, however, to prevent heavy seas from penetrating into the anchorage, the apertures in the jetties were kept very narrow, and the fabric was pierced only at long intervals. Alternately, they were set at an angle to the prevailing wind. A third variant was to have two jetties parallel to one another, and so arranged that the openings in one faced the solid portions of the other, and vice versa.

These blocks, now covered with weed and marine fauna, are arranged in so regular a pattern that it is impossible to mistake them for natural reefs. Their rectilinear shapes and vertical sides convince me that we are here dealing with the work of men's hands, and with Roman work at that. (It would be unforgivable if I did not make some mention here of a book by P. M. Duval, entitled *Cherchel et Tipasa*, 1946, though it is wholly concerned with archaeology on dry land. I will quote one passage: "I have considered it my duty to pay special attention to constructional methods . . . Examples from within the Roman Empire have sometimes been lacking. Archaeologists have been too often content to speak of large, medium, and small buildings, without taking into account that of the last two categories, at least, numerous varieties exist which have remained unnoticed. It seems certain that in the case, for example, of small buildings we are still very far from having exhausted all the possible material at our disposal." What has been left undone on solid ground has been left undone to an even greater extent under water. I noticed among the harbor constructions at Cherchel at least two instances of "small" buildings. We are without the necessary photographic documentation which would make it possible to identify submerged remains. I recommend this as a useful job for unemployed divers. The work might be somewhat thankless, but it would certainly be valuable.)

At the foot of these blocks there are accumulations of stone which may well be the relics of collapsed arches. On one of the blocks Madame Monsenergue discovered a stone fitted into a shallow seating still in its original position.

Between these blocks and the shore the sea bed is, one might almost say, paved with remains and thickly encumbered with ruins. I am not referring to the amphora necks and the earthenware sherds, which we have grown tired of collecting, but to the bases of columns, to flagstones, to a whole wilderness of stones of all dimensions, the presence of which can scarcely be accounted for unless we assume the existence of a fourth harbor.

I am perfectly well aware that a strong argument against its existence might be made from the fact that it would have been exposed to the prevailing wind from the west. But the jetties, which no longer remain, may have given sufficient protection. Besides, it is not at all certain that the western entry was the only one. It is at least possible that this anchorage communicated with the main basin lying in the shelter of the Joinville islet. For centuries Turkish ships entered and left Cherchel by that route quite as often as by the more easterly channel. Drawings made at the time of the occupation, and, alas, only too rare, make that quite plain. There existed in the basin which is now the harbor a westerly passage by which it was just as easy to reach the shelter of the islet as from the east. It is hard to say whether this passage was merely the result of accident or whether it was deliberately contrived by the Romans.

On a map made in 1713 by Michelot, the king's pilot, and now preserved in the Bibliothèque du Service Central Hydrographique de la Marine, the islet of Joinville is shown as linked with the shore. If that were so, it seems probable that there was an anchorage on the west side as well as on the east. It is certain that in summer the prevailing wind is from the northeast.

In 1843, the Marine Commission for the Port of Cherchel advocated the construction of an installation which should consist of "an elliptical basin of 15 hectares, having an entrance facing N-E ¼ N, and running between the two rocks which served as pierheads for the Roman moles." Unfortunately, these documents lack the accompanying plan which would have clarified them.

The ancient name of Caesarea was Iol, which was that of a Phoenician god. The site is almost certainly Phoenician rather than Punic. It is not a cothon, which is an inland port artificially excavated. In the middle of the fourth century it is mentioned in the so-called Periplus of Scylax, together with its harbor, as being a Carthaginian possession. But it must have been a scene of activity long before the Punic occupation. (No archaeological evidence for this has been found, though, at Cherchel. A bronze cymbal has been recovered from the harbor with a Punic inscription dating apparently from the second century, as well as a sarcophagus which shows signs of Phoenician influence, and a number of Egypto-Phoenician scarabs.) The lay of the land was admirably suited to the peculiar layout beloved of the Phoenicians—an island close inshore along either side of which ships could sail according to the wind. An arrangement of this kind is to be seen at Tyre and Sidon, and it was adopted by the Romans when they restored these two harbors—a principal entrance to the south, and another to the west, sheltered from the "sharp and sudden" southerly winds.

It is beyond doubt that, whatever the prevailing winds, the ancients were careful to provide their harbors with two entrances. It is enough to refer here to the three classic examples studied by K. Lehmann-Hartleben—Syracuse, Halicarnassus, and Mytilene.

At Cherchel, the construction of the modern harbor has partially obliterated what submerged traces remain, just as the continued existence of the town on one single site has covered up the relics of many ancient monuments. It is not the abandonment of a site that effaces the marks left by the past, but its continuous occupation. It may well be, however, that we have not yet come to the end of what the sea may give us in the way of evidence. Cagnat, in his *Armée romaine d'Afrique*, reproduced a letter found among the unpublished papers of L. Renier. It is signed D., and it seems rather surprising that this text has furnished the authority for everything written during the past sixty years about the port of Cherchel, and that nobody has troubled to look for evidence in the sea (with the single exception of the Quémard survey, which was hydrographic rather than archaeological). This is what the letter says:

The ancient port occupied precisely the same position as the present one. It was divided into two parts, the outer harbor and an inner one communicating with it by means of an extremely narrow bottleneck discovered in 1847 when the present works were put in hand. . . . This outer harbor consisted of two jetties. The most easterly started from the shore opposite the spot where the Arab Bureau stands, and proceeded in a northwesterly direction, ending at an outcrop of rock. The other, which was much shorter, started from the islet, and ran northeast towards another outcrop which today serves as the extremity of the new jetty. . . . Westwards, and facing the property belonging to Captain Thierry, it is possible to make out the remains of certain substructures in the water. This has led many to believe that there was once an anchorage in that place designed to provide facilities for fishing boats and other light vessels, but this seems doubtful in view of the fact that the coast here is open to the westerly and southwesterly winds, and could never, at any time, have afforded effective shelter. . . .

That may be, but several anchorages at Ostia were far from secure, though that did not prevent their use. The important point is that on the final sentence of this anonymous letter rests the denial so frequently made that there never was a harbor to the west. Sailors are in agreement that the entry to Cherchel is even now extremely tricky when the wind is in the east.

🖎   🖎   🖎

E. F. GAUTIER, in his book *Genseric, roi des Vandales*, reproduces a photograph of Cherchel with the following caption. "The Roman port of Caesarea was situated in the small quadrilateral lying in the lee of the small island on which the lighthouse stands. [In other words, the islet of Joinville.] It is not large enough for modern requirements, and a new jetty has been constructed. Present-day Cherchel is, however, an insignificant township of some 6000 inhabitants, whereas Caesarea was a great and wealthy capital with a population of, possibly, 100,000." It seems surprising that this remark should not have roused doubts in Gautier's mind as to the accuracy of the dimensions attributed to the ancient port. The dimensions given to it by archaeologists seem to accord ill with what we know of Caesarea.

What matters is not the number of inhabitants then and now, but the relative importance of the trade handled in the present century and two thousand years ago. The present harbor accommodates only six or seven trawlers, each of them smaller than the vessels which used it in the Roman period. I have never seen there any cargo boats which could compare with the *corbita* which were in the habit of loading corn and oil at Caesarea.

What was the actual value of this trade? Less, no doubt, than some scholars maintain, but still considerable. "The phrase 'the granary of Rome' remains one of those convenient common-places which are the stock-in-trade of official orators and publicists," writes C. A. Julien in his *Histoire de l'Afrique du Nord*. The two annual crops would seem, indeed, to have been a legend by which Strabo was taken in. The soil was as naturally poor and arid as it is today, but in ancient days there was a well-developed irrigation system, and that, too, in tracts of land which are no longer cultivated. It is generally agreed that Africa supplied one third of Rome's crop consumption. The balance came from Spain, from the region of Narbonne, and from Sicily. Mauretania, in which Caesarea was situated, ranked only second as an exporting district, being inferior to Carthage. Two hundred thousand citizens of Rome received a free monthly issue of a million bushels of cereals. The production of olive oil, which was highly developed, especially in Tripolitania, Tunis, the valleys of Kabylia and Chelif, was used, not for cooking, but for burning and the requirements of the toilet.

If we want to establish a parallel between the sea-borne trade of North Africa in antiquity and that of the present day, it would be fairer to compare Caesarea with, say, Algiers or Oran, both of them great modern ports living on the export of Algerian produce and having the same sort of standing as Caesarea had in the days of the Roman Empire.

But it was not only an important port and a hive of economic activity. It was also a political capital and a center of civilization. It owed its brilliant position to Juba II. It was his creation, just as he was the creation of Augustus. Mention of this Berber prince is not irrelevant. It serves to remind us of the importance of a harbor of which nothing now remains but mud and a scattering of masonry beneath the sea.

King by the grace of Rome of a territory which comprised the whole of Morocco and Algeria, this son of a Numidian monarch whose lands had been confiscated by Caesar was familiar with all the best authors of Greece and Rome. He set himself to outshine the Roman civilization of the first century in all that it could offer of science and literature. Duly obedient to Augustus, he married the daughter of Cleopatra and Antony, that young Cleopatra Selene who had been brought up in the household of Octavia and united in her person the elegancies of Alexandria and the refinements of a Roman education. This was quite enough to go to the head of a Berber whose position as a vanquished enemy of Rome must have been wretched in the extreme.

After the death of his adorable wife, he married an Oriental harpy, for he had no more discrimination in love than taste in letters. When, thanks to a divorce, he got out of this scrape, he was able to indulge his liking for art and books, which was passionate in the extreme. Not content with giving Caesar's name to his capital, and building a temple dedicated to Augustus, he attracted thither a swarm of Greek writers and artists. He established a library in which a number of rather too crude forgeries found a place, and a gallery of sculptures which contained more copies than original works. None of this collecting could have been achieved without a continuous coming and going of ships between Rome, Athens, Alexandria, and Caesarea, a "cultural relations" activity which was additional to the commercial traffic of the port.

It is only necessary to pay a visit to the Cherchel Museum to realize that Juba imported into his kingdom as many marbles from Greece as statues from Egypt; as many Roman mosaicists as minor Greek orators and poets. There must have been a ceaseless to-ing and fro-ing of messengers and visitors, all providing nourishment for the king's self-imposed task of gathering together an indigestible mass of miscellaneous volumes which occupied the full time of an army of secretaries and copyists from every corner of the Mediterranean and all the schools of human thought. Juba was, too, a great traveler, and did not spare himself in the general hurly-burly of his court.

But Caesarea was concerned with more things than trade. It would, for instance, be a mistake to undervalue its strategic importance. When Caligula had the son of Juba II, the young Ptolemy, assassinated, for no better reason than because he wanted the inheritance to devolve upon himself, he found it necessary to land a punitive force in Mauretania to put down the rebellion that followed. (Those interested in this affair should read, in *Le Maroc Antique*, by J. Carcopino, the account of the young Ptolemy's death, and the description of Juba II. What I have said here has been drawn exclusively from this author's masterly pages.) The supplying of these troops by sea presented so great a problem that even the merchant fleets of Britain, says

Dion Cassius, had to be called upon. This fact alone permits one
to suppose that extensive harbor works existed.

☙   ☙   ☙

Iᴛ may be objected that there were other harbors in North Africa.
That is perfectly true, and it is important that they should be
identified. All along the littoral their names and their ruins come
thick and fast, but neither names nor ruins go to prove a degree
of importance which in the case of Caesarea is borne out by both
its situation and its name.

A week's diving, divided between Cherchel and Tipasa, is quite
sufficient to make one realize the difference between a make-do
anchorage and a genuine port of the ancient world.

It was formerly held that the construction at Tipasa consisted
of a quadrilateral lying between the shore and the two small
islands off the headland on which the remains of the Basilica of
Sainte-Salsa can still be seen. As an anchorage it is beneath contempt. No doubt it may once have been more elaborate. There
may, for instance, have been a creek which has since been filled
by the alluvial deposits of a *wadi*, and buried under the sand on
which fishermen have now built their huts. Our Ponts et Chaussées have not been sparing in their use of stone, but their efforts
have served only to create a scene of surprising nudity, consisting
of a quay and a concave protective wall against which the rollers
break. There may have been more than this, but probably nothing
comparable to the harborworks of Caesarea. The same holds
good all along the coast. There are sheltered inlets, to be sure, and
remains of jetties, but I very much doubt whether it is possible
to find traces of any large-scale harbor until one gets to Tengi—
Tangier.

A large harbor will always leave its marks beneath the surface,
except where another, and more modern, harbor has totally
effaced them and engineers have scraped the bottom in order to
make contact with a shelving beach where once an earlier installation existed.

The great merit of R. P. Poidebard's examination of Tyre and
Sidon is that it reveals once and for all the elements upon which
it is possible to establish a scale of size. Before it was completed
many things were in doubt—the development of quays and

basins, the efforts made to protect them from the sea, their area extent and the depth of their foundations—all of them matters of the highest significance in attempting to establish the importance of ancient ports. The plans, the surveys, the photographs made and taken on the Phoenician coast provide us with evidence which cannot be challenged. It not only confirms but greatly exceeds the most generous estimates previously advanced. We know now what the size of a Roman colonial harbor in the second century A.D. really was. We are in a position to see what huge concrete constructions were used to protect the anchorage from incoming rollers, often at some distance from the land; how communication was established between a complex system of basins so designed as to accord with the traditional siting of a place which native experience had submitted to prolonged tests: different channels suited to different winds, the setting of storehouses, tanks, and arsenals, the positioning of harbor craft at the different quays. Sometimes, as at Sidon, there was an arrangement of flushes to prevent silting, taken over from the Phoenicians, who had first installed it. Our modern engineers have never been able to produce anything half so efficient for the purpose.

Everything that P. Poidebard and his assistants found in the sea and on the shores of Phoenicia was Roman. This may have caused them disappointment, for some had hoped, in the landsman's rather simple-minded way, that the sea, like the solid earth, would reveal, in superimposed layers, traces of all the successive occupants. The only thing left to recall the Phoenician past was the choice of site, and the ingenious methods devised for dealing with the various problems of adaptation, the material remains of which are still there for us to see.

Undersea archaeology can offer nothing remotely resembling this fidelity to a chronological succession. The best it can provide is a handful or two of sherds which need to be sorted carefully. There is never, at any given point in any given harbor, evidence relating to more than one century at a time. "Only death preserves the lineaments of youth," a novelist has said. Only death can preserve the features of a harbor. It is from the dead ports of Cherchel that we can gain some idea of what the harbor was like in the days of its Roman youth. Under water the quays do not lie one on top of the other like the many cities on the hills of Troy. To build them, much scraping and cleaning and dredging was

Plate 1. The author at work on an archaeological discovery off Cherchel. He wears a sweater for protection against the cold water. Pounding the hammer on the chisel produces a disagreeable metallic sound.

Plate 2. Madame Monsenergue on the sea bed off the ancient ports of Cherchel, examining enigmatic relics of some unknown age. The object tied to her waist is a pad for sketching or making notes.

Plate 3. Bronze panther now in the Saint-Germain Museum. This Hellenistic statuette was found in 1950 by a helmet diver operating off the coast of Provence. It probably came from a wreck of the First Century, A.D.

Photo Chardcl

Plate 4. The Antheor "stopper." Such discs were frequently used to seal in the corks of amphorae. The lettering is Oscan, and should be read counter-clockwise.

Photo Monsenergue

Plate 5. The author making an underwater sketch.

Photo Dr. Beaucaire

Plate 6. Searching for the remains of submerged
houses in the Saint-Gervais Cove. This is where some
of the most valuable discoveries have been made—
notably an antique altar complete with lamps.

Photo Dr. Beaucaire

Plate 7. This ivory head of Aphrodite belonging to the Hellenistic period, First Century B.C., was found near Fos-sur-Mer and is now in the Vieil Istres Museum.

Photo Musee de la Marine

Plate 8. A lead anchor stock engraved with Medusa's head—a protective symbol of the Roman and Hellenistic eras. It was found off the Cape of Antibes and is now in the Marine Museum in Paris.

Plate 9A. Fragment of an ancient lamp found at Fos-sur-Mer. It is modeled after a ship's prow. The figure is probably a fisherman, and the bird-siren above him gives the article a funeral character.

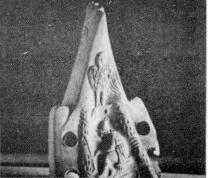

Plate 9B. Fragment of a decorated vase found at Fos-sur-Mer. The figure is Venus surrounded by her attributes—a dove, a shell and a cupid.

Plate 10. Theseus at the bottom of the sea. This group appears at the bottom of a cup now in the Louvre Museum. Theseus, supported by a bearded Triton, is flanked by Athena on his left and Amphitrite on his right. The design pertains to the well-known legend of Minos, who told Theseus that he was not the son of Poseidon. To prove his divine parentage, Theseus threw his ring into the sea and then proceeded to recover it, bringing up from the bottom of the sea not only his ring but also a crown of gold given to him by Amphitrite.

Photo L. Dessault

Plate 11. Aerial photographs of the twin ports of Cherchel.

Photo by the Author

Plate 12. Roman marble columns found in shallow water just outside the modern port of Cherchel.

Plate 13. Aerial photograph of the "Pointe de Lostmarc'h."

Plate 14. Fish swimming around a wreck.

Plate 15. A wreck lying in 23 fathoms.

Photo Monsenergue

Plate 16B. Pierced stone found at Cherchel on the site of the ancient commercial harbor.

Photo Monsenergue

Plate 16A. A Fifth Century Tetradrachm, masterpiece of ancient numismatics. Marine motifs were very common at that period.

necessary. When French engineers set to work to construct the modern port, they did precisely what their Roman predecessors did when they sought to recondition the Phoenician port of Tyre. When, in either case, an existing block of masonry was used because it was conveniently to hand and difficult to move, the builders incorporated it so completely in the new construction that it at once assumed a Roman or a French look. It would need a powerful magnifying glass to discover any trace left by the original laborers or quarrymen, and even if any such trace has been left it is probably on one of the inner faces. Divers in all ages have been careful not to leave such matters to chance. They have their little manias and precautionary methods which do not vary much. When a piece of existing masonry is used, it figures as new work in the account rendered of work done.

ᴗ   ᴗ   ᴗ

I AM only too well aware that this brief study of the underwater remains at Cherchel bristles with inadequacies. There is a deal of evidence, even of archaeological evidence, in the sea upon which a diver can rely, but which would certainly not convince an archaeologist who is not also a diver. Persuaded though I may be by what I saw with my own eyes, I could prove my assertions only by providing the necessary plans and photographs.

But what purpose would be served by that type of documentation? Would all the trouble involved be worth while merely to show that the port of Caesarea was not confined to a quadrilateral situated behind the islet of Joinville? Good sense can tell us that much. The trading fleets which assembled there always at approximately the same time of the year preparatory to carrying food to Rome would have needed a different style of anchorage from that suited to ships of war. It is at least plausible to suppose that the Annona had a harbor as well as a temple.

Much time is necessary for an exhaustive underwater survey. It took R. P. Poidebard and his assistants four years to build up a picture which could be accepted as a faithful representation of the port of Tyre, and four years more to do the same for Sidon. Even so, many of the elements were situated on rocks off the coast, and not beneath the surface. The use of free-divers ought to be able to shorten the time needed for such work. Still, eight

days are not four years, and I do not for a moment claim to have
achieved at Cherchel results even remotely comparable with
those produced in Syria. This I say to encourage those who would
like nothing better than to undertake the task. Perhaps, after
carrying their inquiries beyond the preliminary stage, they may
draw conclusions very different from those that I have here
recorded.

There is no lack of promising sites in this region. Before reaching Cherchel, the traveler, starting from Algiers and moving along
the eastern flank of Cape Zizerine, has only to look down into the
water to find telltale traces beneath the surface. On the cape
itself, stumps of antique columns are now used to mark the
boundary lines of gardens. The path that leads downhill towards
the sea rings hollow under the feet, and on the shore lumps of
concrete can still be seen clinging to the rocks. It is said that there
were once fishponds here, baths, and a temple. Flagstones and
fragments of pillars are visible upon the sea bed. It may be necessary to go deeper, to extend the area of exploration. But life is
short; the sea too wide; the past too rich. . . .

᭙   ᭙   ᭙

THOSE African dives did at least reveal to me the powerful mark
which Rome has left upon the sea. The deep places of the Mediterranean have a Roman look. Almost everywhere the conquerors,
who were never sailors, have left hard and lasting traces of their
passage.

"*Mare nostrum*": yes, indeed, they made this difficult stretch
of water, with its scattered and infrequent ports, their own. But
it was by way of the coast and in terms of masonry that they did
so, and not, like the Greeks, as a result of daring and intuition,
of love, and the gallantry of sails. Their history here was that of
contractors, not of navigators.

Juba is firmly linked to this port, even in the water, even at four
fathoms. Both he and it were sharers in the same "collaboration":
the Berber prince togged out like a Roman, and the Punic harbor crowned with Roman cement, both served the same cause
and were products of the same policies.

On sea and land alike Rome laid a heavy hand. Her traces are
solid rather than beautiful, staggering rather than thrilling. I am

not sure that there is really a great deal worth recovering from
these Cherchel waters—a few columns, perhaps; but there are
already so many columns in its tree-shaded square! What matters
is the eloquent abundance of masonry in the sea, masonry and
concrete, witnesses, all of them, to a grueling task. But only if we
see these things where they lie on the sea bed can we hope to
understand their message. There is room for the casual visitor as
well as for the scholar in the world of undersea archaeology.—
I do not mean that there is no need of scholarship. The blocks
themselves may be of no intrinsic value, but in the mud that lies
beneath them it may well be that there are other traces. The
example of Fos is, in this respect, instructive.

Man's desire is that the dark waters
of death may become the waters
of life, that death and its cold
embrace may be revealed as a
mother's breast. The sea swallows
the sinking sun only to give it
new life in the deep places . . .
Life has never been able to believe
in death.

                    C. G. JUNG

THE "TREASURES" WHICH PLAY SO GREAT A PART IN STORIES OF
adventure beneath the waves, from the days of Glaucus and the
Arabian Nights, to those of Lieutenant Harry Rieseberg, bulk
much less largely in actual fact. When they are not just the product of the literary imagination they demand of those who seek
them more of ruthless determination and less of mere curiosity
than I possess.

Sea gold does not tempt me. I regard diving as a means of
acquiring knowledge, not as a way of collecting loot, nor even of
recovering material objects. What I seek below the surface is
knowledge of man, knowledge of myself, knowledge of those who
have preceded me upon the shore, upon the sea, and even under
it.

That, in its way, is loot, and the time has now come to take
stock.

146

LET me begin by recalling what we owe to those who blazed the trail by exploring sites which, from now on, must forever be regarded as classic examples in their kind—Mahdia, various places in Greece, Tyre, and Sidon.

Mahdia was the first instance on record of a wreck being systematically and successfully examined, the first triumph which undersea archaeology can legitimately claim. It is a spot where sponges and mud abound. It is also a gift which the sea delivered up to us after first cheating the original looters of the leavings of the conquered.

ja   ja   ja

THE undersea discoveries made in Greece deserve a volume to themselves. To a great extent they are outside the scope of this book, and if I mention them at all it is only because I do not want to be accused of leaving anything out.

The most important are those of Anticythera, Artemision, Marathon, and the Piraeus.

It was long ago pointed out that most of the antique bronzes now in our possession have been recovered from the sea. Off the southernmost point of the Peloponnesos, on the reef of Anticythera, in the year 1900, the bronze statue of a youth, measuring almost six feet in height, dating from about 370 B.C., was brought to the surface. In the same general region, to the south of Cape Malea, not far from Cerigotto, there is a rich deposit from which sponge divers have recovered a bronze astrolabe, a number of terra-cotta and glass vases, and some marble statues, all badly eroded as a result of their long sojourn in the sea. They almost certainly come from the wreck of a ship carrying a cargo of works of art.

A bronze Hermes belonging to the period of Praxiteles (now in the National Museum of Athens), was fished up in 1925 from the Bay of Marathon, "a lucky haul made by a caïque."

Another statue of a youth, also in bronze, but lacking its head, probably dating from between 390 and 380 (now in a Berlin museum), was found in the sea near Eleusis, on the coast of Salamis.

In 1926, off Cape Artemision, at the northeast corner of Euboea, another deposit was found which gives every sign of being particularly rich. It was here, as a result of the discovery by fishermen of a bronze arm, that, in 1928, a colossal Zeus was recovered; it is over six feet tall, now in the Athens Museum. It is an original Greek bronze of the fifth century, perhaps the only example we have besides the Charioteer.

Two other bronzes, the forepart of a horse, and a young rider, were also found; it is possible that they were parts of a single group. The wreck was sighted by helmet divers. It lies about six hundred yards from the most northerly point of Euboea, almost opposite Histiaea, at a depth of twenty fathoms.

Some marble reliefs were found in the harbor of Piraeus. They are of especial interest, and represent spirited scenes in which Amazons play a part.

Robert Demangel, Director of the École d'Athènes, called upon some free-divers in Paris for assistance and took them, in 1950, to a number of sites where accidental finds had sent hopes soaring. With the exception, however, of one small silver cup, the harvest consisted for the most part of amphora fragments, leaden anchors, and terra-cotta dishes. It still remains to stage a demonstration of scientific undersea research in Greece.

Since 1950, Professor Dontas, Director of the Hydrobiological Institute at Piraeus, has made an underwater survey of the Bay of Helike and may yet be successful in collecting fresh information about that submerged city. Further finds, too, have been reported from Cape Artemision—"on January 26, 1952, a net belonging to a fisherman named Soulitzes brought up three archaic vases. A very heavy object broke the net before it reached the surface." (I owe this piece of information to Robert Demangel.)

Finally, mention should be made of a recent discovery, not, this time, in Greece but in Italy. Off Terracina a bronze horse of colossal size was brought to the surface by fishermen. It is now in the Thermae Museum at Rome. It seems likely that it formed part of the cargo of a foundered ship.

᭝   ᭝   ᭝

THE investigations carried out at Tyre and Sidon are of a very different character from those undertaken in Greece and Italy. They mark a new stage in marine archaeology. No longer has it been merely a question of fishing for works of art, but of resurrecting, at the cost of prolonged efforts, two Roman harbor installations on the coast of Syria. The results achieved have been the fruit of teamwork carried out with official support, and employing all the traditional means—helmet diving, cartography, draftsmen and engineers of the Ponts et Chaussées. The overriding problem with which the original harbor makers had to deal was that of silting. It was the Phoenicians who found the solution, the Romans who copied it. The principal merit of the modern researches at Tyre and Sidon has been that they prove, beyond the shadow of a doubt, the extent to which the Romans built in the very sea itself during the Imperial Age. Tyre and Sidon have put an end to a deal of archaeological skepticism in the matter of quays, basins, and, especially, of deep-sea breakwaters.

Now for the sites more recently surveyed. Anthéor offers us the wreck of a ship which foundered on the wine route in the course of the first century B.C., and this means that it must have been sailing from Campania to Gaul. Nothing, however, has so far been recovered from it but a small quantity of timber and a great deal of broken pottery. The sea, in this instance, has supplied us with evidence of a rather subtle kind which should delight those who dote on nice distinctions. Anthéor has little to tell us about the Roman annexation of Gaul. At most it indicates the underlying reasons for that heavy-handed achievement, scarcely, if at all, its cause. What those broken amphorae attest is the infiltration of trade, the bustling activity of seamen, the cunning of vine growers—all of them matters which are quite distinct from the conquest itself. In spite of the "heavy tread of the marching legions," what reaches our ears at Anthéor is the sound of an Oscan tongue in which a trace of Greek is audible.

All this we know on the strength of a simple disk of pozzolana found on a submerged site. But it needed the erudition of Heurgon to interpret the meaning of what was found. It was mind, not hands, that made the fruitful clearance in the mass of litter which lay upon the bottom.

Albenga stands for the recovery, for the tearing loose from a watery grave, of hundreds of amphorae. The sheer quantity is overwhelming, and I, for one, would gladly exchange such massive odds and ends for one single piece of reliable information about the wreck, or one good photograph of any of the objects, *in situ.*

At Fos-sur-Mer we have the spectacle of many centuries of history concentrated in the mud of a place lying on one of the great strategic arteries of civilization. Such bringing back to life of many periods from a distant past demands courage, patience, and knowledge. When the work has been done the future will hold promise of still greater victories to come. The Rhône Delta is stuffed full with remains which can tell us much. They are hidden in its many turns and twists, in its deluding secrecies and weaving tentacles. Human life began in the delta before Massalia had ever been founded. An axe found at Fos attests to the long persistence of a local past. The very name Massalia is "Ligurian." The historic unity of the delta has still to be established. Our knowledge must be extended to include the beginnings of Christianity, the sarcophaguses awash upon the shore at Fos, and the ships of St. Louis sailing out from Aigues-Mortes.

Narbonne: the meeting place of mineral convoys, of the route of Herakles and the road from Brittany. But it is more than that. It is the standing proof of the wealth of Gaul and of what could be done by the intelligent operations of an enterprising freedman. At Narbonne we are in the presence of the Golden Age of the Roman Empire, of its least liberal but most colossal aspects—a shipowner's vanity, a courtier's astuteness, but also of the remains of a temple which has not its equal outside Rome. Like the Empire itself, Narbonne was a vast façade.

Saint-Tropez ranks as a triumph for the practitioners of free-diving. It is to them that we owe all the preparatory work of pinpointing identification as well as the rapid adjustment of slings and cables which made possible the recovery of many objects. The operation demanded a great deployment of power. That in fact it turned out to be relatively simple was due to the use of the right technical means. Luck was with us. We might almost call it a *deus ex machina.*

Last of all, Cherchel, which is still in the early stage of reconnaissance. I have been able to record only a diver's-eye view. Cherchel may well confirm the knowledge gained at Tyre and Sidon. We may learn from it what in the water constituted the Roman unity from Syria to Africa. Rome followed in the footsteps of the Phoenicians and the men of Carthage, but conditions varied from place to place. Tyre and Sidon were the "railheads" of the Asiatic caravan routes—more especially, the delivery point of silk during the Empire: Caesarea, which was ruled by a man of letters, and where Annona had a temple, supplied Rome with a large proportion of her bread. "After the death of Carthage," Mommsen has said in a magnificent passage, "it was still necessary to mount guard over the corpse."

It was that necessity which brought into existence the arsenals, the jetties, and the sheltered basins. All that remains of them are blocks of masonry beneath the sea—a harbor maze to which only time, an appalling amount of rubble shifting, and a ruinous expenditure on documentary photographs will provide a clue. (I have not thought it necessary to speak at length in this book of the galleys of Lake Nemi, richly rewarding though their recovery was. The reader would do well to consult the fine work by Guido Ucelli, *Le Nave di Nemi*; Libreria dello Stato, 1950.)

☙ ☙ ☙

I HAVE now explained what it is that gives an individual character to each of these several sites. It remains to show what they all have in common. This, as must be abundantly clear, is the sea.

But it is also man.

The same waves broke against the breakwaters of Tyre and Cherchel. The same mud preserved the Aphrodite of Fos and blocked the entrance to the harbor of Sidon. The same festoons of date-mussels burrowed deep into the marble blocks of Saint-Tropez and the columns of Mahdia. But it was men who fought the storm at Mahdia, at Anthéor, at Albenga, at Saint-Tropez. It was men who transported tons of marble and gallons of wine. They performed tasks and made gestures the traces of which have not been rubbed smooth by the sea but live again in their anchors and their vases.

It was men, too, who hacked out the creeks of Carthage, Mahdia, and Motya, men who made the nails which still hold together the timbers of their ships. In the peaceful waters of their harbors, as in the violence of tempest, men worked to satisfy their longings, to safeguard their lives. In their ships no less than in their temples they expressed themselves, in their sails as in their weapons, in their cargoes as in their laws. Whether on the sea or on the land, their destiny was the same.

It is diving that has taught us all this. When undersea archaeology emerges from its stage of childhood it will provide us with the illustrations to confirm our knowledge.

But is that all?

Is there nothing to be said about the spirit of those ancient mariners? Can no distinction be drawn between the sailor's destiny and the landsman's? Is it impossible for us, in all the long adventure of mankind, to mark off the part played by the human spirit from that played by the sea?

I know that my fellow divers hope so. They rely on me to justify by historical argument the happiness they feel below the surface. Celebrating anew the marriage of Thetis and Peleus, they hunger after all the precedents. I fear that they expect from me something that of right belonged to God the Father in the first hours of creation. They want *me* to divide the earth from the waters, not now materially, but in the spheres of history, psychology, metaphysics, and what you will! I might point out to them that the Divine Work of Creation was not, in itself, wholly successful, since all over the world there exist such halfway houses as bogs and lagoons. Physical frontiers have never been clear-cut, and this seems to me to be even more obvious in the spiritual order of mankind.

I think that where man and water meet there is more to be found than scattered stones and broken pottery. A human truth, buried in the past and in the depths, drowned in mud like a wreck, would be of all trophies the most marvelous. But before we can draw it from the sea there is much alluvial deposit to be shifted. That is a trap into which I would gladly fall, from friendship, and in memory of those many conversations after bouts of diving in which dangerous generalizations flourished, and hasty formulae.

It is, indeed, true that a flicker of man is to be found in the sea, and of the sea in man. "The soul's past is a deep water," says Gaston Bachelard, "nor is it possible to describe a past save in terms of depth." But what one fishes from deep waters and the human soul is ambiguous, half flesh half gravel, and over it all a shimmer of movement, exquisite colors that fade in the light of day.

The difficulties of the "humanist" diver are not so very different from those of the biologist. There is the same richness, the same inability to tease out the confusion and to isolate the facts. There is a risk in the water of confusing gods, trade, and morality as hopelessly as chemical properties, temperature, and "finalism," and all to no purpose. Speaking of certain problems of archaeology, Déchelette makes mention of those "meeting points of the sciences which so easily become the meeting points of errors."

Nevertheless it is there that I have tried to work. A rhythm, a quivering of life seemed to cradle me and keep me there. From the water the past derives a pulse beat which the land refuses. Historians seem to think of history as building itself upwards while remaining stationary in one spot, as being a construction of four walls mounting in rigid and successive courses of centuries and individuals. Speaking of civilizations, they use, uneasily, words drawn from the vocabulary of architecture—fragility, solidity, collapse. In the water we think no longer in terms of building, but of currents, vibrations, and alluvial deposits. Is all this just another case of talking at cross-purposes, a quarrel over words all of which are equally unsuitable? Quite possibly.

It is no secret, however, that oceanographers, biologists, hydrographers, love "cycles" above all things. For them no truth is valuable until they have succeeded in imprisoning it in a closed circuit.

In the water, history, too, revolves. The same circular movement has sucked civilizations and fish alike into the Mediterranean basin. It is the universal law of life's will to survive. Mud is a staging post both for history and for the sea. It collects the symbols which are the very food of religions no less easily than it absorbs the nitrogen by means of which the creatures of the depths evolve. The same mud thrives on dead copepods and on the images of divinity—Aphrodite, born of the sea, whom the sea has restored to us in the silt of the Rhône; Dionysos, descending from the pediment of the Parthenon, calling in at Egypt, and then settling on the rock of Monaco in fourteen fathoms; Sulla looting from Athens her marbles and her bronzes, only to lose them among the Mahdia sponges, whence divers have brought them to the surface—who can fail to recognize in this dance of gods and masterpieces the circuits of carbon, phosphorus, and nitrogen in the great biological cycle of the seas?

The promises made by the sea to biology and history are, perhaps, the same promise—that an end shall be made to what Professor Bertin has called "the science of corpses." Only when one swims under water can one escape both from fish preserved in alcohol in the specimen bottle and those acres of the dead which provide material for archaeology as it is conducted on dry land. The motto of Captain Nemo, who was inclined, I used to think, to indulge in oversimplification, takes on a new meaning— "*Mobilis in mobile.*" I realize now that it admirably describes what should be the task of the historian. Bringing back the sea into his "restricted and conjectural" science is to free that science from the tyranny of a rigid system of stratification, to give it once again fluidity.

And uncertainty, as well. We must learn not to fear either the contradictions which, it well may be, are the very stuff of life, or the freakish whims which are inherent in all human activities.

                    ✥   ✥   ✥

JUST as the sea displays a biological and capricious fertility, so, too, it knows a fertility that is purely human. If it is constantly varying in its volume, in its microscopic forms of life, in its fixed animals, in its currents, in its seasons, in its temperature, so, too, it varies in its coasts and their people, its floating or fixed populations. There are in the sea historical as well as biological "aspects." To all appearances they are equally enigmatic and equally indestructible. One notes them, one describes them, and I fear that it may not be impossible to account for them.

If it comes to that, why should we not regard man as just another type of marine animal? We can decide upon the nature of his minimum requirements; we can take into account his seemingly causeless proliferation, the biological and historical chances to which he is every whit as much exposed as is the living coral and the mollusc. It needs a sharp mind to be certain whether a passage like the following applies to the navigators of Crete and Phoenicia or to the larvae of the plankton: "Those who were lured onwards along the great sea routes were brought in contact with many different types of habitat. They could make their choice: could settle here or there; could thrive, could take root and evolve under the pressure of life-giving competition, and in response to an easy adaptation in such localities as were most favorable to them." That is a quotation from one of the first scientists to examine the problem presented by the distribution of living creatures in the sea, Professor Pruvôt, a biologist.*

I shall never know why the finest collection of *Gorgonia* that I have ever seen was found at La Ciotat, below the Bec de l'Aigle. Was it because of the transparence of the water, the exposure of the rock? The same conditions are to be found together in places where there are no *Gorgonia*. There must be in these animal communities some sort of urge, a determination comparable to that which has led men and peoples to found empires, a constant repetition of opportunity, and, at the heart of the group, some tiny element of gratified desire which we cannot explain.

I shall never know why one of the most remarkable marine communities of all Greece came to birth and prospered at Aegina. Favorable conditions? Advantages of insularity? But there were many other islands, far better placed, the inhabitants of which were not even fishermen! There is no apparent reason why Aegina should have produced conditions favorable to life—even maritime life—unless it be that everything combined to crush it. The English historian Arnold J. Toynbee is of the opinion that nature's "challenge" to man has always been the best stimulus to the growth of human societies. He might well have taken Aegina as an example. Just over fifty miles of sterile rock, a bare minimum of fresh water, stones but no minerals, a shelterless coast bristling with reefs. If the soil was a challenge to cultivation, the sea was a challenge to navigation. The men who settled there were Dorians, that is to say, Indo-Europeans accustomed to move on foot or horseback, who had arrived from the continental plains of Asia. They hollowed out two basins protected by moles, and launched themselves upon the deep.

Their ships went in search of the corn of the Hellespont, of the perfumes of Egypt, and carried these commodities to the West. Says Herodotus: "The greatest profit ever drawn from a single cargo was that realized by Sostratos of Aegina." On that barren rock, where the soil was unsuitable for the production of ceramics, pots were endlessly produced which the island sailors

* G. Pruvôt: "Principes de distribution géographique des animaux"; *Année Biologique*, 1896.

traded through the length and breadth of the Mediterranean. Aegina remained the Χντρόπωλις, the "seller of pots" (there is here a play on the words πόλις, "city," and πωλέιν, "to traffic"), until such time as iron and copper, brought back by her ships, enabled her to fashion pans and lamps of metal—an industry peculiar to Aegina.

But what part in all this did the sea play? It is easy enough to register the presence of a rather sordid determination to "do business," as well as no little courage, but what sort of virtue did the waves contribute? This rocky island was the home of perhaps the only one of all the Greek cities which never knew tyranny. Her history presents a continuing picture of social freedom, of a balance struck between individual interests, until at last Athens, sick of finding Aegina in her way on all the highways of the sea, brutally crushed her. She had, however, recognized the principle of the freedom of the seas for others as well as for herself: she had designated her own harbor a "free port" and thrown it open to all ships, no matter to whom they might belong. Aegina was a port of call which all Greece could use for purposes of provisioning and protection. Her coins bore the effigy of the turtle, which, in Egyptian paintings, is the symbol of marine life. The sailors of the island were not content merely to sell their pots and pans. They knew how to appreciate the meaning of a sign.

There, where a sea animal had prospered, the species still lives on. Not often does life die out forever in the nourishing waters. Aegina even now lives off the sea, but off its depths. Her inhabitants today are not only sailors but divers, too, both free and helmeted. They are the best sponge divers to be found in the whole of Greece. In spite of Athens, in spite of Barbarossa, Morosini and the Turks, an ancient local tradition has remained firmly fixed, like a branch of *Gorgonia*, to that rocky isle.

¥   ¥   ¥

IN those happy days when Taine was explaining history in terms of "environment" nothing would have seemed easier than to say where, why, how a type of man as necessary to civilization as the sailor came into being. Unfortunately we have found out that it is not the suitability of a coast line that produces sailors, ease of communications, navigators; nor the profusion of fish, fishermen.

The Phoenicians, who were the foremost sailors of antiquity, lived on the least indented coast it is possible to imagine. Their harbors, always threatened by encroaching sand, were the artificial creations of men's hands, and had to be protected against silting by ingenious and complicated constructions. The coast of North Africa, where they set up their colonies, was just as bad. Greek sea power was developed, not among the inlets and peninsulas of the Peloponnesos, but in Ionia, on the bastioned coast of Asia Minor, where today the Turks have no maritime population at all.

"Nowhere," wrote Camille Vallaux, "is there a more complex coast line than that of Chalcidice, yet the people of that promontory had neither harbor nor navy, and never have had, down to the present day. The narrow peninsula of Hagion-Oros contains nothing but the monasteries of Mount Athos and their monks." *

If maritime skill is not dependent on geography, may it not at least be hereditary? It would be dangerous to bank on that. Arnold J. Toynbee has pointed out that the Aegean refugees who, during the first millennium B.C., set foot in Asia and were the ancestors of the Philistines, abandoned all maritime activities, preferring instead to dispute with the Israelites the fertile plains of Esdraelon and Sephala. Those ancient sea rovers fought to the death for a prize that was wholly continental and agricultural.

We are apt to think of the Normans of Sicily as sailors, but nothing is further from the truth. Their ships were manned by crews from Sicily and Calabria, but they themselves no longer had the skill necessary to command them. Grandsons of Vikings though they were, they had completely forgotten the sea. Their weapon of choice was cavalry. It was as mounted men, and thanks to a new system of shock tactics, that they won their victories. When Roger II needed an admiral to carry out the conquest of Tunisia, he took into his service George of Antioch, whose father had fought for the Zirides of Mahdia, a Levantine without a country, the son of a Christian woman and a Moslem, and to him he gave complete freedom of action.

❧   ❧   ❧

SICILY and Corsica are two islands the destinies of which were

* Camille Vallaux: *La Mer.*

wholly different. Sicily has been, turn and turn about, Phoenician, Greek, Carthaginian, Roman, Vandal, Byzantine, Arab, Norman, Angevin, Aragonese, Imperial, Savoyard, Austrian, and Italian—a place of call on the sea routes, a breeding place of art, science, and religion, but always the home of a maritime community. Corsica witnessed the same, or a very similar, succession of peoples: Phoenicians, Etruscans, Phocaeans, Greeks, Carthaginians, Romans, Vandals, Byzantines, Arabs, Genoese, and Pisans. Nevertheless, it played practically no part in the history of gods and technical inventions. It has remained a place of scrub and boar hunting, of goats and poor soil. Its deeply indented coasts look onto an empty sea. There has never been a seagoing population in Corsica. Even today it can count only 380 fishing boats, scarcely the complement of a small Breton harbor. (This is no discovery of mine. Camille Vallaux and Lucien Febure drew attention to it a long time ago.)

Still, there was little to choose between the importance of these two islands in the ancient world. Sicily might have its corn and wine, but Corsica was rich in the timber which is indispensable to ship building. It is on record that Genseric sent there for material to supply the carpenters whom he had brigaded at Carthage.

If islands always breed a race of sailors, England should be an outstanding example. On the contrary, it was only late in their history that Englishmen took to the sea. King Alfred, in his struggle against the Vikings, had to turn to the continent for crews. He enlisted them in Frisia. For a long time England believed that her future lay in France, and was slow to realize that her true element was the sea. That is why the Hundred Years' War lasted for three hundred (1154-1453). "Before discovering that she was an archipelago with a future on the ocean," wrote Dupont Ferrier (*Formation de l'État Français*), "England was convinced that France was her true field of action, and that chiefly for feudal reasons." The last sentence throws a flood of light upon the confusion caused in the lives of peoples when they turn away, in the course of historical evolution, from their natural element, the sea. Those responsible for that break were the Romans, St. Benedict, St. Columba, and the Arabs.

It is only too easy to account, as several historians have done, for the fact that the Romans were not a seafaring people by pointing out that their civilization grew up behind an unindented

coast line which had no natural harbor. If that were so, how can
we explain the maritime expansion of the Etruscans? Caere,
with its two harbors, was not so very far from Ostia—scarcely
more than thirty miles.

≈   ≈   ≈

SEAS rich in fish no more make fishermen than do natural
harbors make sailors.

The Levantine boats of the Gulf of Gabes may be Greek, but
the trawlers of Cherchel, on which I have eaten *bouillabaisse*,
are from Marseille, Malta, and even Brittany. They drag their
trawls at a depth of between 200 and 250 fathoms. The continental plateau has little to do with the matter. In times past
there were "Turkish" fishermen at Cherchel—as is made quite
clear by the official reports of the Marine Commissions set up
immediately after the conquest. Should we, perhaps, be on safer
ground if we regarded seafaring in these parts simply as a heritage
of the Berbers, the Byzantines, and the men of Phoenicia? I am
not prepared to give an opinion. Whatever the reason may be,
the old impulse has vanished. My friend Taïeb was forever painting and washing his boat drawn up on the sandy shore. Nostalgia
perhaps. . . .

≈   ≈   ≈

IT would be a mistake, too, to flatter the sea by attributing to it
the gift of positive virtues. On the rocky soil of Aegina ten thousand slaves, brought from all the corners of the Mediterranean,
were regularly at work. Chios and Delos were slave markets. The
maritime civilizations of the Greeks were the parents of industrial
slavery. It was something that even Egypt had known nothing of.
Not a very satisfactory balance sheet, this, even if we add to the
credit side Phoenicia, where the alphabet may have been invented, and Carthage, which, on the whole, had pretty low
moral standards. "Tyrannical, savage, and suspicious," writes
Ch. A. Julien, speaking of Carthage (*Histoire de l'Afrique du
Nord*, p. 84), "her merchant princes composed a caste which
closely resembled—as closely as an elder sister may resemble a
younger—the Venetian nobility, minus its taste and its culture."

It is tempting to think of the human race throughout its history as being divided into two main groups—the landsmen and the seafarers. But Alexander, the horseman *par excellence,* with his dream of universal empire and his Indian adventure, approximated far more closely to the sailor type. I once drew up a scheme of world history arranged in two panels separated by the sea: Nineveh and Croesus, Athens and Sparta, Xerxes and Themistocles, Napoleon and England, Churchill and Hitler. Xerxes was the central motif. Seated on his marble throne at the meeting point of two continents, the Asiatic despot, stiff in his Oriental robes, and incapable of building and maintaining a fleet, enlisted a number of Ionian and Phoenician sailors and, with them, struck a long-prepared but ill-fated blow at the West. It was left for a handful of Greeks to teach him what Aeschylus calls "the cost of inordinate ambition." He was reduced to chastising the sea. But already, on the very eve of Salamis, the whole population of Athens was ready with loins girded to abandon their city. Similarly, in 1940, Churchill was prepared to leave England and carry on the fight from a base somewhere in the Empire. At the heart of every thalassocracy there lurks the potential nomad.

Love of liberty rather than love of home—is that, in the last analysis, what the sea teaches?

But to draw a sharp dividing line between civilizations based on sea power and civilizations based on agriculture is to show oneself a little too simple-minded. The two are complementary. Almost all human communities have turned both soil and sea to account. It was so with the Cretans, it was so with the Phoenicians, it was so with Carthage, famed as much for her olive groves, vines, and livestock as for the quality of her ships. Carthage invented agricultural implements which the peasants of Latium subsequently learned to use. The Romans translated the twenty-eight books of the *Treatise on Agriculture* which was written by Mago, a Carthaginian.

It would be wiser to avoid all simple, clear-cut generalizations: better not to speak of imperfectly defined "civilizations," of the doubtful effects of "moral influences," of a line of demarcation between farmers and seafarers. There is one thing, and one thing only, in man that we can lay to the credit of the sea—his spirit.

I am not speaking now of material conquests or of technical achievements, but of mystical communion and the gift of faith.

And how could it be otherwise? How should this expanse of waters which men found at the far end of their earliest migrations not weigh heavily on their still virgin souls, their still impressionable minds?

To make my meaning clear, let me briefly describe one last trip of mine—and this time *not* beneath the surface of the sea.

🐦   🐦   🐦

LAST autumn I was staying for a short time in Brittany. I had gone there to carry out some diving operations at Roscoff with Professor Drach, director of the local laboratory of marine biology. Some day I may tell in detail the story of those days of hard work and companionship. As things turned out, neither sea nor weather happened to be favorable. From Drach's office, as from the stalls of a theatre, we could watch the gray-backed combers driving in from the horizon. L'Ile Verte lay drenched in rain. Resigned to our fate, we turned for amusement to the twin eye-pieces of the various tanks in which scraps of living matter, torn from that same sea which dashed against the windows, lay now imprisoned in a beam of electric light. A sea-urchin moved its pink, stalklike attachments, displaying its ambulacrum from which grew yellow suckers, its mauve-colored prickles. A sea-fan opened its hundred mouths and swelled its translucent flesh. In these glass-sided cages crabs moved for our entertainment. Dogfish in the throes of an uneasy childbirth danced an acrobatic ballet, showing their white bellies in rhythmic movement. Scallops, desperately afraid of a starfish, rushed madly in all directions, dashing themselves in terror against the glass walls of their prison. It was as though all these creatures were deliberately displaying a cross-section of their lives in order to console us for the ocean's treachery. For the ocean, indeed, had played us false. The scene was filled with the fury of rain and wind and waves.

But next afternoon, about four o'clock, the weather cleared. The tide was low, and diving impossible. I took advantage of the changed conditions to drag my friends to Cape Sizun. I knew that I should find there traces of the prehistoric folk who had settled at the extreme edge of the continent of Europe on cliffs that plunge straight into the sea. Thither we made our way.

Beyond the last village, where sheep and dogs covered with

dried filth were floundering in the mud, we came on a lane which was no better than an open sewer, leading to the sea, to the wide horizon, between stone walls. There the waste land began, a place of thistles and wild flowers growing low on the ground, a bumpy stretch of heath inexplicably cut up by crumbling walls. It was impossible to believe that any animal, any wretched donkey, had ever cropped this grass, that any peasant should have troubled to enclose so miserable a pasturage, where winds and sea mists were the only masters. Squalls caught us before we reached the headland or got so much as a glimpse of the sea. We struggled on until we reached the outer ditch of a settlement where once had lived a nameless people, where once some anonymous civilization had flourished.

A double line of trenches cut the cape off from the land. Through a gap in the middle we entered these defenses, and found ourselves between towering earthworks. On either side the vertical cliffs dropped sheer for hundreds of yards to the sea, or rather, to the foaming chasm.

As we moved onwards to the extreme end of the spur, we came within sight of the bare rock—a curious rock of clearly defined planes, shaped blocks, and the foundations of ancient shanties.

At last we reached the point. We tried to make our way down to sea level, where the rollers were battering the cliffs, but all in vain, the shore was inaccessible.

What folk were they who had lived on these "fortified headlands"? They are numerous all over Brittany. Were these entrenched settlements designed to face the sea or to turn their backs upon it? Were those who lived there fishermen or farmers? (P. R. Giot, Assistant Director of the 4th District of Prehistoric Antiquities, who first determined the layout of the fortified headland of Lostmarc'h, saw in it "one of the characteristic camps of the Armorican Gauls." In the single Bay of Douarnenez, there are two similar settlements: Castelmeur and Château en Beuzec.)

We gazed at the tormented, thundering, foaming waters in which, on that day, not one of us would have risked his life. Somebody spoke the word "Acropolis." A Western Acropolis: a Celtic Acropolis, seeking its safety in the water, at the very heart of a furious sea. A Pantheon without marble. I had had to come to this place to understand the price paid by man for his discov-

ery of the sea—a discovery which marked one of the outstanding
episodes of his adventure.

We are the heirs of those threatened dreamers who hoped so
much of the sea in this world and the next. Fear and faith, the
infinity of water, the infinity of the beyond—these things have
been linked in our imaginations for thousands of years.

Driven by necessity, it has been said, men ventured out to sea,
and, straddling a tree trunk, invented the arts of navigation. The
truth is probably more subtle. It seems to me that Gaston Bachelard has a truer view when (in *L'eau et les rêves*) he describes prehistoric man sending forth his dead as scouts onto the waves,
that intermediate country between the worlds of the living and
the gods, the antechamber of mysteries, the frontier zone of
humanity's great secret. According to him, "the first sailor was
the first living man who showed himself as equal in courage to
the dead."

On the corners of the western façade of the Temple of Aescu-
lapius at Epidaurus, are set the figures of two women mounted
on horses. They are nereids, and their steeds are sea horses. Classical Greece never forgot the last journey as it was envisaged by
prehistoric man. The nereids of Epidaurus, flanking the Goddess
of Life, the Goddess of the Cock, are there to escort the souls of
the elect over the sea to the Happy Isles. (The idea of the Happy
Isles seems to have existed in pre-Hellenic times.) "The whole
pagan world of antiquity," writes Charles Picard, "saw them thus,
riding the ocean of men's dreams, ready to take the souls of the
blessed into the secret haven of salvation." *

Maybe man's image of the afterlife was based upon his vision
of the sea.

The spumy distance of the Breton tides, the sea with its color
of molten lead, the shadowy forms of stretching, close-packed,
fleshy weeds forever reaching upwards from the ocean depths, of
such was the drowned *lucus*—that Sacred Wood of human souls
through which there roamed fear and a ghostly vagueness. Thus
came into being the funerary religion of these men of Armorica,
which, too nebulous to provide a family of featured gods,
assembled on the frontiers of the sea gigantic stones and the bodies of the buried to do service to the most oppressive and exacting

* *Manuel d'Archéologie grecque*, III, 335.

worship of the dead that humanity has ever known. It expressed the mysterious adventure of the troubled seas, of swimmers and divers blinded by the spray and paralyzed in the darkness of deep waters.

But there is another side to the picture. From a clear and sunlit sea emerged the gods made in man's image: the divinities of Crete.

They stood for a triumph no less important than the craft of metalworking, the invention of writing. They brought a liberation of the spirit. To the shapeless mystery by which till then man had been oppressed, the Cretans of the second millennium gave a name and an intelligible form. In this way was art freed, and human thought, from the animal conceptions of the Oriental pantheon.

When the Indo-Europeans, those landlubber tamers of horses, reached the Mediterranean, they had, as we know, no word for sea. Nor had they one for a statue: βρέτας and κολοσσός are both pre-Hellenic. "A study of linguistics shows us," says Marie Delcourt (in *Les Grands Sanctuaires de la Grèce*), "that many of the denizens of Olympus—except always Zeus—had names which cannot satisfactorily be associated with Greek."

The Cretans rid not only the earth but also the sea of monsters. A people of divers, they exorcised the depths, and knew nothing of "panic" fear. They found safety in fable and in art. The Cretans depicted octopuses on their vases, and in their verses poets created heroes. To draw, to name, is to conquer, is to fix the unknown within known limits.

Theseus, so closely linked with Minos, sought for a golden ring at the bottom of the sea to prove that he was Neptune's son. The secret of fable and the sea's secret were thus transmitted simultaneously to the Hellenes.

But the lesson holds good only for clear water. The Middle Ages of the West again saw monsters where the Cretans had found themes for their artists and heroes for their poets. Even Victor Hugo evokes an octopus far larger than any to be found off the coasts of Europe.

＊ ＊ ＊

EXORCISM, clear-mindedness, rationalism, these, I think, can be

set to the credit of the Aegean Sea, without too greatly forcing
or romanticizing the truth. It would be hard to deny the influen-
tial part played by the sea. If she cannot give us the answer to
every problem, we can at least claim one virtue for her, that of
"reducing." I have seen it for myself in the course of much diving.
There have been times when I have deliberately called to it for
help. The sea washes a man clean. It fines him down. In other
words, may we say, it *spiritualizes* him. That truth, perhaps, was
realized three or four thousand years ago. "Bathing in the Sea"
played a part in the Eleusinian Mysteries as a rite of "Royal Ini-
tiation." There is little doubt now that those Mysteries had an
Aegean origin.

What, in any case, cannot be denied is that the sea was responsible for a kneading together of cults, for a migration of symbols.
Universal religions are necessarily compromises—compromises
between faith and reason, between ritual superstitions and moral
fervor. For the establishing of these syntheses of peace a sea
breeze is necessary, and the international melting pot of harbors.

Of this truth Egypt forms the best example. It is to her that
we owe, in such matters, the overriding, the most "modern," creations of the spirit—a belief in personal survival, and the separa-
tion of good from evil. But it was at Byblos, the city of Adonis,
that Isis went in search of the body of Osiris. Before the Phoenicians, the Kefti, the Sabaeans and the Jews; after them, the Greeks
of Naucratis, and the Hindus—all played their part in a long
metaphysical interchange, the lines of which met and mingled at
the Egyptian crossroads of the ancient world. The religious creation of Egypt was the child of her harbors. It was from Alexandria
that the cult of Isis, the forerunner of Christianity, set out upon
the conquest of the Mediterranean; and there it was that the
hope of salvation—*soteria*—was born. In Alexandria the religion
of Dionysos took form, and thence, too, the Gospels set off
towards the West. Alexandria looking on the sea.

Like copper, like tin, like poetry, like the axe of the Labyrinth
and the swords of Huelva, faith traveled on board ship. The God
of Asine and Taenarum, the ancestor of Poseidon, with whom
Athena had to dispute her patronage of the Acropolis, walked on
the waters before ever Jesus did.

The earliest iconographies of Christ are redolent of the sea.
He is shown surrounded by fish and by anchors. (While work

was being done on the graving dock at Marseille in 1837, the oldest Christian inscription known in Gaul, or in the world, was found. It dates from the year 64, and makes mention of the martyrdom of Volusianus. It is ornamented with an anchor. It is now in the Borély Museum.)

The Cretan Dyctina, Lady of Waves and Mountains, the Good Goddess, χρηστή and πελάγιδ, who had an altar at Arles, is today called Notre-Dame de la Garde. The name of the Good Mother was written in Greek, more than two thousand years ago, on the Rock of Castelan. (An inscription to the Mother-Goddesses, written in large Greek characters, has been found cut into a rock in the neighborhood of Istres. The paintings in the Catacombs are not, as was long thought, the work of Roman artists, but of Greek. It was the seafaring peoples who spread both faith and art.)

As to the mystic symbols born of the sea—the spiral, the fish, the Sea-Fan, and the anchor—they are endlessly persistent. They are older than gold, older than minted money. "A symbol," Jacques Bousquet has said, "costs humanity as much labor to produce as is expended by a plant in the putting forth of a new characteristic." That is why humanity rarely lets a symbol die. It is the sea that is the faithful preserver of such things, even when the symbol has nothing to do with her, but is by origin wholly of the land. At Lepanto (1571), the Turks saw the standard of the two-headed eagle floating above Don John of Austria's galley. It had once adorned their own blazons. This old Sumerian emblem, found originally on the banks of the Euphrates, had taken three or four thousand years to cross the Mediterranean from end to end. Associated once with Babylonian Gilgamesh, it was now accompanying the natural son of Charles V into battle. Its meaning had not changed: it had always stood for strength.

9.　　　　　　　A Diving Suit for Clio

*. . . for History is not only a
science on the march, it is also a
science in its infancy.*
　　　　　　　　　MARC BLOCH

"WHAT WOULD HAVE BECOME OF HISTORY WITHOUT ARCHAE-
ology?" writes Raymond Lantier. "Each restoration of a buried
civilization gives us a new perspective, and lights a beacon for the
future." *

It is, I think, in undersea exploration that we may hope to find
these "new perspectives" and these "beacons." In a hundred years
from now, perhaps, men will hold it as a paradox that scholars
should have claimed to have found the truths of history at a time
when the archaeological evidence lying at the bottom of the sea
was still inaccessible. History deprived of the testimony of the sea
must be history incomplete. As to the extent of this testimony,
the world is more or less at one. It can scarcely be doubted that
sea-borne trade has been intensively carried on over thousands of
years. Certainly no one would dream of denying the existence
of the great continental tracks—many of them very long—or of

* *Revue Archéologique*, January-March, 1951, p. 77.

caravans, and extremely numerous caravans at that. But ports were built before the land trade routes were trodden. The sail was known before harness for draft animals was even imagined. Of those ports, however, we know nothing, of their ships, or of the sailors who manned them.

For it is not "knowing" merely to have at our disposal a few phrases from Vitruvius on the subject of harbor works, a few mosaics and bas-reliefs depicting ships, some linguistic comments about sailors. The matters which formed the essentials of life in the ancient world are relegated today to the background of history.

As to diving, which is inseparable from the problems of navigation, of harbor architecture, of naval victories, of religious beliefs, it has not yet been promoted to the dignity of history. It has remained within the sphere of anecdote: it belongs to the world of historic trivia.

Of what relates to the facts of the story of mankind, we have collected, so far, only such traces as can be found on land. The task of surveying the seaboard has not yet been completed. We have not even reached a point at which it is possible to enumerate all the harbors of the ancient world, or to determine their development in time and place. Interest, certainly, has been expressed in the most important of them, but only, as a rule, so that scholars may indulge in vain discussions based on manuscripts. There is no general agreement about the site of Troy, about the full extent of Pharos, about the ports of Carthage, or the precise location of Corbilo and Tartessus.

There are hundreds of Mediterranean ports which call for a thorough underwater survey. We lack good monographs, studies, and papers devoted to submerged remains, of the kind that swarmed into print at the end of the nineteenth century on the subject of land sites. Such an undertaking needs only a little encouragement, and this, doubtless, will be given by official archaeology. But teams will have to be enlisted, and men trained to make the necessary investigations. The task will be no light one.

Is there any reason to think that the example of Fos-sur-Mer, about which, four years ago, we had at our disposal only information culled from books, is in any way exceptional, or that no less rewarding results might be achieved in many other places? The coins of Ampurias and Rhoda were widely diffused throughout Gaul. They have been dug up as far north as the Loire and occur more frequently and in greater numbers than the coins of Greece. But has anybody told us how those two ports were built?

No. Have any diving operations been undertaken? Have any fragments of pottery been recovered from the sea bed? No.

Accurate information about these matters would be all the more interesting seeing that Jannoray, in a recent study, has pointed out the existence of a relationship between these towns on the eastern coast of Spain and Ensérune. But at Ensérune, too, nobody has yet troubled to examine the underwater remains, nor tried to find out whether or no a harbor existed on the Vendres Lagoon. If this were done, it might be possible to explain a local prosperity which, so far, has remained something of a puzzle.

Archaeologists and historians are hesitant about taking the sea into consideration. The reason is not so much timidity and wariness when confronting a world with the problems of which they are unfamiliar. Marc Bloch once spoke about "an education in historic sensibility."

"Whether consciously or not," he wrote, "it is always from our everyday experience . . . that, in the last resort, we borrow the elements which enable us to reconstitute the past . . . The only piece of machinery upon which we can call when we try to move backwards up the stream of time functions within our brains, by making use of the materials supplied by past generations . . ." *

Should we not find it simpler to feel within us that "stirring of human life which we can restore to ancient texts only by dint of hard labor," if we made an effort to relive its marine life of antiquity?

It is possible to give examples of what I mean: examples of intuitions and of errors, both closely involved with the historian's *sensibility*. Here are two.

Allmer, when he was studying the inscriptions on the amphorae found at Vienne (Isère), wrote, in 1902: ". . . it is unlikely that these large and heavy amphorae could have come from very far." We know now that, in fact, they came from Baetica, being trans-

* *Apologie pour l'Histoire*, pp. 14, 22.

ported by sea and river craft. The mistake arose because, when Allmer made that remark, little was known about the possibilities of maritime trade at the period in question. The movement of these "large and heavy amphorae" was, indeed, highly unlikely, so long as one thought only in terms of land routes. The conclusions of the archaeologist have here been falsified because he was not sufficiently "sensitive" to the evidence of his eyes, simply because he was not prepared to accept what his eyes told him—as a doctor might say, he had not been sufficiently "sensitized" to react to the marine impression.

Take another example. It needed the work done underwater at Mahdia, and the discovery of twelve large marble urns, to compel archaeologists to revise one of their most obstinate dogmas. Until then it had always been assumed that objects of this type, the most famous example being the Borghese Vase at the Louvre, were the products of Athenian artists resident in Rome. Faced, however, by the unimpeachable evidence of the Mahdia wreck, they were forced to admit that marble vases, five feet high and three wide, were, in fact, exported from Athens by the dozen, and in a brand-new state, during the first century B.C. The lesson was taken to heart, and many of the "neo-Attic" reliefs are now held to have been executed at Athens and not at Rome.

Lessons of this type are always recurring. The discovery and indentification of the Carrara blocks at Saint-Tropez, for instance, offer convincing proof that a marble lintel, weighing thirty-eight tons, could perfectly easily make a long voyage.

⚔ ⚔ ⚔

WHEN it comes to the writing of history, it is not enough to rely on land archaeology. On land men move about. Towns, fields, crops, and roads are in a constant state of flux. The only things that remain in one spot are those that live on in men's hearts, and those that happen to have fallen into the sea.

Sailors from places which no longer play a part in official history still live on in their ships, their anchors, their amphorae, their customers, their friendships, their sailing routes, and their ports of call. The evidence, no matter how small it may be, lies in the sea in the form of wrecks, pottery, and, especially, anchors. The pierced stones, for instance, τρητὸιλίθοι or λίθιναι, which have been found at Marseille, in Greece, and at Cherchel, may well serve to define the time limits of an epoch and give the character of a certain type of navigation. A day, no doubt, will come when we shall be able to write its history. It is possible that the stone anchors in the form of a pyramid, βαίτυλοι, belong to another seafaring tradition.

The Roman ports of Italy are of Etruscan and Greek origin. Those of Spain were Etruscan, Phoenician, Punic before they became Romanized. Rome's African harbors were ports of call for Phoenicians and Carthaginians. But the web of evidence has holes in it. To fill them, we have only, perhaps, to search the sea. Is the discovery of a few stone anchors a matter of no great importance to history? On the contrary, it may quite easily lead to one of those changes in perspective prophesied by Lantier. There is a feeling already abroad that Greece began the conquest of her conqueror long before she was vanquished. It may be that the evidence for that statement lies a few fathoms deep off the coast of Italy.

We shall never understand Rome unless we take into account the political bequest of Campania and the maritime activity between Greece, Sicily, and Greater Greece. Jacques Heurgon has shown how the Campanians, in the persons of Atilii and Regulus, garnered the heritage of the Sicilian tyrants and, in the third century, bequeathed it to Rome. Sea power is one of the keys to history.

It was not under the leadership of those much vaunted drivers of the plow, Cincinnatus and Manius Curius, that Rome rose to greatness. "Pigheaded peasants and men with the limited outlook of the soldier," writes Albert Grenier, "could never have been the founders of a great people." It was as the result of the pressure exercised by a foreign "plebs" that Rome was forced to forge the instruments of her greatness—her money system, her fleet, her ports, her law—all of them late creations. In navigation the Romans never amounted to much: crews were composed of sailors who had roamed the Mediterranean for many centuries—Greeks, Illyrians, Syrians.

It has generally been held that the sea civilization of Crete collapsed entirely round about 1400 B.C. But the "piracy" which dominated the Aegean and was so irritating a thorn in the side of Rhodes was for centuries based on Crete. The Seleucids did not fail to call upon these pirates for help. Mithridates was wise enough to seek them out when, firmly established in Athens, he made war against the Romans. Pompey, too, decided to enlist, rather than conquer, them.

These irregulars, like their Barbary successors, prove the long continuance of a certain type of seafarer who valued liberty more than a settled home, and life on shipboard above life in cities, and practiced now piracy, now trade. The ship in their hands was not unlike Joseph Prudhomme's saber, which came in useful for defending established authority but could, at need, be used to overturn it. The race of Mediterranean seamen was the hard core of all the great empires of antiquity—not excluding that of Rome.

But Greece provided Rome not only with sailors but with divers, too. The Roman *urinatores* were the heirs of an Aegean tradition which could claim to have won its spurs in many fights— in the siege of Syracuse and that of Tyre, as well as in the exploits of Scyllias of Scione and his daughter. (I have spoken of this in *The Undersea Adventure*, pp. 37 ff.) It is significant that the last evidence we have on the subject of diving in the ancient world comes from a Byzantine source. Vegetius speaks of it in one of the chapters of his *De re militari*. For many centuries the practice of navigation was closely bound up with a knowledge of the depths.

When the Empire fell, these men who had raised it up and provided it with food, prolonged its memory. It is quite wrong to think that after the collapse of Rome the whole of the ancient world came crashing down. The skeleton had been Romanized, but the flesh that clothed it was that of twenty different peoples who drew their lifeblood from the sea. Even when its frontiers shrank, even when it was living under constant threat, a civilization which had always depended more on the sea than on the soil could scarcely vanish altogether, or only as the Minoan civilization had vanished—through a process of reincarnation. Through the length and breadth of the Mediterranean there was more than one port ready to receive it as a friend and to continue its tradition.

Proof of this is to be found in Constantine's decision to move the imperial residence to the shores of the Bosporus, and in St. Augustine, expounding in Africa the form of a Christian Roman community. The instance of Byzantium is little likely to be contested, but that of Africa has been somewhat neglected. Only by forcing the evidence can we regard Western Europe and, in particular, Gaul, as the heir of Rome. Rome's eldest and most beloved daughter was North Africa. It was the great staging post in the onward movement of Christianity. The Catholic, Apostolic, and Roman Church was established in North Africa; in North Africa with its frontage on the sea. With its harbors, its resources, and its sailors, North Africa became the very keystone of the Empire when the fabric of Christendom was built. It was in a hybrid Latin, showing Punic influences, that the earliest version of the Old and New Testaments was produced and, under the deceptive name of *Italia Vetus*, was to serve for a long time to come as the Bible of the West. Latin was still being spoken in Africa in the eleventh century, and there were still five bishops in the country. (El Idrissi assures us that Latin was being spoken at Gafsa in the middle of the twelfth century. In 1053, on the eve of the Crusades, the Bishop of Mahdia claimed precedence over the Bishop of Carthage.) The halting place of God was where the shipmen plied. Jesus journeyed by way of the same ports as Isis.

✠   ✠   ✠

THE longevity of Rome is different as seen from the land and as seen from the sea. The Mediterranean was still a Roman lake, even when Rome fell. Military force and barbarian violence did not at once prevail against the long stretches of a Hellenized and Latinized coast, against the intense vitality of a long-organized system of intellectual and commercial relations, against the traditions of trade, the equipment of harbors, the armament of ships. For years after the Roman Empire had collapsed, its inhabitants were still handling the naval plant of a civilization which was not dead.

Marseille passed into the hands of Goths and Burgundians, of Visigoths and Ostrogoths. At one time she was shared between Sigebert and Gontran, and thus was partly Austrasian, partly Burgundian. But never, through all those vicissitudes, did she fail to keep open her communications with Egypt, Syria, and Constantinople.

So dense was the web of interests between Marseille, Carthage, ·

Alexandria, Antioch, and Byzantium, that the barbarians could not help but be caught in the trap set for them by civilization and the sea.

Besides, the sea was the best protection available to the civilized world. That was a truth of which the peoples of that age were well aware. A law promulgated at Constantinople on September 4, 419, decreed the death penalty for anyone who should instruct the barbarians in matters pertaining to the sea, of which, so far, they knew nothing.

Genseric set out to conquer Africa in May, 429. He sailed from Julia Traducta, probably the modern Tarifa, rather more than twenty-six miles from Cadiz, the Gadir of the Phoenicians. It was the fishermen of Andalusia who betrayed Mediterranean civilization. Genseric's horsemen could not transform themselves overnight into sailors. Andalusia had been Hannibal's "fief," and the link with Africa was, for its sailors, a matter of ancient tradition (and long remained so. It has been pointed out that the limits of the Arab conquest were almost identical with those of the Punic occupation). This Andalusian fleet, which carried to Africa the invading troops of the Vandals, was succeeded by a Punic fleet recruited in Carthage. The difference between them cannot have been very great.

But the occupation of Africa, the existence of a fleet under Vandal control, even the conquest of Rome, did not break the unity of the Mediterranean. The peace of 476 marked the end of the Empire and a recrudescence of Carthaginian sea trade.

The trap had been sprung, and the most dangerous of the barbarians, those who had thrust furthest, had let themselves be caught. The western Mediterranean was to remain Byzantine for more than a century and a half, until, indeed, the capture of Carthage by the Arabs in 698. It had once more become a Roman lake.

⚑   ⚑   ⚑

THE maritime unity of the Mediterranean might have continued to our own day. What shattered it was the coming of the horsemen. A wave of mounted Arabs, sweeping from east to west, was sufficient to deprive the West of that African "platform" with which it had lived in a relationship of give and take for 1500

years. It was thus that the outpost of Roman life and culture
eventually disappeared. "From then on the bridges were down
between Africa and Christian Europe," says Gaudefroy-Demom-
bynes (in *les Institutions Musulmanes*), "Africa lived thereafter
with her eyes on Baghdad and Cairo." Henri Pirenne (in *Charlemagne et Mahomet*) points out that "By occupying Sicily, Islam
cut Byzantium off from the West, just when Europe was grasping
the Byzantine lesson."

I know that these two statements are only approximately true,
since, on the one hand, Christendom remained firmly implanted
on the soil of Africa down to the twelfth century, and, on the
other, the flow of sea-borne trade between the Orient and the
West never wholly ceased. But it is in terms of "approximation"
that the destinies of nations take their form. There will always be
room for discussion to rage round the *incidents* of history during
this period of recession—the arrival of a roll of papyrus at Marseille, the existence of this or that Syrian middleman, the fact
that men could travel to Jerusalem even before the days of the
Crusades. But these things do not really weigh in the balance
against the mass of the evidence. Spain was conquered. Though
France cleared her territories of the enemy there was always a
threat hanging over Provence. The Port of Marseille was empty.
Down to the middle of the seventh century Marseille was still
minting money with the effigies of the Byzantine Emperors. But
a day came when she ceased to do so, and when that happened,
life had been squeezed out of the West: darkness and silence
descended. No longer was the Mediterranean a seaway for wealth,
inventions, and religions. From then on it was a menacing sea.
Dangers lurked in its waters—first the Arabs, later, the Normans.
It had become a frontier—the most dangerous of all frontiers.
Never had that been so since the time of the Ligurians. The
towns retreated to the interior and climbed to the hilltops,
where the ancient *oppida* awaited them, which had trodden the
same path centuries before.

The West, already driven back upon herself, was now reduced
within the measure of her own boundaries. She forgot the liberalism which had been born of trade, the art on which, for so long,
Hellenism had set her mark, and the monetary system of Europe.
The farmer of the seventh century had become quite literally a
disinherited man. He became a dispossessed dweller in the

wilderness, not because the barbarian invasions had stripped him, not because the fall of Rome had beaten him to his knees so that he could not rise, but because he had lost the Mediterranean.

The heart of the West, which once had beat in Rome, moved northwards to the valley of the Meuse, to the valley of the Seine.

It will always be a cause for wonder that Haroun-al-Raschid sent a clock to Charlemagne. "It was rather," said Gautier, "like offering a phonograph to a Negro chief."

Why?

Haroun-al-Raschid had a fleet. He was the world's broker, heir to the civilizations of Greece and Rome, of the traditions of commercial liberalism, even of Hellenistic science. These things could fall only into the lap of a maritime empire. Only where the sea pulsed and the surges pounded, bringing to the surface the sediments of the deeps, could the way to a new life be opened.

The West had become petrified. At a single blow it had lost its communications with the ancient cultures, and with the sea. Not only did the Abbasids have Aristotle translated into Arabic: they patrolled the route to India.

That Gregory the Great should deliberately have broken with the literature of the ancient world is significant. More significant still is the vigor of the monastic order founded by St. Benedict at Monte Cassino (529), for its central rule was that the monks should work in the fields. The Church intended that men should be firmly fixed in a peasant existence. To be strictly accurate, this rooting of men in the earth had begun somewhat earlier. "On the country estates the custom was introduced of entering the names of the *servi rustici* on the census lists, so that they became bound to the land and could be sold only with it. That was the law in the fourth century." So wrote Camille Jullian, who found this innovation enchanting. "They were serfs not of the master but the soil." But all that really amounted to was that their servitude was the more firmly fixed.

The doctrine of St. Benedict and of his disciple, St. Columba, was novel only by reason of the moral, the religious value now attributed to work upon the land. The *Regula Monachorum* says: "If the poverty of the soil and the tending of the crops cause them to labor without respite, let them not be offended, for they will be true monks only if they live by the work of their hands." One would search in vain for such teaching in the Gospels, in oriental monasticism, in St. Paul or St. Augustine. (In the *City of God* we read: "If, then, the Brethren would dwell together in harmony, let them not love the earth.") Jesus, coming from Smyrna, by way of Carthage, had allowed himself to be caught in the snare of the soil.

One can scarcely speak of "feudalism" prior to the tenth century, and historians have never really found a name for what happened in France from the time of Clovis to that of Robert the Pious, from 511 to 1030. The best they have been able to do is to coin a word expressly for the purpose, "La Francia" in contradistinction to "La Romania." The reason for their helplessness is that it is difficult to define a situation of which the sole outstanding characteristic is negative, is a "lack." For five long centuries Europe was deprived of sea water, as an organism may be so completely deprived of calcium as to become debilitated. Even today, as I have already pointed out in a previous book, our vocabulary, our ignorance of marine life, our failure to understand the nature of the deep places of the sea, shows how heavy a weight of misapprehension lies upon the whole of Western civilization. Contrary to the generally accepted view, we have failed, in the course of fifteen hundred years, to renew our links with our ancient heritage, for the simple reason that the Moslem world did not transmit it to us in its totality.

🐦   🐦   🐦

WERE it but admitted that the sea could, in some way, come to the aid of history, one would be only too glad to think that she could solve the Moslem enigma. The history of Islam, as it has been taught to us, is confused, contradictory, and well nigh incomprehensible. It is limited almost entirely to the Arabs, and their name, so freely bandied about, refers sometimes to sailors and traders, as at Djedda, sometimes to horsemen, as in the Maghrib. They figure as the destroyers of Roman Africa, and as the builders of Baghdad, as playing the part of pillagers in the West, and of poets and scholars in the East, as the men who burned the Library at Alexandria, and illuminated the "Hizb" of the Koran.

Should we, by introducing the sea into this disorder, give ourselves a chance of seeing the facts more clearly? Perhaps.

In the course of the seventh century, these Arabs succeeded in
making the whole of the western Mediterranean their own. This
they did with lightning speed. Were they, then, sailors? By no
means. It was on horseback that they achieved the conquest of
the Maghrib. Did they come, as the Vandals came, to turn the
Mediterranean once more into a civilized lake, to make of it
"almost a family affair," as Pirenne puts it? Far from it. They
kept to the shore. There is no record of an Arab naval victory.
Their attack on Constantinople was a costly failure. Carthage,
no doubt, could have provided them, as it had provided Genseric,
with ships and crews. But Carthage had other fish to fry. The
pirates who preyed upon the coasts of Christendom, who pillaged
Brindisi and Tarentum, who burned the Abbey of Monte Cassino and occupied Le Freinet (Fraxinetum)—La Garde Freinet—
may have been Moslems—they most certainly were not Arabs.
(The Saracens landed at Saint-Tropez round about 884. It was
not until 972 that their power was broken by William, Count of
Provence.) It is much more probable that they were the leavings
of Genseric's old crews, men from Andalusia and Carthage. The
Greeks had already raided Marseille in 848. Piracy was not necessarily an Arab occupation.

The Barbary pirates were men of a number of different races—
Greeks, Spaniards, Provençales, and Levantines. There was even
among them a Jew and a Visconti of Milan. (The Jew became a
rais and took the name of El Hadj Mohammed el Islam. The Hus-
seinite dynasty was founded by a rais who was the son of a Cretan
father and a Moorish woman. Mourad Bey, king of Tunis, was a
renegade Genoese of Corsican origin. Barbarossa was born at Les-
bos of a Roumeliote father and a Christian mother. That did not
prevent him from taking the name of Khaireddine—"The Bless-
ing of Religion.") But how many Arabs can be counted among
them? These Moslems, moreover, did not speak Arabic, but Sabir
—lingua francese—lingua franca.

A Moslem fleet did, however, undoubtedly exist. Its origins
were actually pre-Islamic. To tease out this tangled skein we must
do more than pull on the Mediterranean threads. It is between
the Red Sea and India that we shall find the central knot. On the

eastern coast of the Red Sea lived the only fish-eating Arabs
known to history. They were sailors, pirates, traders, but there is
good reason for thinking that they never left Arabia except to
indulge in freebooting or to travel to India and back. It was the
Bedouins, the nomads of the desert, who, sick of their poverty
and wretchedness, answered the call of the Prophet and rode out
from their homeland to conquer the world. The sailors stayed at
home and reaped the harvest brought them by the traveling pil-
grims.

Many things have been said of the Mediterranean, but never
that it extended as far as India. Close to what Lesseps called the
"new Bosporus," though it was, in fact, a very old one, lie the
crossroads of civilization—not of Eastern civilization, not of
Western civilization, but of the whole of human history. For
thousands of years a road had passed that way, which was the
golden river of the Mediterranean. There had been a more or less
secret interchange between Eastern Europe and India, and it was
that interchange which had provided the lifeblood of antiquity.
The Mediterranean world had drunk deep of India's wealth. It
had dreamed dreams, and it had known the road along which
dreamland might be reached.—"From the end of the fourth century B.C., down to the time of the Sassanids, Greek and Latin
characters figured in *graffiti*, in inscriptions on stone, and in a
number of texts preserved on parchment. The oldest Iranian
monument, the epitaph of a Greek from Sinope who died at Susa,
may well be earlier than the conquests of Alexander." *

Or, rather, the two roads, one running down the Persian Gulf,
the other down the Red Sea—the Mesopotamian road and the
Arab road. The Mesopotamian had been the road of Croesus
and of Cyrus, the "Royal Road" from Sardis. But before Cyrus
the destinies of Sumer and Mohenjo Daro had been so closely
intermingled that it is impossible for us now to be certain which
of the two civilizations gave birth to the other.

The route that lay along the Persian Gulf was Iranian from
the days of Cyrus the Great to those of Yazdajird III, through
all the lifetime of the Achaemenid dynasty, and all that of the Sassanids, from 558 B.C. to 651 A.D., more than a thousand years.
Twice, first under Cambyses, and later under Darius, Persia con-

* Huart and Delaporte: *L'Iran antique*, p. 24.

trolled Egypt, too, that is to say, the second route running down
the Red Sea.

It would be scarcely true to maintain that it was Egyptian.
Alexandria, Arsinoe, Myos Hormos, Berenice were no more than
staging posts upon it. The road to India was in the hands of the
Mineans, the Himyarites, the Sabaeans, the pre-Islamic Arabs,
whom the Egyptians, the Greeks, and the Romans attempted
to supplant. It was the country of incense, the spice road, the
storehouse of aromatics: the Land of Punt, whither fared the
merchants of the ancient world in the second century B.C. from
as far afield as Massalia to collect their goods.

Fragments of a contract dating from the second century B.C.,
concerning a journey to the Land of Punt undertaken by five
travelers, one of whom was a Massaliet, have been found in the
wrappings of a mummy. Among the guarantors were three capi-
talists from Massalia.

The question whether the Land of Punt, to which the 18th
dynasty of the Pharaohs sent fleets, should be located on the
Arabian or the African coast has not yet been answered. The
incense trees and the animals which figure in the bas-reliefs of
Deir el Bahari, and refer to these expeditions of the fifteenth century B.C., are of an Arabian rather than an African type. Whatever the exact position of the Land of Punt may have been, there
can be no doubt that trade with it dates from very far back. The
first Egyptian expedition sent to bring back incense dates from
the twenty-eighth century B.C.

It should be remembered that South Arabian coins have been
found, dating from the third and second centuries B.C. They are
copies of Athenian originals, and bear the head of Athena with
the owl.

It was to be foreseen that when the Arabian and Iranian currents should unite under the banner of the Prophet, when the
two routes should be controlled by one authority, the flood of
gold from the Far East would achieve its highest yield. The
fusion, when it came, could not have been more complete. "The
Abbasid who, in the eighth century, overturned the Omayyad
dynasty, was, it is true, a descendant of the Imam Ali, the
Prophet's nephew, but he was also, through the female line, a
descendant of the last of the Sassanid kings." It was this half-

breed who acted as the instrument of the power and civilization which go by the name of Arab.

The Abbasids who, according to Darmesteter, "were true Sassanids of Arab blood," had behind them a long tradition, maritime, civilizing, and Hindu. Their tolerance went back as far as Cyrus, just as the "Satrapy of India" went back to Darius. E. F. Gautier has tried to explain the tolerant attitude of Islam. According to him, it was the outcome of Arab indifference where the infidel was concerned, and even of a certain degree of contempt. That might be true today, but in the time of the Abbasid Caliphate there may perhaps have been as an operative factor a memory of Cyrus restoring her gods to Babylon, and to the Hebrews their sacred ornaments.

It was as the outcome of no mere caprice, but in obedience to a highly self-conscious political planning—which had nothing Arab about it—that the Abbasid Caliphs decided to make Baghdad their capital. They abandoned Damascus and the close proximity of the desert, preferring a site where Tigris reached its nearest point to Euphrates before turning down towards the Persian Gulf and India. This explains why it is that "Arab" numerals are, in reality, Hindu, as, too, is muslin and so-called Damascus steel.

There is no such thing as the Arab "miracle." There are survivals, many of which are due to the sea. At the crossroads of civilization, which the Bedouins reached in the seventh century, Byzantium, India, and Egypt met. At the head of the Persian Gulf, in the Port of Siraf, on the island of Kish, a thousand years of familiarity with the monsoon and the Indies were concentrated. The Arretine pottery found near Pondicherry, the Roman coins dug up on Indian soil, the Temple of Augustus at Mysore— all these things bear witness to the long continuance of that maritime route on which the Arabs had laid their hands. (The Cabiris of Ptolemy is situated at the mouth of the Kaviri. The river craft of Bengal show a surprising resemblance to those of the Middle Empire in Egypt.)

Sailors, ships, and naval science had long combined to produce this liaison. It was no more a Moslem creation than Eastern civilization was an Arab "miracle."

We find proof of this liaison in a people living at the far other end of the great route, in the ports of Southern India, where

they served as a link between the East and Far East. They were
a halfway-house people. Perhaps in prehistoric times they had
watched ships coming from the West, and had loaded them for
the return journey with what their own ships had brought from
China and Ceylon. These Tamils, who perhaps preserve in their
traditions a memory of what life once was like in the Mediterranean, were Dravidians, "pre-Aryans." They have a very old
literature of no little importance. Its basis is a collection of 1600
poems, from which we learn that the name given by the Tamils
to the men of the sea who came out of the West and landed
among them, was "Ionians"—Yona, Yonaka, Yavana. This appel-
lation they used from the fourth, and even perhaps the sixth century B.C. for all who reached them by that one particular route.
The sailors with whom they became familiar between the eighth
and the fifteenth centuries, whom we call Arabs, they called
"Saunaga," which is merely an altered form of "Yavana." This
Tamil civilization was quite as old as, if not older than, that of
the Arabs. If it were possible to estimate the extent of the debt
owed by each to the other, there is little doubt that the Tamils
would prove to be by far the bigger creditors. One of their kings,
Pandya, had sent an embassy to Augustus. They had known, at
one and the same time, the civilization of the West and the
civilization of China—thanks to their familiarity with the sea.
(Professor Meile, of the École des Langues Orientales, has
pointed out that the Persians had a word *bandar*, meaning a port
and its adjacent town—Bender Abbas, etc.—of uncertain origin,
but closely akin to the archaic Tamil word *pandar*, used in the
sense of a port, though its true meaning is, rather: "warehouse,"
"storage place," "dock." It is difficult to say which was borrowed
from the other, but it is certainly a word which belongs to the
tradition of Indo-Persian maritime civilization.)

Like the Cretans, the Tamils were great divers, the foremost
pearl divers in the world. Even today, on the eastern coast of
India, Tamil schoolbooks for use by children describe the breathing exercises which were used in the training of divers. We know
the important part played in the life of India by this breathing
technique, the religious and mystical use made of it. We should
not, therefore, be surprised that it formed the basis of the achievements of the Tamil divers. . . . It may even be that breath control used for professional ends *preceded* its employment as a

religious exercise, since the Dravidian civilization is certainly
earlier than that of the Brahmins of India.

The junks which, in the tenth, eleventh, and twelfth centuries
carried the trade between China, India, and the Persian Gulf,
contained a number of Tamil divers whose duty it was to inspect
the hulls and to carry out repairs by daubing holes and cracks
with a composition made of sesame and wax.

It was along this route, from the Persian Gulf and India, that
in the course of the twelfth century the compass traveled, an
instrument which the Chinese had devised, though they used it
only for journeying by land. The nautical science of the period
seems to have spread outward from the port of Barygaza, a ship-
building center lying to the north of Bombay, in the neighborhood of Surat. It has been identified with the modern Broach,
not far from Oujjaïn, where the Gupta culture came to full
flower at the meeting point of Iranian, Scythian, Graeco-Roman
and Far Eastern influences.

This Arab-Persian interlude echoes, or rather, continues, that
of the Aegean. There is the same constant activity, the same
abundance, the same political and religious tolerance. The "buzi"
—light—draft vessels (in the thirteenth century the merchants of
Marseille possessed "buzzes" which are frequently mentioned in
legal documents of the period) and the "junks," enormous ships
with a complicated rig, and equipped with hinged rudders, "such
as no Arab could ever have contrived, let alone handled," brought
into the port of Siraf, and thence to the island of Kish, cargoes of
fabulous wealth, and those charts which, adapted to the Mediterranean, gave birth to the earliest, illustrated, books of sailing
instructions. (The Normans of Sicily played a part in adapting
Arab-Persian science to the Mediterranean.)

🐦   🐦   🐦

THIS bringing together of Tamil technique, Sassanid tradition,
the heritage of Greece and Egypt, Byzantine influences, and the
sailors of Carthage and Andalusia puts into our hands most of
the threads of the Arab enigma. It only remains to add to that
total a sword—the Turkish sword. Nomad horsemen had for
brothers sailors who never moved from their native land, while

other sailors spread under the name of Arab a civilization which
had already existed for a thousand years.

Nevertheless, the interlude remains a thing to wonder at,
though in a sense rather different from that usually meant. It
provides the best evidence one could hope to find of the advantages inherent in the sea. One has only to consider the extraordinary combination of chances which made it possible for the
Caliphate of Baghdad, at one brief moment of history, to act as
the trustee of civilization, including its ancient manuscripts.
Everything that came to it, whether from East or West, came by
way of the sea: knowledge of navigation, commercial liberalism,
religious toleration, the skills of art and science. All these things,
mustered under the banner of Islam, were destined to make the
slow round of the Mediterranean, and to wake the West, late in
the day, to a realization of its great future.

As a stranger to the ancient heritage, Europe set off on foot
for the First Crusade. That adventure, and it is no use blinking
the fact, was just simply a barbarian raid on civilization. The Crusaders were the debtors of the Infidels. But one thing, in the
course of it, was lost—the secret of diving, a secret more important, perhaps, for the future of evolution than historians are
inclined to realize. The Saracens, who, in this matter as in many
others, had inherited the Greek tradition, did not impart it to
the West, not even through Venice as intermediary, though
Venice was privy to many other secrets. A military detachment
of swimmers took food into Saint-Jean d'Acre when the Crusaders besieged it. Even as late as the fourteenth century Ibn Batou-
tah came across a "sultan" at Sinope who was a skilled swimmer
and, with his own hands, pierced the hulls of the Byzantine ships
with a sharp iron spike, thus showing himself to be a worthy
successor to Scyllias of Scione: whereas, in 1522, at Venice, the
Doge, at considerable inconvenience to himself, saw two divers
descend into the sea with the aid of a great metal pot, an exploit
which would have surprised no contemporary of Aristotle!

A knowledge of the sea depths had once been part and parcel
of the art of navigation, and it long remained the prerogative of
Moslem pilots who, in order to discover the nature of the area
in which they were to work, drew to the surface, by sounding,
what amounted to a complete sample of the bed, from the composition of which, and from a study of the animals it contained,

they could plot their exact position. The navies-to-be of the West knew nothing of such practices. As a result of employing a Moslem pilot on his journey to the Indies, Vasco da Gama bequeathed to Portugal weeds and corals and shells which, after an interval of four thousand years, seem to repeat the motifs of Minoan art, *plus* an Indian flavor, but *minus* the experience which a diver gains. The Knights of Christ might be great sailors, but they knew nothing of the sea's deep places. More trawl lines than octopuses hang in the windows of Thomar, and such shells as there are were mostly picked up on the beach.

Atlantic navigation was born. I am not at all sure whether it has ever been made sufficiently clear how much this differed from the sailing of the Mediterranean which preceded it. It bred human character, it made demands on men which no longer had anything in common with the Aegean, Ionian, and Phoenician tradition. Swimming and diving were excluded from it. Those activities ceased to matter on voyages so long that, for weeks together, ships were out of sight of land. The coasting trips of traders had given place to vast expeditions undertaken by adventurers. Character was what mattered, not intelligence, and the operations were more in the nature of raids, *razzias*, like those of Spain upon the New World. Gone was the civilization which had sought strength and inspiration in the very bosom of the sea.

※   ※   ※

I HAVE done my best to draw up, as honestly as possible, the balance sheet of the sea. If I have refrained from putting to its credit virtues which may be debatable, I have felt myself dutybound to recognize the mark it set on the sensibility of nations and of individuals.

The ancient world achieved the conquest of the sea, of its depths as well as its surface. The gains were enormous and various. There is symbolical significance in the fact that we have not yet succeeded in deciphering the writing incised by the Cretans, four thousand years ago, on tablets of clay in the form of flat fish. Two secrets were lost at one and the same time. "Those who could not swim and those who could not read were objects of equal mockery in Greece," writes Charles Picard. That is the formula of a human situation which is entirely foreign to Western Europe no matter how loudly it may claim to have harvested the heritage of the past. Paul Perdrizet spoke of the "superb feeling expressed by Greek art for the sea's majesty." That feeling is alien to us. We have barely got beyond the stage of shrimping nets and paintings on seashells. We have not yet entered into possession of the world of the deep. We may have introduced beneath the surface a few men equipped with rubber suits, or imprisoned in blind submarine craft, but that does not mean that we have made our own an element which the ancients were already on the way to annexing.

As to the sailor—who occupies a relatively small space in our modern life—he is now no more than a mechanic whose soul and spirit is but distantly engaged. It is difficult to see what he gains from floating in a steel hulk with his eyes on a pressure gauge, and the headphones of a radio clamped to his ears. The water is more strange to him than the sky, less familiar than the ether.

We should not overmuch count on him to bring safely into port those intellectual and technical treasures, the combination of which, born of the sea, once made up the gift of civilization.

"A sailor who never dives," J. Y. Cousteau has said, "is like the driver of a motor bus who passes the Louvre twenty times a day but has never been inside the museum." True enough. But that word "museum" gives me an uncomfortable feeling. It has so little in common with the promise of the sea. It is not so much our past as our future that we must look for there, if we are to be true to the message of humanity which reaches us from three, from four thousand years ago.

10.

Conclusion: The Stake

Life in the bosom of the waters remains linked with the memory of lost happiness.

CHARLES MAURON

Does DIVING HELP UNDERSTANDING? WHEN IT COMES TO THE writing of the history of man does one see with a clearer vision in the sea than on the land? That is the supreme question with which this book has been concerned. Some may think that I have had recourse to a pretty solid slab of erudition before coming to grips with it. No matter. The essential thing, from my point of view, has been to concentrate the reader's attention on marine perspectives. My especial hope has been to convince him that an activity which is considered praiseworthy in the case of a biologist like Professor Drach might be seen to be no less so in that of those who profess the "humane sciences." For it is more difficult to evoke the past than to observe life. Those who would give themselves every possible chance in that task of conjectural reconstruction might do well to enlist the resources which psychology and sensibility can give them, especially of those that have become foreign to us. In the periods of antiquity millions of men established a tight knot of association between themselves and the great sea depths. That knot we have allowed to go slack. It seems to be obvious that our understanding of distant ages must depend upon the degree to which historians are familiar with the sea. Navigation in the ancient world was only very faintly connected with what we, today, call by the same name. This holds true just as much of navigation on the surface as of exploration beneath it. No historian, so far as I am aware, has ever mentioned a wind which blows in August across the Aegean and can, even today, waft a vessel of medium tonnage from the Cyclades to Alexandria in forty-eight hours. It is called the "Meltem" and alone suffices to explain the relations existing between Crete and Egypt in the great ages.

How is it possible to understand Glaucus, Theseus, the frescoes of Knossos, the octopuses on the golden cup of Medea, if we confine ourselves to the surface and cannot by personal experience measure the importance of discovering the depths?

Who would dream of discussing Italian painting without evoking the Umbrian scene and the light of Venice? If we seek to discuss Crete, and even classical Greece, it is essential that we realize the harmony that once existed in both places between human sensibility and the sea—right down to its bed. The subject is well worth the expenditure of much labor. It is not only art that is in question, but that capital, that investment, of humanity which we have not yet exhausted.

Is that all? Far from it.

Familiarity with the great waters helps the understanding because it provides one of the keys which unlock the door of the unconscious. Let me give an example, drawn from my own experience, of what I mean. Once again it is an account of one particular dive. For years now, I, like many others, have been trying to define what that special, that very precious, appeal is that the Mediterranean can have for our sensibility. Gide had that in mind when, in the course of a sea crossing, he noted down in his *Journal:* "Overwhelming impression of *glory.*" It was this glory that I found, ten fathoms down, more radiant there by far in the water, caught in a cage of crystal, than ever it could be beneath the sky.

It was at La Moulinière, a submerged shelf off Le Brusc. Lying there at anchor, we were rolling badly on a deceptively blue sea.

We hurried into our diving gear and, once under the surface, came on the delight of utter stillness. We dived, and found ourselves in a world of sun and water imprisoned in a mirror. Thousands of spear points thrust down through a density of sea unmoved by any wave. They were not arrows, and not golden, but seemed like silver threads obliquely stretched.

We slid down the gleaming rays to their very source, ten fathoms deep: an upside-down sun lay there on the bottom. All its beams spread like a fan from a central point—the furthest zone of submerged shadow. But when, instinctively seeking one another's company, we got there, we found nothing but a rock drowned in blue night from which, now, the spears of light drove up above our heads.

There is in the Louvre a picture by Claude Lorrain called *Cleopatra Disembarking at Tarsus*. Take a good look at it. Dazzling sunlight suffuses a conventional classic landscape, overwhelming it, crushing it. In the foreground the vertical masts of a ship serve but to give full value to the radiant glory which fills the sky. Not fire, not arrows shot from the empyrean, but thousands of rays. We have but to turn that picture upside down, to set foot for a moment on that baked and swarthy shore, to plunge into a sky which has become water. At once we find ourselves diving toward the imprisoned sun.

Elsewhere than in the water, too, we can silently force an entry into a solidified universe. We can do it by visiting the scene in which the *Virgin of the Rocks* is seated, or by wandering among the peaks where the *Gioconda* smiles. That blue light, those torn and jagged cliffs belong far more to the world that lies beneath the sea than to any of our upper air. I have seen it at Cap Brun at ten fathoms. As to the landscape in which the Virgin, the Infant Jesus, and St. Anne have been pursuing their mystic colloquy for four hundred years, I know it, too. I visited it once somewhere off the peninsula of Léoube.

But what, you may ask, does all this amount to? Does it mean that Leonardo da Vinci practiced the art of diving? It may be that he did. With such a man all things are possible—the more so since his biographers assure us that he invented a machine to enable men to breathe under water, just as he invented another by means of which they could fly in the air. What matters here, however, is the choice that Leonardo made. When he needed a setting wholly compact of poetry, a scene suited to a presentation of the spiritual at its highest degree of perfection, he elected to borrow it from the sea.

There are in Chinese painting just such landscapes of fantasy. They belong beneath the water. There would seem, indeed, to be a close relationship, always on the verge of spontaneous expression, between human poetry and the deep sea. Man's spirit, especially when it works unfettered, floats among visions of sea things. It is visions of the sea that waking dreamers build, who have never seen it with their bodily eyes.

Here, taken from among many others, is a waking dream for which I am indebted to a psychiatrist, Robert Desoille.

"The dream begins with a feeling in the dreamer that she is descending into ocean caverns. Lydia is conscious of an extremely rapid plunge downwards between walls which, at first, are metallic blue, turning, later, to a subtle shade of green. After a while she sees a golden light and says: 'I seem to be submerged in a luminous vibration. It is a light which has lain, through all the ages, condensed just there, in union with the sun, but in a great depth of water. . . .'" Reading that, I am reminded of my own impression when I dived at La Moulinière.

It seems, therefore, that between the inner secrecies of the sea and those of the human spirit there is a mysterious harmony which finds expression in art and in dreams. Is that sense of harmony a heritage from our aquatic ancestors? If, as Jung holds, consciousness is a relatively late offshoot of the unconscious mind, may it not find delight in rediscovering a world in which it has been a wanderer for thousands of years? The happiness we find in the sea, the joy with which Leonardo da Vinci painted those drowned scenes, the waking dream of the troubled Lydia, all these things may, perhaps, have a close connection with the annelids, the molluscs, the marine vertebrates which are the distant forebears of our race. Ceaselessly each human embryo reforms in its own body the useless gills which wither as it grows older, the kidney of the lamprey, the fish's heart. If that can happen, why should not the mind of man conjure up, in his moments of liberation, images of fluid movement, of an element in which to speed, in which to hang suspended—the heritage which has come to him less from the sky than from the sea, which in him is not so much the mark of an angel as that of the fish that once he was—perhaps?

That is why susceptibility to the influences of the sea is not the worst equipment one can have for the writing of history. From the Cretan potters to Claude Lorrain those influences have characterized the golden ages of the Mediterranean, and have been closely knit with ways of thinking, living, and praying which the land cannot provide.

"I will stop you from being the sea's lover!" cried a genuine chip-of-the-old-block Spartan to an Athenian admiral. In those words we hear the snarl of the landsman, and in it a confession of humiliation. One does not talk like that unless one is conscious in one's own heart of a bitterness which comes with the realization that, no matter what one may do, one cannot belong to a race of seafarers. It is the cry of the disappointed lover: "If I can't have you, then nobody shall!"—the commonplace of all crimes of passion, the small change of all newspaper paragraphs. Why? Because the sea influences peoples only through the halfway house of the individual heart. Before ever it can be the secret of social equilibrium or economic liberalism, it must first and foremost point the way to the joy of life.

For five centuries the ravaged West did not have a mistress, but only masters. It dragged out a wretched existence, and when at last it emerged from the dark night of history, the link which it renewed once more with the sea was that of the landsman, a love which did not go below the surface.

And yet, we can scarcely say that our life is linked with the land. A layer of solid comfort, an acquired habit of using blind tools, has cut us off from the external world. Only by means of machines can we make contact with the four elements: with tractors we plow the earth, in airplanes we explore the air, and fire we confine in boilers. A steel hull, the sides of a ship which is as high as a wall, separate us from the life of the sea. Man and the world have been divorced.

Life is no longer difficult. Nevertheless, we feel it to be threatened, and there is nothing much we can do about it. We are the beneficiaries of an enormous, of a fragile, "Meccano." Meccano and fragility are but a century old—the Century of Progress. Happy those men of the Palaeolithic Age who gained a soul in the struggle to live, by learning endurance, courage, moral strength, the power to observe, logic and faith. We, the heirs of all the ages, are nothing but lazy humbugs, men who are content to tinker with life and to forget its essentials. And so it has come about that, in a world rationalized to the last inch, chance plays a greater part than ever before—the chances of social life, the chances of family life, the chances of education, the chances of human relations—the chances of a falling bomb.

Of the four elements, one at least, water, can be incorporated once again in the human adventure. There was a time long ago when it was a great discovery. Has it lost its virtue? Is there nothing of value to be learned from that past, the relics and fragments of which I have been so busily stirring?

For me the stake of this sea victory is no less than twentieth-century man, a creature so richly equipped with tools, yet so confused, so fragile. In the deep places of the waters he can find a refuge.

The sea, in its best moments, can offer more of peace than any land. Without fuss, now, or any mighty preparations, we can go down into it, and there enjoy such tranquil hours as come to the suburban householder in his garden, with gorgonians for rose trees, and bream for birds. The blue serenity of mornings in the Ile de France wraps the diver as he hangs motionless. It is my belief that we may come to love the sea as in the past we never loved the air, the sky, the clouds, and the light of dawn and dusk.

This dwelling in a gleaming crystal, this bath of silence into which our bodies slide, has the power to relax us utterly, flesh, heart, and mind. Peace reaches to us through our envelope of skin, our landsman's covering. In a moment we move from one world to another and, greatest of all blessings, we can take our universe with us and bathe it in the blue light which is the most efficient of all cleansing preparations.

Already, up there on the surface, the skeptics, the cavilers, the fanatics are busy commenting, each in his own way, upon the great adventure. "Just another form of snobbery," say some, "a literary affectation, a new sport"; and others, "a revelation." Maybe it is still too soon to say exactly what it is.

What I know most clearly on the subject I will try to tell. To break through the mirror is to recapture the world of childhood, the world of the cradle which once we knew. In an unknown universe, among sand and rocks and floating creatures, we, floating, too, in a medium eight hundred times heavier than air, must learn to live a second life. It is a challenge to which the human spirit cannot remain indifferent. From the world of waters we must wrest our sea personality, as from the world of earth the child must wrest his human one. What wealth—or what perils—lie in wait for us? As yet I do not know. And of what use is all this to us today? What shall it profit a man that he shall find again the pathway of the deep? What shall it profit him to be a diver, unless it be that there, as elsewhere, he may seek the proper balance of his human state?

Some may think that I have traveled far from my starting point. But on this journey through the realms of archaeology and sea, I have remained ever faithful to man—as was my purpose.

᭰   ᭰   ᭰

AND now, just one word more, of ending and of self-excuse. I have left the deep waters behind me. The only part left for me now to play is that of the demonstrator with the magic lantern, of an impresario of the sea, playing with adjectives.

I have been treating of a miracle through the medium of books and quotations, with much citing of Greek and Latin, just as one of Molière's doctors might have done. But is that my fault? I was blamed, in the politest possible way, on a former occasion, for having quoted rather too frequently from Paul Valéry, for having called all the world of poetry to my rescue. I did that because I needed help. There are people who, when they travel, carry all the great authors with them: Lamartine when they go to the East, Stendhal when they go to Italy. I envy those who can draw from themselves all that they need, like those Neapolitan shepherd boys who end up as operatic tenors. But this "adventure" of mine is not a matter of singing: rather, it is a story of deaf-mutes. Deaf-mutes, when they address those who are ignorant of their language, take refuge in a terrible pantomime, a frightful sequence of signs and grimaces. I have been reduced to just such a necessity on emerging from my "land of silence"— have been forced to transcribe laboriously a strange reality, have had to employ images borrowed from the poets, and subtle or fantastic analogies. This I have done because I wanted desperately to be honest, and not to falsify a world which is not yet a place of common knowledge. Future generations, no doubt, will smile at my efforts. By that time the world of the waters will be a familiar experience. But a beginning had to be made somewhere. The fact remains that all these artifices are apt to land one in the grand style, so that one catches oneself in the act of phrase-making, like those who, when talking to foreigners, suddenly realize that, while trying to make themselves understood, they have been guilty of shouting. That, I am afraid, is one of the inescapable laws of the literary calling.

Let me say, too, that when one is diving the past weighs heavy sometimes on one's hands. The effort to lift stones under water means that one has to scrape one's belly on the bottom. The mud rises all around; the sky loses its brightness; the mind falls a prey to a form of excitement which is not good. It is well that divers should be set on their guard against vanity—which is the commonest characteristic of the amateur archaeologist. One must be cautious in one's use of books lest the sea be darkened by too much ink. Not that I would wish to play traitor to my arsenal of weapons, that higgledy-piggledy bric-a-brac from museums and junk shops, redolent of the stench of sacristies for the service of dead gods; cults nibbled by molluscs, fragments of pottery over-laid with the spaghetti of sea worms; words floating beneath the surface which must be brought back to life again like half-drowned men—the Yonaka of the Tamils, the puzzle of Tauroen-tum, Ceyreste and its lyre. I long to be alone once more in the sea, the empty sea, far from the concrete blocks that look like gigantic pieces of nougat, unhaunted by phantoms, and not beset by Aeginetan pots nor any amphorae: alone in the sea whose riches bring me satisfaction absolute.

Appendices

Variations in the
Mean Sea Level

THIS is a question of direct concern to all archaeologists. At the beginning of the present century Déchelette and Camille Jullian consulted a number of specialists in oceanography. The view most widely accepted at that time was that, in the historic period, there had been no variation in the mean sea level, but only local modifications determined by the conformation of the coast line.

Recent archaeological investigations, however, in the eastern Mediterranean and, more especially, those carried out in Syria by Poidebard and Schaeffer, have once more drawn the attention of workers in the field to this problem.

Contenau in his book on the Phoenician civilization gave it as his opinion that

to the arguments generally advanced to prove the importance of the Aegean to the cultures of the ancient world, can now be added the fact that many harbors were constructed which were later destroyed as the result either of invasions or of natural cataclysms. Such was the

fate of the Aegean port of Pharos in Egypt, and also of many harbors
now submerged in consequence of a rise in the level of the Mediterranean in historic times—of Phalasarna, for instance, on the west coast
of Crete (quays lying eighteen feet below the present level), and of
Nauplia, near Argos (six feet). It would seem that the Aegeans built
a whole series of harbors at a time when the level was some seven and
a half feet below that of the sea as we know it today. The rise must
have occurred suddenly at some time towards the end of the Bronze
Age.

Contenau quotes in support of his opinion a book by A. Souleyre, *Les
niveaux marins de la plaine de Bône,* and maintains that "mere flat denial does nothing to solve the question. It must be examined afresh." I
have not myself consulted Souleyre's publication. But I have found in
Erwin Marec's *Hippone,* p. 11, the following passage: "Excavations have
revealed little material dating back to this distant period except the foundations of a massive wall, apparently cyclopaean, at points where the
level seems to have been different from what it is now. This confirms the
existence and importance of certain oscillatory movements in the Mediterranean anterior to the Christian era."

The problem is one of the highest importance to undersea archaeology.
On its solution depend any hopes we may have of finding harbors and
port installations beneath the surface.

I can give no view about this "sudden rise of the level." A submarine
geological survey might discover traces on the coastal face of the continental land mass, and we may find ourselves in possession of the necessary
evidence.

What we do know with absolute certainty is that the level, both of the
Mediterranean and of the Atlantic, has constantly risen since around
1890, in which year the first observations were made. If we ignore all
purely seasonal variations, we find that the rise works out at an average
of considerably under half an inch every ten years for the Mediterranean,
and slightly more than three quarters of an inch for the European coast
line of the Atlantic. If this movement was as continuous in the past as
it has shown itself to be during the sixty years since 1890, that would fully
account for the submersion of all the Aegean harbors now lying between
eighteen and six and a half feet below the surface. (It is extremely difficult
to establish vertical measurements in water. How those in question were
calculated I do not know, nor what underwater base was taken. If it
turns out to have been masses of sunken masonry belonging to quays, these
should most certainly be inspected.)

But was the rise as now established for the modern period the same in
the past? Yes, say the specialists, and support their assertion by reference
to the cause, which has not varied. This rise in the sea level, according to
them, was due to the melting of the Polar and the Alpine icecaps. During

one of the warm periods of the globe, masses of ice accumulated at certain points slowly dissolved, thereby increasing the volume of water in the oceans.

Certain local conditions have disguised this phenomenon. Thus, the Scandinavian Peninsula, which sank by something like two thousand feet in the course of the last Ice Age, ten thousand years ago, under the weight then imposed upon it, started to rise again as soon as the ice melted. At the present time it shows a rise of fifteen hundred feet, seven hundred and fifty of them before the end of the Ice Age, and a further seven hundred and fifty since. The land level now rises at the rate of three feet in a hundred years. Heiskanen showed in 1939, basing his calculation on anomalies in weight, that this rise must continue for another six hundred feet before a state of equilibrium will have been reached. But the fact that the Scandinavian movement has been constant justifies us in assuming that the rise in the sea level was continuous in ancient days, if, that is to say, the explanation put forward by the scientists is correct.

It is, however, only fair to mention an alternative theory suggested by an engineer, Jules Legrand, who has taken a great interest in these questions. According to him, there was "a period of between twelve hundred and thirteen hundred years during which the level of the sea remained static." This he attributes to "the delaying action produced by the viscous fluid lying beneath the solid crust of the globe."

The question, in this case, is closely connected with terrestrial physics, a science which depends upon gravimetry and is far removed from archaeology. But, having touched upon it, to however small an extent, I do feel that this matter of the Mediterranean level is one which archaeology cannot neglect. All we need to know is whether the variation was continuous or cyclical, and what was its cause.

It may well be that archaeology will provide terrestrial physics with just the proof it needs, if, that is, it can produce a sufficient number of accurately dated monuments, the evidence of which cannot be open to doubt.

Jean Legrand maintained that a definite argument could be established from the examination of certain buildings constructed on the coast. A study of the archives kept in the Direction des Travaux du Génie de Marseille has shown, it seems, that the square tower of the Fort Saint-Jean, the foundations of which now lie in six feet of water, was originally built on a site above sea level, and without the use of caissons. A similar condition might be found to exist in the case of Fort Saint-Louis at Toulon. Deductions of this type are always delicate, and a great number of instances will have to be collected before any definite conclusion can be drawn.

The evidence at Fos and at Olbia is not wholly conclusive. A rise in the water level, if it could be proved, would, of course, explain how it comes about that, in both places, the archaeologists have found part of the constructions submerged. This may, however, be due to landslides which would not necessarily imply any change in the level of the sea. On the other hand, these ancient buildings may from the very first have been erected on underwater foundations, or on foundations which lay very close to the water's edge.

Finally, we know that in 1946, at Marseille, the remains of the Greek harbor, dating from the sixth century B.C., were brought to light. According to the hydrographical engineers, we could conclude from this fact that the level of the Mediterranean has not varied at all in 2600 years. (It is worth while remembering that, in 1906, L. Cayeux believed that he could prove the fixity of the Mediterranean level during the historic period from the evidence brought to light by his examination of an ancient quay in the port of Delos.)

It becomes clear how fragile, and sometimes contradictory, are the facts at our disposal in the realms both of oceanography and archaeology. It does not follow, however, that the problem is insoluble or that we shall be forced to abandon it. I think, on the contrary, that those who are looking for solution would be well advised to collect observations of many different kinds which might, in the long run, lead to the truth in this particular field of research.

Amphorae

In view of the great number of amphorae which still remain to be found, varying widely in shape and in degree of antiquity, the reader may, perhaps, welcome some observations of a general nature on the subject of these very ancient receptacles which Albert Grenier includes among "marine stones."

Jars made of baked clay are among the commonest form of container used in the Mediterranean area. They date back a very long way, and representations of them have been found even on the cylindrical seals of the proto-Elamite period. The Minoans used them for storing liquids, such as wine and oil, and also fish preserved in brine, vegetables, and even cereals. We are justified in drawing a distinction between the large-sized jars employed as permanent fixtures in shops—the *dolia* of the Romans, and the smaller amphorae used for purposes of transportation. The *dolia* were flat-bottomed and without handles. The amphorae had looped handles and tapered to a point, which enabled them to be thrust into the earth. In the Roman period the *dolium* was designed to hold

201

20 amphorae = 1 *culleus* = 120 gallons. The amphora unit of measurement was the ancient *quadrantal* = 80 livres = 25.79 liters.

✠   ✠   ✠

The prize awarded to the victor at the Panathenaic Games was an amphora of fine oil, and it is possible that the wide diffusion of this form of container throughout the Mediterranean area originally derived from this fact. According to Glotz' *Greek History*, "the winners of horse races and gymnastic contests were presented with Panathenaic amphorae, each one of which held 72 κοτύλι (34 56 points) of precious oil. These amphorae, whether full or empty, were much treasured by collectors all over the Mediterranean."

The interest attaching to the very large number of amphorae found in Gaul, Africa, and at the bottom of the sea, lies in the fact that they provide us with chronological data, whether by reason of the marks which appear on them, or of the evolution of their shapes. Since, too, it has been found possible to attribute certain types to the carriage of wine during the Roman period, while others seem to have been reserved for oil, we can draw from them important evidence bearing on the economic life of antiquity. But anything like a comprehensive survey on these lines is still only in its early stages.

✠   ✠   ✠

The first classification of amphora shapes was made by the German archaeologist Dressel. He drew up a chart on which each separate model was numbered, and this compilation of numerals is still used for identifying the different types.

This classification, however, stands in need of a good deal of revision. Edgar Pélichet has been able to study in the Nyon Museum (Switzerland), of which he is the director, a collection of amphorae of many different shapes, and as a result of his researches has added three additional types to the forty-five already described by Dressel. He has also pointed out that Dressel's classification is by no means entirely satisfactory from the point of view of chronology. "For instance, Type 20, known to have been in existence in the first century B.C., persisted all through the Roman period."

As I myself have had occasion to notice, certain types which were long in use underwent some slight modification, especially in the shape of the "lip" in which the neck terminated. A study of this detail might produce some interesting chronological evidence. Monsieur Pélichet has compiled a basic chart of lip forms, and this could be carried a good deal further as a result of recent finds made both on land and in the sea. A comparison

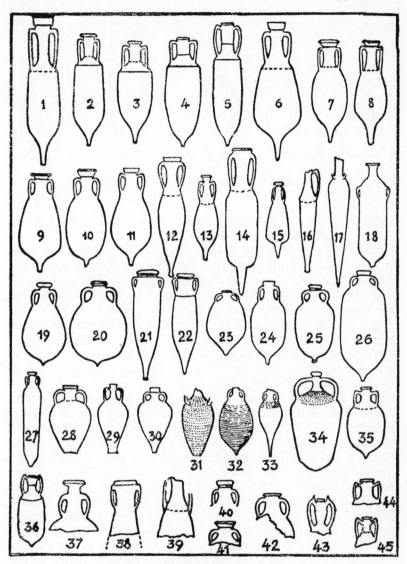

DRESSEL'S CLASSIFICATION OF AMPHORAE
ACCORDING TO SHAPE.

of the lips of amphorae from Albenga and Anthéor would be extremely
instructive. In drawing up any new classification, however, the different
places of origin should be taken into account. It is possible that the many

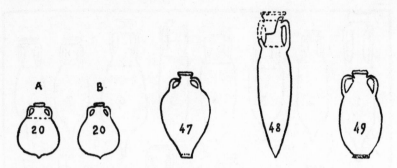

PELICHET'S ADDITIONS TO DRESSEL'S CLASSIFICATIONS.

scattered workshops in which these amphorae were produced did not always show the same degree of evolution.

I have said that the amphorae of Dressel's type 1 found at Albenga and Anthéor, dating from the end of the Republic and the early years of the Empire, were for a long time known as "Gallic," for the simple reason that specimens were found in great quantities on French soil. They are the typical form of wine container used in importations from Sicily or Campania. Chemical analysis has shown that the material from which they are made reveals volcanic traces from Etna and Vesuvius.

The importation of this type of amphora into Gaul stops short in the first and second centuries A.D. The second-century amphorae found in Gaul, though almost equal in quantity, are spherical in shape. They were used for oil and not for wine, and came from Baetica. As the result of a careful study of the marks, Emile Thevenot has been able to trace the manufacture of these amphorae to several places in the valley of the Guadalquivir. Hirschfeld, the editor of the *Corpus des Inscriptions de la Gaule*, was of the opinion that there might have been an amphora factory at Vienne (Isère)—"the wine from that district was famous in Rome from the first century onward, and the great number of fragmented amphorae found in the capital would seem to indicate a considerable output of these receptacles." It is doubtful today whether this hypothesis can be maintained. Most of the sherds found at Vienne are of oil containers originating in Baetica and, no doubt, transported to Narbonne by sea. Grenier had already noted that a number of the marks on the Vienne amphorae have also turned up on the Monte Testaccio.

On the other hand, when Gaul became an exporter of wine, in the middle of the first century, her merchants used the traditional receptacles, as is proved by the amphorae (Dressel's types 2 and 3) found in the camp of the Praetorian Guard in Rome, all of them originating in the region of Narbonne. The movement of traffic had been reversed.

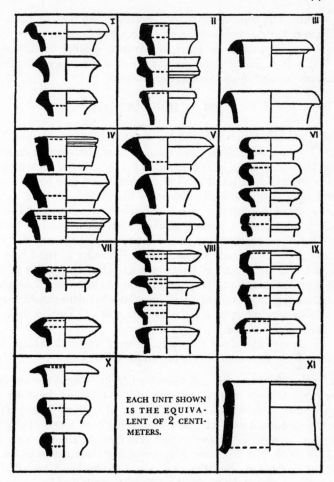

CHRONOLOGICAL INDICATIONS FROM AMPHORA LIPS.
(ACCORDING TO E. PELICHET.)

Chronological indications from amphora lips (according to E. Pélichet):
I. End of the Republic; II. 20 B.C. to 20 A.D.; III. 7 B.C. to 53 A.D.;
IV. 10 to 20 A.D.; V. 41 to 53 A.D.; VI. Middle of the first century A.D.;
VII. End of the first century A.D.; VIII. 120 to 160 A.D.; IX. End of second century A.D.; X. 190 to 260 A.D.; XI. End of third and sixth centuries A.D.

It is worth pointing out that the fragments of an amphora found by Henri Broussard not far from the Anthéor site belongs to a type having a wide opening and a thin lip fairly similar to Dressel's type 38, though

the lips differ. The general appearance, however, and the size, are much
the same as in the amphorae found off the coast of Carthagena, in Spain,
and published by Juan J. de Jauregui (*Archivo español de Arqeologia*,
1948, No. 70). A similar fragment was found at Fos, and published in
the *Bulletin du Club Alpin Sous-Marin* (1948).

☙ ☙ ☙

While I am still concerned with the question of shapes, I should like
to stress the confusion which has resulted from the close resemblance
between Dressel's types 5, 45, 44, and 43. I list these in the apparent order
of their relationship. It is not at all clear whether we have here a case of
one basic type which was long followed by the makers—as I am inclined
to believe—or of the revival of an ancient form. "An example of Dressel's
type 5," writes Grenier (*Manuel*, p. 635), "has been found at Haltern.
It must, therefore, antedate the end of the reign of Augustus. We know
that this camp, which was a staging post in the valley of the Lippe, was
abandoned after the defeat of Varus in 9 A.D. Hence the great value of
the finds made there, from the point of view of chronology." Amphorae
of this same type have turned up at Fos. To what date should they be
assigned? Are we dealing with Dressel's type 5 or 45? Further finds may
throw light on this puzzle.

We know very little about the manufacture of an article which played
so great a part in the economic life of antiquity. Pélichet says:

> The ancient authors were not concerned to know how the amphorae
> were made. Objects so large and with such wide bodies could not have
> been thrown or molded like other articles of pottery. This problem,
> however, is not without interest. No trace has been found of the tools
> necessary for such a massive output. They must certainly have been
> made of wood, but they have disappeared. An examination of the jars
> leads us to conclude that the work was done by hand, and that the
> various parts—point, body, shoulder, handles, neck, and lip—were con-
> structed separately and then assembled before firing. After they had
> thus been brought roughly into shape, smoothing tools and cloths
> were used to impart a polished surface, and to disguise the joints on
> the inside.

An examination of the big spherical amphorae belonging to type 20
(oil containers) suggests that another method was sometimes used. The
large body of the jar was molded round a core formed of a coil of rope
wrapped in cloth; and when the molding process was completed, the core
could be removed by drawing the rope out through the mouth.

Something, in conclusion, must be said of the marks found on the
amphorae. They are of many different kinds, and vary according to type.

At the base of one of the handles belonging to a wine jar (Dressel's type 1) from Anthéor, I discovered a mark which has not yet been deciphered. Such marks are always imprinted on the neck. This is so in the case of the jars found at Mont Beuvray—the ancient Bibracte—at Alesia, and especially at Les Bolards (Nuits-Saint-Georges), where Thevenot found eleven marks, all on the necks of amphorae, three of which are exact counterparts of those unearthed at Mont-Beuvray.

These marks, stamped into the clay while it was still soft in the case of the wine containers, also appear on the spherical oil jars, where they are on the handles. The marks are sometimes those of the makers, sometimes of the proprietors of the vineyards or olive groves. Quite often the maker and the proprietor must have been one and the same person.

Dressel made a special study of the fragments from Monte Testaccio, at Rome, close to the ancient port of the Tiber. This mound, rather more than a hundred feet tall, and between nine hundred and twelve hundred in length, is entirely composed of amphora fragments accumulated in the course of many hundreds of years. All those which it has been found possible to date fall within the period 140 to 251 A.D. Such of the inscriptions as have been deciphered furnished Dressel with enough material to fill one half of a volume of the *Corpus* of Latin inscriptions. It seems to have been established that the majority of these fragments are of oil jars sent from Baetica.

In addition to the makers' marks stamped on the necks or the handles, the amphorae in many cases carried the names of the Consuls in office in that year, and this enables us to date them with precision. These are written with a brush dipped in ink. The same method is used for inscribing names which are those either of the owner or importer. Some of them indicate the nature of the contents, followed by the name of the grower. Instances have also been found in which the weight when shipped and the weight on arrival is shown, the latter being sometimes preceded by the letter R with a stroke through it, indicating that the contents have been checked and found correct. To this is also added, quite often, the signature of the slave or "hand" who did the checking. (To identify the position on the amphorae of these inscriptions, Dressel listed a number of "zones" to which he gave the letters α, β, γ, δ, ϵ. This division has been generally accepted.

At the end of the nineteenth century, an English archaeologist, G. E. Bonsor, who explored on foot both banks of the Guadalquivir—the ancient Baetis—identified, between Cordova and Seville, more than a hundred pottery workshops where amphorae were made. He collected the names of nearly three hundred makers. Some of these were in a big way of business, as is shown by the fact that one of them, Flavius Charisianus, the grandson of a certain Quintus Fulvius Rusticus, whose workshop Bonsor found, was, as patron and pontifex of Arva, honored with a statue. Under Septimius Severus many of these workshops were directly controlled by the Emperor. It was at this time that the exportation of oil from Baetica reached a high level, and that the sherds of the Monte Testaccio were accumulated. It was, in fact, Septimius Severus who established a free distribution of oil to the Roman people—"a custom which, in spite of certain vicissitudes, lasted until the days of Constantine."

In Rome the oil merchants formed an association, which was certainly not among the least important of such bodies, as may be seen from the fact that at one moment it had as Patron M. Peronius Honoratus, a Roman knight of high rank, who was *procurator a rationibus*, prefect in charge of the Annona, and prefect of Egypt. The association chose as its patron in Gaul another knight, who was *diffusor olearius*, a shipowner on the Saône, and patron of the Shipowners' Association. It is clear from this that commercial relationships were very complicated, and that the names appearing on the amphorae may be expected to throw much light on the subject.

☙   ☙   ☙

THE great volume of the ancient evidence of this kind makes study difficult. It is to be hoped that undersea archaeology, by renewing an interest in the amphorae, may make a more accurate classification possible, as well as a regrouping of all the inscriptions bearing on the subject. Very little work is needed to provide us with a system of dating which will be no less valuable for land archaeology than for its submarine brother. A further examination of the inscriptions might well furnish the names of producers, shipowners, and ports of lading in such numbers as to make it possible for us to establish a general picture of commerce in the ancient world. This would be as valuable for economic history as for the history of navigation.

Anchors

APPARENTLY it was only from the seventh century B.C. onwards that ships in the Mediterranean carried anchors. The earliest mention of an anchor occurs in Alcaeus.

Anchors in the primitive periods seem to have been of stone. A document dating from the second century A.D. contains a curious passage bearing on the subject. I refer to the *Periplus Maris Euxini,* the report of an inspection carried out by Arrian, the Imperial Legate of Cappadocia, and submitted by him to Hadrian. In it he states that at the mouth of the river Phasis, in the Black Sea, he saw the statue of a goddess:

"In this place," he goes on, "one of the anchors of the ship *Argo* is exhibited. But, since it is of iron, my own opinion is that it cannot be ancient. . . . Very old fragments of another anchor, this time of stone, are also on view, and these, it seems to me, are more likely to be the remnants of the anchor of the *Argo*."

Homer speaks of a pierced stone (τρητὸς λίθος), but whether this was an anchor or one of the stones of a quay with a hole in it we do not know. Poidebard found in the island of Saïda, and in that of Rouad, holes made
209

4000 YEARS UNDER THE SEA

in the rock, the obvious use of which was the making fast of ships' cables.
Talking of these he employs the Homeric term τρητὸς λίθs. I myself
found on the sea bed off Cherchel a pierced stone, a photograph of which
appears in this book. It is identical in appearance with stones found by
Chénevée in Greece, which have been classified as "sockets in which
masts were stepped." It seems to me to be a matter of extreme difficulty
to date finds of this kind with any degree of accuracy. The objects concerned are what the Provençal fisherfolk call *mouilles,* or mooring blocks.
These have a long tradition behind them in the Mediterranean. There is,
however, no proof that the examples known to us are, in fact, ancient.

J. N. Svoronos * distinguishes between two different types of stone
anchor. He writes: "Primitive anchors were of stone (λιθίναι) in the shape
of a pyramid (βαίτυλος), either pierced at the top, or with handles, for
the attachment of the cable." These stones were also known as ἑυναί
as opposed to the anchor proper, 'άγκυρα.

Leaden anchors have been studied by Moll and by Magon. There seems
to be no doubt at all that the part of the anchors in our possession is in
every case the stock. One of them was found, still *in situ,* in the mud of
Lake Nemi. It consisted of a wooden shank, some sixteen and a half feet
long, terminating in a leaden stock of the now familiar pattern.

Here is a list of the ancient stocks found in the Mediterranean. It is
almost certainly incomplete. These objects are of interest only by reason
of the marks or inscriptions which they bear. An analysis of the lead
might furnish us with evidence about the deposits worked in the ancient
world.

MARTIGUES, Verdon Quarter. October, 1875. Length: a trifle over 6
   feet. Weight: approximately 650 lbs.
CARRY-LE-ROUET, 1888 (Borély Museum, Marseille). Length: just
   over 6 feet.
MAHDIA, 1909 and 1911. Two anchors, now in the Tunis Museum.
   Length: 6¼ and 6⅓ feet.
MAHDIA, 1949. Two anchors, one with the G.R.S., the other in the
   Toulon Museum. A fifth anchor, the heaviest of the group, had to
   be left at the bottom. Its length would appear to be between 11½
   and 15 feet.
CARTHAGENA, 1905. Two anchors, now in the Carthagena Museum,
   one of them just over 5 feet, the other just over 3, in length. Several
   other examples have been found in the same coastal region, near
   Cape Palos. One of these, over 6¼ feet long, weighed over 1570 lbs.
   Several carried inscriptions, some of them in Greek, addressed to
   Zeus Cassios, the savior, and to Aphrodite; others, in Latin charac-

* "Stylides, ancres hierae"; *Journal Inter. d'Arch.,* XVI, 1914, p. 110.

ters, were manufacturers' marks: L. V. Lupo and L. Ageili. L. Lmaxsumi. These examples seem to have been dispersed. Two other anchors were found at Malaga.

ANTIBES, 1949. An anchor found by Denéréaz, rather over 3½ feet.

ANTIBES, 1949, now in the Musée de la Marine, Paris. An anchor found by Dr. Chénevée. Length: 5¾ feet. On three sides there is a Gorgon's head.

LA FOURMIGUE DU LAVANDOU, 1951. Found by Giraud (Borély Museum, Marseille). Length: rather over 3½ feet.

PORT DE BOUC, 1951. Found by a Ponts et Chaussées dredger (Musée d'Istres). Length: rather over 3½ feet.

The Club de la Mer de Juan-les-Pins has found a number of ancient anchor-stocks, weighing 22, 66, 176½, 220½, 264½, and 882 pounds. On two of these the mortise and tenon joints were still in place.

Similar stocks, varying in size, are to be seen in the Madrid and Barcelona Museums.

The British Museum possesses three examples from Cyrene. On two of these, which are of almost precisely the same weight (452 lbs.), there is an inscription to Zeùs ὕπατος. Another, from the island of Syme, off the coast of Caria (Southwest Turkey), has inscribed the word Σώτειρα. It is now in the Athens Museum.

Cecil Torr took these inscriptions to be the names of the ships to which the anchors belonged. Svoronos, on the other hand, reads them as invocations for protection. This would be in keeping with the sacred character of the anchor as an object, which must have made of it an important vehicle of beliefs. Zeus, Supreme God and Savior (ὕπατος ὀωτήρ), "was the god whose cult was widely spread among the harbors of the Greek world, especially at the Piraeus, as the tutelary divinity and protector of ships." *

🇾 🇾 🇾

AN ancient iron anchor has been found at Cherchel. It is now in the museum of that town. Another anchor, also of iron, has been found at Etaples.

* Svoronos: *op. cit.*, p. 105.

Numismatics and the Sea

I⊤ has seemed to me that it might not be wholly without value to point out the nature of the assistance likely to be received from the science of numismatics by anybody bent on studying the relationship existing between man and the sea. Historians and archaeologists have already drawn on it extensively, and certainly it should not be neglected by those who take an interest in the part played by the life of the sea in the ancient world.

From the very earliest days the Greeks made use of minted coins as a means of expanding their sea power and of achieving a bloodless conquest of the barbarian lands. We, today, can have but a faint idea of what that invention must have meant in the hands of the Ἔμποροι and Κάπηλι. We do not at first grasp the manner and degree in which it was linked with the sea.

This "weapon" of the sixth century was by no means heavy. The *obolos* (0.55 to 0.70 grams) represented the 24th part of a *stater*. It was a tiny coin made of electrum, a rough alloy of gold and silver. The obverse carried a design—a sea horse, a Gorgon, the head of a lion, or a seal. On the reverse, in the earliest forms, there was no decoration more elaborate than a simple, or sometimes a partitioned, square sunk into the metal. "Coins of this type have been found on the banks of the Durance, at Cavaillon, Orgon, and Saint-Rémy," writes R. Busquet, "as well as on the eastern coast of Spain . . . In February, 1867, a hoard of them— 2130 pieces, all dating from the sixth century—was discovered in a clay pot buried in the ground at a spot known as Les Barres, not far from Auriol."

It is quite clear that the minted money of the Greeks reflected to a large extent the seafaring activities of the civilized world throughout the course of eight centuries. It can, therefore, furnish us with specific evidence about the importance and nature of sea-borne traffic, the greater or less part taken in it by each city, the expansion and nature of trade, and the myths born of the sea, all of them symbolized by marine animals. The first electrum coins were issued by the coastal cities—Miletus, Ephesus, Phocaea—and on all these coins marine animals appear.

Perhaps I may be allowed to preface my remarks on this subject by pointing out that the effigies on the coins, and the adornments on the various objects of ships' equipment, often take the form of the same symbols. The Gorgon's head, which appears on the coinage of Athens and Neapolis, and on the silver pieces of Etruria and of a great variety of cities, is found (four or five hundred years later) on the stock of an anchor discovered off Cap d'Antibes (now in the Musée de la Marine, Paris). The Zeus Cassios on the anchor which was fished up off Cape Palos (now in the Carthagena Museum) appears also on the coins of Seleucia and Corcyra (Corfu). The knuckle bones of the Carry-le-Rouet anchor (Borély Museum, Marseille) appear at an earlier date on coins minted in Athens. It should be noted that we possess very few ship's accessories carrying either inscriptions or adornments. Later discoveries, to be brought to light, I hope, when undersea archaeology has progressed beyond its present stage, will possibly make available even more suggestive comparisons.

The establishment of a fact of this nature proves clearly the persistence, or the wide dispersion throughout the Mediterranean area, of certain apotropaic images. It is worth while to determine the part they played in the life of the sea.

The science of numismatics may be even more useful to us. It has already enabled us to establish with accuracy the place not only of navigation, but of marine images in the life of Greece. It is a matter of no small importance to find upon coins of various kinds representations of the galley of Samos and that of Sidon, of anchors, of fishermen's nets, and of the very curve of the harbor at Zancle—the ancient Messina. The markings of these coins serve also to remind us of what I have called "a susceptibility to marine influences," with all that such susceptibility implies of knowledge of, and familiarity with, forms of sea life—which we, today, lack. They speak a language which is incomprehensible to our contemporaries: the dolphin of Tarentum, the tunny of Cyzicus, the crab of Agrigentum (the earliest silver pieces issued at Marseille, about 460 B.C., bear the effigy of a crab on the reverse), the murex of Segesta, the "cardium edule" of Corcyra, the octopus of Messina, and its fellow of Posidonia, the cuttlefish of Coressia, the mussel of Kyme (Campania) —all these had for the Greeks an evocative power which they do not have for us. Modern numismatists need the assistance of a naturalist to help them identify these fish, crustaceans, and molluscs. Perhaps only my fellow divers are capable of appreciating the beauty of the great elongated cockleshell which is shown on a coin of Gryneion, and the very appearance of which continental Europe has now forgotten. It is the *Pinna nobilis*, the silky fibers of which were once used for weaving sacred garments. Today we gather it in handfuls from the sandy bottoms.

This "marine susceptibility" found expression of an extremely subtle kind on the coinages of Greece. The designer had only to portray a cockleshell beneath a hovering eagle to bring a shore to mind, and so to create an eagle of the sea. With a few undulating lines he could indicate the presence of waves. His art, so to speak, was a piece of significant dialogue carried on between the artist and a more than usually instructed public.

Just how far did this taste of the Greeks for marine fauna go? Should we give to all these symbols the same importance and the same value? There are undoubtedly distinctions which cannot be ignored, and we must be very careful to avoid the danger of forcing this fascinating subject to yield more than it may normally be expected to do. In the first place, nothing like all the monetary types carry marine symbols. It is well to be frank and to admit that those which do may account for perhaps one third of all the Greek coins in the great collections, in the British Museum, for example, and the Bibliothèque Nationale. But even that is a high proportion and deserves consideration. Many of the designs, however, call to mind animals of the dry land: the bull of Samos, the stag and the bee of Ephesus, the lion of Miletus, etc.

Furthermore, we must distinguish among these heraldic blazons of the cities ($\pi\alpha\rho\acute{\alpha}\sigma\eta\mu\text{ov}$) those which have a religious significance, those which bear witness to commercial activity having to do with the sea, those inspired by a mere play on words, like the seal ($\varphi\acute{\omega}\kappa\eta$) of Phocaea, and those which may genuinely be considered as expressing the kind of "susceptibility" of which I have been speaking. It is quite certain that the delphin of Tarentum, on which the hero Taras rides, has a mythical and religious significance and expresses in a fabulous, even magical, form the maritime, commercial, and technical pre-eminence of that city. The

tunny of Cyzicus is simpler. It was reproduced on staters of electrum up
to the time of Alexander, and served primarily to "publicize" the famous
fishing grounds to which the place owed its prosperity. It is to be assumed that the meaning of the symbol was obvious, and this prosperity,
drawn from the sea, real enough, since the currency was everywhere accepted and enjoyed a long-lasting popularity. But much of this marine
symbolism may have had a deeper meaning. All that we know of ancient
coins justifies us in the belief that many of the types had a propaganda,
and even an advertising, value. They served less as reminders of a religious
cult than as commercial trademarks.

It is important to realize that the great sanctuaries, such as Delos and
Delphi, where the peoples of Greece periodically met together, were not
only religious centers but "trade fairs" as well. The temples served as
banks, and the oracles were agencies through which commercial and marine information was spread. It was a distinct advantage for a city to
possess a currency which stood at a premium in those places and could,
through the symbolism of its coinage, make a clear claim to some sort
of commercial monopoly. The tunny of Cyzicus was not the only image
of this kind. The silphium shown on the reverse of the gold pieces of
Cyrene was an advertisement for that marvelous plant which ships from
all over the Mediterranean went to seek on the coast of Cyrenaica, where
even the king himself did not disdain to keep a careful eye on its weighing and loading. As to the galleys shown on the coins of Sidon, they
may have been intended to remind possible customers of the fact that
the Phoenician fleet, which so often hired itself out with its crews for
expeditions and conquests, specialized in maritime operations of many
kinds. We should read these symbols not only in terms of civic pride, but
sometimes also as a means of serving the ends of well-organized self-
interest.

Is that all? If so many Greek cities showed sea beasts upon their coinage, may it not have been that they intended to underline the fact that
they were not strangers to the sea? Such familiarity had, since the days
of the great Aegean heritage, taken on a somewhat flattering significance.
There can be no doubt that, for many centuries, skill in navigation was
synonymous with prosperity, and that it was no bad thing to announce
this on the local coins. But were not these octopuses, these shellfish, these
molluscs also for the contemporary public a proof of civilization? For
more than a thousand years the inhabitants of the Aegean had represented
these creatures on vases and engraved stones and had acquired a degree
of prosperity, a standard of living, an accumulation of wealth and art
of which the Greeks and Phoenicians had been joint heirs. The Myce-
naean vases had traveled round the Mediterranean, carrying far afield
the very image of the fairest sea civilization that the world has known.

It is perhaps legitimate to see in that fact one of the reasons which urged the Greeks to reproduce upon their coins cuttlefish, molluscs, and even seaweed. A concern for prestige was at work to reinforce the desire to announce a certain technical pre-eminence; navigation in those days was the occupation which displayed the highest technical skill. It was, in fact, the equivalent of our modern air services.

This being so, one of the most interesting of all the currencies of the ancient world would seem to be that of Syracuse. On its coins were combined ears of corn and the four dolphins, reigned over by the Goddess of the Waters, Arethusa, for whose features the maidens of Sicily had served as models. On the reverse could be seen the blood horses of the great landowners, drawing a chariot. The whole curiously complex destiny of Sicily was there made visible in a few grammes of silver. The ears of corn bore witness to the fertility of an island which, during the Persian wars, had undertaken to provide all the food needed by the Greek armies. But the ambiguous character of Arethusa had its meaning. Goddess of Rivers and Fresh Water, she had passed through the deep places of the sea without being contaminated by them. She was the true symbol of an island in which the races, the skills, the myths of many peoples met. To the products of the earth she had added the resources of the sea, yet had preserved her purity. It is matter for wonder that so many subtle truths could be expressed with such concision, and in a language which the whole civilized world could understand.

꙳   ꙳   ꙳

I FLATTER myself that I have tracked down an analogy between the science of numismatics and that "humane oceanography" which may be established at some future date. Both have this in common, that they open perspectives into the past which are very different from those provided by history and based on texts alone. Both silently mark out the salient points in the pacific and commercial activities of peoples, and show, over great stretches of time and by the evidence of small things, the achievement of influences, exchanges, and expansions. They reflect general trends rather than single events, though these, too, they handle with clarity and brilliance. For instance, they can deal convincingly with the first gold coins minted in Athens during the great financial slump of 407, and with the wreck of Mahdia, which revealed to us the loot collected by Sulla in Athens. The science of numismatics, and the exploration of the deep seas, present us with proofs of the same general type, concrete, not much open to doubt, and limited in time. Maritime activity, and the issues of currency, follow the same general graph, are affected by the same successes and the same forms of decadence. Their common denominator is economic prosperity. It must, I think, be admitted that the discovery of a hoard of coins has something in common with that of a wreck and, by dint of ingenious deduction and careful examination, can provide us with accurate analogies bearing on the general economic situation of a given period, the social and commercial relations then obtaining, and even, at times, the language spoken or the fashions in favor. For instance, the enormous twenty-stater piece struck in India, and bearing the effigy of Eucratides, shows the extent to which Hellenism and the Greek tongue had spread. But undersea archaeology is rich in similar evidence. The stoppers of Anthéor are indisputable proof that Oscan was spoken in Campania in the first century B.C.

♛   ♛   ♛

IF additional proof be needed of the mighty revolution imposed by Rome on the civilized world, numismatics can furnish it. It will be seen that this revolution was not confined to economics and politics, but also affected the general susceptibilities of mankind. Of all the many types of coin for the designs of which the Greeks had ransacked the sea, only one survived in Roman hands—the prow of a war galley, eloquent of battle and domination rather than of familiarity with the creatures of the deep. In the great mass of Roman coins the most various objects are utilized as emblems—elephants and zebus, Troy in flames, the features of ephemeral emperors, walls of cities, a view of London in 296, but never more a cuttlefish, never more a mollusc. A land power had battened on the world, repudiating the maritime heritage of the Aegean. It triumphed by means of its legions, and left to Greeks and Syrians the handling of its ships.

Notes on a Search Conducted by Commandant J. Y. Cousteau off Marseille

DURING the autumn and winter of 1952-1953, Commandant J. Y. Cousteau was engaged in the examination of an ancient wreck lying off Marseille. He used to the full the facilities offered by the oceanographic vessel *Calypso*, equipped in accordance with his instructions, and enjoyed the advantage of a subsidy provided by the Ministry of National Education. He was also given a great deal of help by the various public services of Marseille.

The site on which he was working lies at a depth of between eighteen and twenty-one fathoms, at the base of a rocky islet—the Le Grand Congloué—close to the Ile Maïre. The proximity of these two places enabled him to use the islet as a base for material and personnel. To clear the ground he made use of a very powerful compressed-air suction pump. A team of experienced free-divers was responsible for the work on the sea bed.

This was a case in which conditions were perfect. The depth of water was not excessive; there was a land base close at hand; adequate material

218

and financial resources were available, and official support for the enterprise was forthcoming. Furthermore, it became clear from the preliminary examination that the wreck had not, apparently, broken up, and that she had been carrying a cargo of no little importance, consisting of a very large number of wine amphorae.

As soon as the initial clearance had been accomplished, the divers concentrated their efforts on raising the amphorae. Over three thousand were brought to the surface. I am told on good authority that several thousand still remain at the bottom. The dimensions of this ancient cargo vessel must, therefore, have been considerable. Some of the amphorae are Greek, others Campanian. The latter were stamped with the letters S. E. S., which indicate the ownership of a certain Sestus. This man is known to have come originally from Fregellae, in the Bay of Naples, and to have settled at Delos round about the year 240 B.C.

The ship was also carrying a quantity of black-glaze Campanian ware. The hundreds of fragments recovered belong to some thirty different shapes, all of them of a well-known commercial pattern.

The objects thus collected will be lodged in the Musée Archéologique at Marseille.

None of the archaeologists worked with the divers. They confined their activities to staying on the surface and receiving the finds brought up by the divers.

So far, no particularly interesting information is to hand about the ship itself, or about its equipment. No specialist in naval archaeology went down with the divers.

For the first time in an operation of this nature, underwater television was used, and a submerged loudspeaker was installed by means of which instructions were issued to the men at work on the sea bed.

Bibliography

This Bibliography is limited to works which have a direct bearing on undersea archaeology.

Dr. Beaucaire: *Les fouilles sous-marines de Fos-sur-Mer* (*Bulletin de la Société des Amis du Vieil Istres*, December, 1949)

A. Beltran: *Ojetos romanos de Plomo en el Museo de Cartagena y sus inscriptiones* (*Memorias de los Museos arqueologicos provinciales*, VIII, 1947-1948, pp. 200-209)

A. Beltran: *Découvertes sous-marines en Espagne* (*Publicaciones del Seminario de Arqeologia y numismatica aragonesa*, III, Saragossa, 1952.) I have not been able to consult this work, which was still in the press while I was engaged on this volume. The author kindly informed me of its existence. It deals with all the objects found off the coasts of Spain.

F. Benoît: *Le vieux port de Marseille, bouchon d'amphore des Saintes-Maries, Olbia* (*Gallia*, 1948, VI, I, pp. 207, 213-214)

F. Benoît: *Antibes, Anthéor, Saint-Tropez* (*Gallia*, 1950: 1952, pp. 129-130)

Fernand Benoît: *Jas d'ancre à tête de Méduse* (*Bulletin du Club Alpin Sous-Marin*, 1950)

Fernand Benoît: *Jas d'ancre à tête de Méduse* (*Revue Archéologique,* April-June, 1951, XXXVII, pp. 223-228)

H. G. Beyen: *La statue d'Artemision* (The Hague, 1930)

H. G. Beyen and W. Vollgraff: *Argos et Sicyone* (The Hague, 1947)

R. Cagnat: *Les fouilles sous-marines de Mahdia* (*Revue de l'Art*, 1911, I, pp. 321 ff.)

R. Cagnat: *Mahdia* (*Annales du Musée Guimet*, XXXVI, 1912, pp. 91 ff.)

R. Cagnat: *A travers le monde romain*, 1912, pp. 240 ff. [Mahdia]

J. Carpopino: *Sylla et les fouilles sous-marines de Mahdia* (*Mélanges offerts à Nicolas Iorga*, 1933)

P. Cavvadias: *Comptes rendus de l'Académie des Inscriptions* (1901, pp. 58-63)

E. Condroyer: *L'exploration sous-marine de la Galère de Mahdia* (*Neptunia*, 4e trimestre, 1948, No. 12)

J. Coupry: *Recherches sous-marines à Olbia* (*Bulletin du Club Alpin Sous-Marin*, 1949)

J. Coupry: *L'exploration sous-marine* (*Science et Vie*, September 1950, No. 396)

R. Dain: *Inscriptions attiques trouvées à Mahdia* (*Revue des Études Grecques*, XLIV, 1931, pp. 290 ff.)

A. Danovaro: *Le Nave di Nemi* (*Neptunia*, 3e trimestre, 1950, No. 19)

R. Demangel: *Fouilles et Recherches sous-marines en Grèce* (*Bulletin de Correspondance Héllenique*, 1950, pp. 271-273)

R. Demangel: *Deux chantiers d'archéologie sous-marine ouverts en Grèce par les Français* (*Figaro Littéraire*, March 31, 1951)

R. Damangel: *L'avenir de l'archéologie est sous les mers* (*Figaro Littéraire*, September 29 and October 5, 1951)

R. Demangel: *Une ville grecque engloutie, Helike* (*Bulletin van de Vereniging tot Bevordering des Kennis van de Antieke Beschaving te's-Gravenhage*, Leyden, 1952)

Philippe Diolé: *The Undersea Adventure* (New York: Julian Messner, 1953)

Ph. Diolé: *De la protection des sites sous-marins* (*Neptunia*, 1er trimestre, 1950, No. 17)

Ph. Diolé: *Fouilles sous-marines* (*Neptunia*, 1er trimestre, 1951, No. 21)

Dr. Donnadieu: *Découverte d'une ancre antique* (*Bulletin du Club Alpin Sous-Marin*, 1949)

S. Gagnière: *Bouchon d'amphore trouvé aux Saintes-Maries-de-la-Mer* (*Cahiers d'Histoire et d'Archéologie*, 1948, pp. 113 ff.)

A. Grenier: *Manuel d'Archéologie gallo-romaine*, VI, pp. 473-642

J. Heurgon: *Les Lassii pompéiens et l'importation des vins italiens en Gaule* (*La Parole del passato*, 1952)

Juan J. de Jauregui: *Exploraciones submarinas a Cartegena e San Pedro del Pinatar* (*Archivo esp. de Arqueologia*, XXI, 70)

Juan J. de Jauregui and A. Beltra. : *Acerca de unas anclas romanas del Museo de Cartagena* (*Boletin arquɔlogico del Sudeste Espanol*, Nos. 4, 7, January-December 1946)

G. Jondet: *Les ports submergés de l'ancienne île de Pharos* (*Bulletin de l'Institut égyptien*, IX, 1914)

G. Jondet: *Bulletin de la Société archéologique d'Alexandrie*, 1919

C. Jouhannaud-Raynal: *L'archéologie sous-marine* (*Camping Plein-air*, January, 1950)

G. Karo: "Art Salvaged from the Sea" (*Archaeology*, December 1948, pp. 179-185)

Karouzos: Αρχαιολογικὸν Δελτίον, XIII, p. 40

L. Lacoste and C. Quémard: *Les ports antiques d'Algérie* (*La Revue Maritime*, December, 1932, pp. 760-788)

N. Lamboglia: *Il Museo Navale Romano di Albenga* (*Rivista Ingauna e Intemelia*, 1950, Nos. 3-4)

R. Lantier: *Panthère en bronze trouvée en mer près de Monaco* (*Monuments Piot*, XLV, 1952)

Lechat: *Revue des Etudes Anciennes*, XII, 1910, p. 350; XIII, 1911, pp. 140 ff. (Mahdia)

J. Le Gall: *Un modèle réduit de navire marchand romain* (*Mélanges Charles Picard* II; *Revue Archéologique*, XXXI-XXXII, pp. 607-617)

K. Lehmann-Hartleben: *Die antiken Hafenanlagen des Mittelmeeres* (Leipzig, 1923)

L. Magon: *Essai de reconstitution de l'ancre du Musée de Marseille* (*Revenue Archéologique*, 1894, II, pp. 220-230)

A. Merlin: *Comptes rendus de l'Académie des Inscriptions*, 1908, pp. 245 ff., 286 ff., 532 ff.; 1909, pp. 650 ff.; 1910, pp. 585 ff.; 1911, pp. 206 ff., 556 ff.; 1913, pp. 469 ff.

A. Merlin: *Monuments Piot*, XVII, pp. 52-56; XVIII, pp. 5-17.

A. Merlin and L. Poinssot: *Klio*, IX, 1909, p. 260.

A. Merlin: *Les fouilles sous-marines de Mahdia* (*La Revue Tunisienne*, 1911, pp. 113 ff.)

A. Merlin: *Lingots et ancres trouvés en mer près de Mahdia* (*Mélanges offerts à René Cagnat*, 1912)

A. Merlin and R. Lantier: *Catalogue du Musée Alaoui*, 2nd Supplement
A. Merlin and L. Poinssot: *Guide du Musée Alaoui*, 3rd edition, pp. 50-67
A. Merlin and L. Poinssot: *Marbres trouvés en mer près de Mahdia*
  (*Revue Archéologique*, 1911, II, pp. 92-126)
A. Merlin and L. Poinssot: *Statuettes trouvées en mer près de Mahdia*
  (*Mémoires de la Société des Antiquaires de France*, LXX, 1911)
A. Merlin and L. Poinssot: *Epotides de bronze trouvées en mer* (*Le
  Congrès International d'Archéologie*, Alger, 1930, pp. 227-241)
George Mylonas: *The Bronze Statue from Artemision* (*American Journal
  of Archaeology*, 1941, p. 90; 1944, p. 143)

ΟΙΚΟΝΟΜΟS: *Praktika of the Academy of Athens*, 1928, p. 750
ΟΙΚΟΝΟΜΟS: *Monuments Piot*, 30, 1929, pp. 15-24

Charles Picard: *Manuel d'Archéologie grecque: La sculpture, Période
  classique, 5e siècle*, p. 62 (*Artemision*); *4e siècle*, p. 301 (*Ephèbe du
  Musée de Berlin*); *4e siècle*, p. 270 (*Ephèbe d'Anticythère*); *4e siècle*,
  p. 500 (*Hermes de Marathon*); *5e siècle*, p. 394 (*Reliefs du Pirée*)
Charles Picard: *Revue de l'Art*, April, 1926 (*Marathon*), Id. November,
  1926, pp. 241-244
Charles Picard: *Acropole*, 1926, pp. 40-42 (*Marathon*)
Charles Picard: *Chronique de la Sculpture Etrusco latine* (*Revue des
  Études Latines*, VIII, 1930, p. 360 [*Mahdia*])
Charles Picard: *Comptes rendus de l'Académie des Inscriptions*, 1946,
  pp. 671-676 (*Boethos*)
Charles Picard: *Ornements de lits en bronze* (*Revue Archéologique*,
  1947, I, pp. 200 ff. (*Agôn et Hermès*)
Charles Picard: *Observations sur la groupe du Musée du Bardo signé de
  Boethos* (*Carthago*, 1952)

S. Reinach: *Courrier de l'Art antique* (*Gazette des Beaux Arts*, 1901,
  I, p. 203; 1928, II, p. 215; 1930, I, p. 141)
A. K. Rhomaios: Αρχαιολογικὸν Δελτίον 9, 1924-1925 (1927), pp. 145 ff.,
  pls. 2-5 (*Marathon*)
A. K. Rhomaios: *Antike Denkmaeler*, 4, 1929, 3-4, pp. 54 ff., pls. 30-37
G. M. A. Richter: *Archaic Greek Art against its Historical Background*
  (New York: Oxford University Press, 1949)

H. Schrader: *Forschungen und Fortschritte* (Berlin, June 20th, 1931, No.
  18, p. 249 [*Reliefs at the Piraeus*])
J. N. Svoronos: *Die Funde von Antikythera* (Das Athenen National-
  Museum, 1908)

J. N. Svoronos: *Stylides, ancres hierae, aphlasta, stoloi, akrostolia, embola, proembola et totems marins* (*Journal international d'Archéologie numismatique*, XVI, 1914, pp. 81-152)

Ph. Taillez: *La "Galère" de Mahdia* (*La Revue Maritime*, May, 1949, pp. 573-585)

Guido Ucelli: *Le Nave di Nemi* (Libreria dello Stato, Rome, 1950)

R. Weill: *Les ports antéhelléniques de la côte d'Alexandrie et l'Empire crétois* (*Bulletin Institut français d'Archéologie orientale*, XII, 1919)

Antiquity, December, 1930, pp. 405-414
Bulletin de Correspondence hellénique: Recherches sousmarines en Grece, 1951, p. 198
Gallia, Legislation archéologique, VIII, 1950, 1952, pp. 248-252

Index

(Note. — "q." quoted.)

225